The
ULTIMATE
Equine
Legal & Business
Advisor

by George G. Johnson, Jr.
and Tracy D. Dowson

Copyright 2003 Pica Publishing

Printed in the United States of America

p. cm.

Includes index

ISBN 0-963-0558-1-X (pbk)

1. Horse industry - United States - Law and legislation
2. Horse industry - Marketing, Public Relations, Business
        I. Johnson Jr., George G.
        II. Dowson, Tracy D.

Pica Publishing
5785 Horseradish Gulch Road
Golden, CO 80403-8107
1-800-279-2001 ext. 209
TracyPica@aol.com

ACKNOWLEDGEMENTS

"I dedicate this book with love and gratitude to my wife, Beth, who has tolerated me and been my number one supporter for over 40 years."

George G. Johnson, Jr.

My special thanks to Dean, for his ongoing support. To my parents, Vic and Kay Rowe, for teaching to ask questions and do my best. To real trainers like Mark Boyle and Nancy Goodwin for shairing their stories. To contributors: Gary Schoun, Colorado Brand Board; Connie Kimbrel, Table Mountain Ranch; Jefferson County Horse Council, Mike Shanahan President; Brigitte Nadon, artist; Sandi Pence, Dancing Horses and the entire McConnell Family.

Tracy Dowson

"Think when we speak of horses that you see them, printing their proud hooves in th' receiving earth.'

Henry V,

William

Shakespeare

TABLE OF CONTENTS

"A horse is the projection of peoples' dreams about themselves, strong, powerful, beautiful and it has the capability of giving us escape."

 FOREWORD

Remember when life was a whole lot simpler? People — especially horsepersons — lived by the Cowboy Code and a person's word was enough. As we enter the 21st century, few have heard of the Code or even believe that your word is your bond.

Something else has changed in today'ís world. If you have a participating connection with the horse industry — it's not a matter of if you will be sued — it's a matter of when. Today about the best you can do is to prevent yourself from being successfully sued.

Every person who is considering entering the world of horses needs professional advisors.

George Johnson and Tracy Dowson are experienced and knowledgeable advisors to many horsepersons. They have created a way of passing their cumulative knowledge on in this book, *The Ultimate Equine Legal and Business Advisor.*

This book could be used as a textbook for an Equine Business course, like the ones I taught at several universities during my teaching career. It brings under one cover the myriad of things that must be considered by horsepersons in today's complex and litigious society. The book teaches us, "The most important role of a lawyer is to practice preventative law."

The best defense against litigation is an awareness of potential blind spots and problems in the "inherently dangerous" horse industry. Accidents will happen. Thinking ahead and exercising reasonable care (including the reading of this book) can help prevent consequences that are difficult to live with. For example, an understanding of the words "bailment," "liability" and "negligence" can help you avoid dangerous and costly consequences.

A better understanding of legal and business etiquette will help us all be better horsepersons and help us forge a stronger and more enjoyable connection with our equine friends in a disconnected world.

> Doug Butler, PhD, CJF, FWCF
> LaPorte, Colorado

"A horse gallops with his lungs, perseveres with his heart and wins with his character."

Doug Butler is a life-long horseman and farrier. He received his PhD from Cornell University in Equine Nutrition and Veterinary Anatomy. He is a Certified Journeyman Farrier and a Fellow of The Worshipful Company of Farriers of England. Doug has won state, national and international horseshoeing and shoemaking contests.

Dr. Butler taught horsemanship and horse business at several universities for 30 years and has presented seminars in 46 states and 8 foreign countries. He was a founding board member of the Colorado Horse Development Authority and served for 7 years. He has written several textbooks on farrier science and craftsmanship, including *The Principles of Horseshoeing, Shoeing in Your Right Mind*, and *Six-Figure Shoeing*, and produced 21 instructional videos. He is a member of the National Speaker's Association and presents a keynote program that forges firm foundations for living in the 21st century with the Cowboy Code.

ABOUT THE AUTHORS

George G. Johnson, Jr.

George G. Johnson, Jr., shares his 36 years of experience and knowledge of equine law with readers inside these pages. Johnson was the senior attorney, with more experience and years in practice than any other attorney interviewed in *Horse and Rider* magazine, August 1997, Equine Specialty Attorneys, page 108. We just like to say he's seasoned.

"The Horse. Here is nobility without conceit, friendship without envy, beauty without vanity. A willing servant, yet no slave."

The wide range of topics in this book will be able to help everyone in the horse industry, from the first time horse owner who is learning what paperwork is involved in the purchase of their new horse, to the experienced horse owner who needs to clearly understand the "two of seven presumption," as the IRS sees it.

This book can also act as a primer to any person wishing to pursue a professional career in the horse industry. Professionals and "back-yard" horse owners need this information. State horse councils are working on everything from limiting the liability of horse owners to promoting the industry and developing horse related parks. These leaders, along with every horse owner,will change the future of this industry and this book will offer the professional knowledge needed to make the right choices.

Many horsemen have already become aquainted with Johnson as he is also the author of, *In The Balance, The Horseman's Guide to Legal Issues*. His magazine articles have been seen in such publications as *Western Horseman*, and his nationally syndicated columns are in: *Maverick Press, The Arizona Horse Connection, National Horsepeddler, Modern Horse Breeding, Walking Horse Report, Horse World* and *Saddle Horse Report*.

Many people have heard him speak at; the American Horse Council, Annual Convention (1997), Horse Expos and

Colleges accross the nation. Johnson has served as a past president of the Denver Agricultural and Livestock Club and has been active as a volunteer coordinator for the Denver National Western Stock Show. He is a past president of the Denver Dumb Friends League Animal Shelter and past president of the Colorado Foundation for Agriculture.

Johnson is licensed to practice law in Colorado, Texas, the United States Supreme Court, and the United States Court of Appeals Tenth Circuit. Most recently he was the senior partner of the Johnson Law Firm in Denver, Colorado.

Although, there is a chapter on contracts, no single form could possibly fit every person's situation, so you will not find the "one size fits all" forms within these pages. Johnson points out that these ready to use forms can cause more problems than they solve because of the various laws in each state and the need to customize agreements to each person's individual needs.

His personal experience with horses ranges from former rodeo cowboy, breeding and training horses, herding cattle and trail riding.

George Johnson is now the International Arabian Horse Association's Judges & Stewards Commissioner. He will be using his years of experience as an equine attorney in his new position. Johnson outlines his ambitions as the new Commissioner in an interview published in the April/May 2001 issue of *International Arabian Horse*. In this new position he will shape guidelines for all future competition.

Tracy D. Dowson

After graduating from Colorado State University in 1983 with a degree in Technical Journalism, with concentration in Public Relations, Dowson gained journalistic experience as a newspaper editor for a weekly newspaper in Wyoming. Her advertising experience began when she worked as an advertising copywriter for a major corporation's in-house marketing division. This is where she wrote "Advertising:

Effective Strategies for Your R.O.I.", managed the cooperative advertising program and worked with exciting public relations events, such as being a coordinator of a corporate's sponsorship for the Olympic Games.

Dowson gained community relations experience working for a large metro chamber of commerce, developing programs to benefit the business community and writing business development articles.

Later she became a division manager for a publishing company in Boulder, Colorado, directing a staff of 15 people.

Dowson began Pica Publishing in 1988. Pica Publishing offers her the opportunity to travel to trade shows like Equitana and Rocky Mountain Horse Expo, work with clients to develop their marketing plans and to speak to various groups helping horse owners become successful in their endeavours. Dowson believes in continuing education and has taken upper level courses in accounting, management and advertising. For several years you may have seen her columns in; *Maverick Press, Arizona Horse Connection, Horse World*, and many other horse publications. Pica Publishing is the only company dedicated to the success of horse owners and the development of business products for the horse industry including books, software and agreement forms.

Dowson is a third generation horseman and was raised on a small boarding and training facility in Golden, Colorado, where at age ten she began showing horses for other people. She has shown and trained most disciplines from saddleseat to rodeo and has taken lessons from an international dressage master. She has shown at a national level and has even driven professionally for Denver Carriage. Dowson is very active in many horse related organizations and served as president of Jefferson County Horse Council for three years. At one time she held judges cards for class three and 4-H, but returned to amateur status to enjoy showing her own family horses and spend more time with her son, Roy. Roy is a mutton bustin' champion in his own right.

She shares her passion with her husband, Dean, who stays out of the show ring, but enjoys trail riding.

"I just want to make the horse industry stronger - one horse owner at a time."

FORMS OF EQUINE BUSINESSES

In the horse business, as in any other enterprise, there are three basic business types. This is also known as the structure of the business. The three basic types or forms of business are; sole proprietorships, partnerships, and both C and S forms of corporations. In some states, a newer form of business, the limited liability company is also available. Limited partnerships are another business form, but they are more common in real estate transactions and their use in equine industry is rare. The entrepreneur starting a business should examine the characteristics of each form available and determine which is best suited to their needs.

Generally, people in the horse business must consider the same factors as other business owners in determining the type of business form. Factors to consider include:
- Tax aspects of each business form
- Ease of ownership transfer
- Limitations on liability
- The entrepreneur's willingness to adhere to the required conditions of the business form, especially corporations.

Good planning during the start-up phase of a business is essential and professionals should be consulted. In fact, a good business plan should budget for these costs at the onset. Not only should an experienced attorney be consulted, but also a qualified accountant should also be a part of the team. (You will find further discussion in Chapter seven, *Equine Business and Taxes*.) Proper and careful tax planning should be done at the earliest possible stages of any horse enterprise. When selecting the legal structure or form of business, the business owner will need to make special note of all requirements of each form. This helps to ensure that the available benefits will be derived from the legal structure chosen.

Sole Proprietorships
As the name implies, a "sole proprietorship" is when one person owns an entire business. It is literally a "one man show" and it is probably the most common form of busi-

"While one person hesitates because he feels inferior, the other is busy making mistakes and becoming superior."

Henry C. Link

ness in the horse industry. The main advantages of a sole proprietorship are the simplicity and lack of outside interference. Many people in the horse business describe themselves only as horse trainers, breeders, etc., and not business executives. Generally, they do not want others telling them how to run their businesses; nor do they want to be accountable to partners or shareholders. A sole proprietorship is well-suited to horse-related businesses because it is the most flexible form of business and requires less "red tape" than the other forms of business.

One of the major advantages of the sole proprietorship form of business can also be one of its greatest disadvantages—its simplicity. Too much simplicity, especially in the financial area, can damage a sole proprietorship. Horse businesses are very expensive and require a great deal of capital. The primary legal characteristic of a sole proprietorship is that the proprietor is personally liable for all business debts; therefore if the business is unable to meet its financial obligations, the creditors may pursue the personal assets of the proprietor. A sole proprietor is generally limited to financing the business by either contributing his own funds or by borrowing money. There are no other investors, no one else to share in the losses, expenses or taxes. When loans are taken out from banks or other lending institutions they, require periodic payments regardless of whether the business is making money. As the name implies, sole proprietorships have one owner and are thus not suitable for more than one owner, such as a husband and wife.

All profits and losses of the business pass through and are reported directly on the proprietor's personal income tax return. No matter how appealing the simplicity, privacy and flexibility of a sole proprietorship close examination and long-range planning might show that another business structure is more appropriate.

Partnerships
Another form of business in the horse industry is the "partnership." This involves two or more persons agreeing to be partners in a business venture. Partnerships range in scope from literal "one-horse-deals" to those operating the largest horse farms in the country. There are no formal legal

requirements for establishing a general partnership; however, preparation of a formal Partnership Agreement serves as a legal document between the partners and is highly advisable.

A partnership is generally financed in two ways: First, the partners may make contributions of capital. These contributions become partnership property and are subject to the claims of creditors of the business. Second, the partnership can borrow money. Again, this requires the partnership to make periodic payments to the lender, regardless of the partnership's ability to pay. As with sole proprietorships, the partnership form of business has advantages and disadvantages.

On the advantage side, partnerships can be relatively simple in both structure and administration. Unlike corporations, no government approval is required of a partnership prior to starting the venture. The formal agreement should be written according to accepted business standards at the start of the business partnership.

Although from a tax standpoint partnerships appear to be quite simple, looks can be deceiving. The basic scheme of taxing partnerships is that each partner is taxed on his/her share of income and can deduct their share of expenses. For example, in an equal partnership of two partners, each is taxed on half of the partnership income and can take half of the partnership's deductions or losses. The partnership itself pays no taxes but is required to file informational tax returns annually with the Internal Revenue Service. In Chapter Seven Equine Businesses and Taxes, some of the problems concerning determination of "profit" and "business versus hobby" show that even a seemingly simple tax scheme can be full of difficulties and pitfalls.

Another advantage of a partnership is the ability to raise capital. By bringing others into the partnership, additional financial resources are available to the venture. Also, in a partnership there is an ability to spread the risk of loss. Unlike the "Lone Ranger" aspect of sole proprietorships, partners bear losses and expenses together, which can be considered a prudent business practice.

A major disadvantage of the partnership form of business, however is that it can be like a marriage—easy to get into and expensive to get out of. Unless the partnership is properly documented with a written agreement, providing for dissolution of the partnership, it can become a bonanza for lawyers, accountants, appraisers and others. With professional help and planning, many problems can be avoided. This is the time to ask a lot of questions and make sure that any professional with whom you are working to form the partnership is knowledgeable and is familiar with your business circumstances and needs.

Often times, a partnership is formed among family members. This formation is convenient; however, business agreements between family members can have its own set of problems. Each member may have his or her own reason for getting into the business and the differences between members can cause unresolvable problems. Each member of the partnership should agree on a common goal. This goal may be raising the best horses possible, making a profit, training youth or whatever – as long as the members agree on a common goal and how to reach that goal. Once the goal is agreed upon, the partnership can then work on business plans and other arrangements necessary to accomplish that goal. It is critical for a partnership to agree on a common goal before the business can succeed. Also, conventional business practices like a formal accounting system and organized records, along with open lines of communication seems to ease some of the obstacles.

Probably the biggest disadvantage of the partnership form of business is the ability of each partner to bind the partnership to specific obligations. In the eyes of the law, each partner is an agent of the partnership with full power and authority to speak for and bind the partnership. Unfortunately, it is common for partners to make commitments on behalf of the partnership, which are not in the best interests of the entity or the other partners. This can lead to very serious problems, both within the partnership and with outsiders with whom the commitments have been made.

In a partnership, there is no limit to a partner's liability, as in a corporation. Instead, there is a potential for a broadened exposure to liability. The effects of becoming a partner in the wrong partnership, or with the wrong partners, can spell financial disaster. Not only can one lose his investment in the partnership; he can expose his other assets to loss if the partnership becomes obligated to outsiders for those losses. To avoid this exposure of personal net worth to possible loss, many people in the horse industry prefer the corporate form of business.

Corporations

Corporations are creatures of the law and require government approval before starting the venture. A corporation is formed by filing proposed Articles of Incorporation usually with the office of the Secretary of State, in the state chosen to be the state of incorporation. A Certificate of Incorporation is subsequently issued by the Secretary of State, and the corporation is then in official existence and can start doing business.

The legal description states that the corporation is owned by its shareholders and is run by a board of directors elected by the shareholders. The board of directors appoints the officers of the corporation, who actually run the day-to-day business of the enterprise. Anyone receiving compensation from the corporation, including working officers, is considered an employee for the purposes of state and federal income tax withholding, unemployment insurance and worker's compensation. (Chapter five, *Employer Requirements,* will explain the complex requirements of hiring employees.)

Both legal and accounting participation and advice are required when forming, organizing and utilizing corporations. They are usually more expensive to create and maintain than a partnership.

Depending on the state of incorporation, reports must be prepared and filed every one or two years to the state and a fee paid to maintain the corporation in good standing. Look in the telephone book for the local Chamber of Commerce, Small Business Administration or Office of Regulatory Reform. All can help with licenses and permits for a new or expanding business. These organizations also help with federal and state tax requirements for your type of business, unemployment insurance, worker's compensation and registering your business name.

A major advantage of the corporate form of business is the limited liability of the shareholders. Unlike partners, shareholders have to risk only the amount of their investment in the corporation. Except where the "corporate veil" is successfully pierced the most they can lose is what they put into the venture.

Another advantage of a corporation over the other business forms is that in most cases it has perpetual existence, giving it the power to survive the death of any owner. If a sole proprietor dies, so does the proprietorship, often requiring sale or liquidation of the assets. In the case of a partnership, the death of one of the partners dissolves the partnership, often requiring liquidation and distribution of the deceased partner's share to the estate (although, a well-drafted partnership agreement can address this event to ease the burden on the survivors). From the standpoint of its legal existence, a corporation survives the death of one or more of the shareholders and continues.

The size of your equine operation and source of financing will determine what type of form the business will take.

As in the case of its perpetual existence, a major advantage of a corporation is the ease of ownership transfer through the sale of stock. Rather than selling the business or reforming a partnership structure, all or any portion of the ownership of a corporation can easily be sold or transferred through the sale or transfer of stock in the corporation. Also, subject to state and federal securities laws and regulations, additional capital can be raised by selling stock in the corporation. A Corporation can accommodate a larger number of shareholders, further providing a broader base of capital and greatly spreading all risks.

The structured legal requirements governing the activities and administration of a corporation often assist in making business decisions. This is viewed by many as a major advantage of corporations. Also, the rules and guidelines are more clearly established. The centralized management of a corporation, through its board of directors and officers, has legally mandated rights and duties. Where partners might encounter difficulty in defining their responsibilities, officers and directors of a corporation have more clearly defined roles in managing the business.

The corporate form of business is not without its disadvantages. One of the most common problems encountered in a corporation is the legal formality. The law requires meetings, minutes, stock certificates, bylaws, and other corporate records. A corporation requires annual updating of its activities and maintaining current, up-to-date records. The protection to shareholders offered by the corporate form of business can be lost when the "corporate veil" is successfully pierced. When this occurs, the corporate form of business is disregarded and shareholders can be held personally liable for the obligations of the corporation regardless of the amount of their investment in the entity. Usually where the so-called "corporate veil" is pierced, fraud and self-dealing by the shareholders and the directors is involved. The theory of "piercing the corporate veil" or the "alter ego" theory was well stated by the Colorado Supreme Court as follows:

> ". . . to establish the alter ego doctrine it must be shown the stockholder's disregard of the corporate entity made it a mere instrumentality for transactions of their own affairs; that there is such a unity of interest in ownership that the separate personalities of the corporations and the owners no longer exist; and to adhere to the doctrine of corporate entity would promote injustice and protect fraud."

Although this doctrine is seldom applied, it is very often alleged when a closely held corporation is sued. It is thus very important that the corporate house be kept in order.

Also, the fact that a corporation is more closely supervised by regulatory bodies - such as state agencies and, in some cases, the Securities and Exchange Commission - is seen as a disadvantage.

A corporation may acquire the capital necessary to begin and continue operation of the business by two different means. *Equity financing* involves issuing shares of stock, that represents an ownership interest in the business, in exchange for cash, property, labor or services rendered. The primary advantage of equity financing to a corporation is that the corporation is not required to repay the principal or interest; instead, the shareholder acquires an interest in the business and a share of future profits. In addition, since the investment received by the corporation constitutes equity, it may be used by the corporation for purposes of acquiring additional capital.

On the other hand, the investor who becomes a shareholder in exchange for his/her investment has no guarantee of repayment. If the corporation is successful in the future, the shareholder may receive periodic distributions of the corporation's profits in the form of dividends. Dividends are taxable to the shareholder as ordinary income. If the corporation repurchases its shares from the shareholders, the profit from that event is also taxable to the shareholders.

Remember that corporations are more expensive to administer, due to the increased formal requirements of maintaining the corporate structure.

There are two types of corporations that are different only in how they are taxed under the Internal Revenue Code. With the exception of how they are taxed, both forms of corporations are treated the same by corporations laws. These types are the C Corporation and the S or Subchapter S Corporation.

C Corporations

The C Corporation gets its name from the fact that it is taxed under Subchapter C of the Internal Revenue Code. C Corporations are subject to double taxation where profits are taxed at the corporate level and dividends are taxed at the shareholder level. Since this type of corporation is subject to double taxation, whenever possible, it is avoided in the horse industry. However, when a corporation cannot qualify as a Subchapter S Corporation, the C designation is the only option available. The major advantage of the S Corporation is that the double taxation disadvantage is eliminated.

S Corporations

Under the S Corporation structure, the officers elect to be taxed like a partnership under the Internal Revenue Code. The corporation itself is not taxed, but each shareholder is taxed on his/her pro rata share of income minus expenses. The Internal Revenue Code sets strict standards for qualifying and electing to be taxed as a Subchapter S Corporation. For instance, all shareholders must agree to elect Subchapter S status. This form of business is limited to 75 shareholders who must be U.S. citizens, or can be students from out of the country (aliens). Another corporation cannot own the stock of the corporation. There are other requirements regarding the class of stock and earnings, which should be fully explained to all potential stockholders. Subchapter S Corporations are quite common in the horse industry. Certainly, like the previous forms of business, corporations have their advantages and disadvantages.

"You can always learn something from every instructor."

Tracy Dowson

Limited Liability Company

Recently the majority of states have enacted legislation that created a new type of business, the Limited Liability Company (LLC). The legislation gives the owner of a business, including horse businesses, an entirely new option in the formation of a business. The LLC is neither a corporation nor a partnership, but offers some of the advantages of both types of business structures without being burdened by some of their disadvantages. The Limited Liability Company is a unique business entity. Like Subchapter S Corporations, the LLC combines the tax benefits with the limited liability benefits of a corporation.

An LLC is formed when one or more persons files Articles of Organization with the Secretary of State. These Articles are very similar to corporate Articles of Incorporation and include the name of the LLC; the period of its duration; name and address of its registered agent; the names and addresses of the initial manager or managers; and, if desired, any delayed effective date of its creation. The name must contain the words "limited liability company" or the abbreviation thereof, LLC.

The owners of an LLC are called "members." They have certain voting rights, including: the right to unanimously approve transfers of interests by other members; the right to vote for managers of the LLC; and, if the articles so provide, the right to unanimously consent to continuation of the LLC on the death, retirement, expulsion, resignation, bankruptcy, or dissolution of a member. The members have the right to any other matter provided in the operating agreement; all votes require a majority or unanimous vote, consent, or agreement of the members. New members may be admitted only upon the unanimous written consent of all existing members. One or more managers who are elected annually by a vote of the members manage the LLC. The operating agreement is much like a partnership agreement; it may contain provisions concerning such matters as the purposes of the LLC, the election and duties of the managers, sharing of profits and losses, distributions, etc. A properly drafted operating agreement should state how the company is to be managed, and how profits and losses will be allocated among the members of the LLC.

Probably the most significant characteristic of an LLC is that of limited liability. The legislation contains a specific provision that the members and managers are not liable "under a judgment, decree, or order of a court, or in any other manner, for a debt, obligation, or liability of the limited liability company." However, as with corporations, a member is personally liable to the LLC to perform any promise or contribute cash or property. Also, when an LLC's liabilities exceed its assets and the liability extends for a period of six years after such improper distribution is made, members must return any distributions they received from the LLC. Another six year period of a member's liability is imposed for the amount of the member's contribution that was returned - only to the extent necessary to discharge liabilities that existed during the period the contribution was held by the LLC. Legislation provides that the doctrine of "piercing the corporate veil" is applicable to LLCs as it presently applies to corporations. This gives creditors the right, in certain cases where the entity is a sham, to proceed directly against members for the debts, obligations, and liabilities of the entity. In the case of both corporations and LLCs, "piercing the corporate veil" or the "alter ego status" of an officer or director of a corporation, or a member in the case of a LLC is often difficult, but not impossible to prove. The factors that determine whether or not the member(s) (or corporate officers or directors) are personally liable for the debts of the business generally are directed to how the business was conducted and how the particular member personally benefited from the status of the business. The questions that determine the applicability of "piercing the veil" or "alter ego status" include the following:

- incomplete organization of the LLC
- the member's assumption of personal liability on business obligations
- failure to act as a proper LLC business
- treatment by the member of the assets of the business as his own
- the member co-mingling business and personal funds or assets
- member's use of the LLC as a conduit for his personal business
- the member's use of LLC to procure goods or services for himself

These and other factors that show that the LLC is a sham or a mere shell rather than a legitimate business disqualify the protective nature of the business and make the members personally liable for the LLC's debts to its creditors.

Limited Liability Companies enjoy the same tax treatment as partnerships. Like a partnership, the LLC is not a separate taxable entity between its members and the government, and income as well as losses flow directly from the LLC to its members/owners without subjecting them to double taxation as in the case of non-partnership for the purpose of state income taxation.

While including many of the benefits of a Subchapter S Corporation, the LLC does not include the stringent requirements for membership that a Subchapter S Corporation imposes on its stockholders. For example, an LLC is allowed an unlimited number of members where as a Subchapter S Corporation is limited to 75 shareholders. Also, membership in an LLC is not limited to United States citizens, where as a Subchapter S Corporation may not have foreign shareholders.

The LLC is a new and appealing alternative to conventional forms of equine businesses. It grants both limited liability and favorable tax treatment, while avoiding many of the restrictive requirements imposed on Subchapter S Corporations. Never the less, LLCs are relatively new legal entities created by lack of uniformity in state law, confusion and unfamiliarly can create problems. While an LLC may not be appropriate in every equine business situation, the fact of its existence and availability makes it a consideration for many horsemen.

Syndications

A syndication is similar to a partnership between two or more persons regarding the ownership of a stallion, broodmares, race or show horses. It relates more to forms of ownership and/or management of particular horse(s) rather than a distinct form of doing business. A syndication is a written agreement through which each partner will benefit from his/her share of ownership of the animal. This benefit may be breeding rights or a share of the winnings. The details should always be clearly spelled out in a written contract. A syndication can legally take one of two forms: a partnership or co-ownership.

A co-ownership is less likely, because a co-owner may not sell breeding rights. Caution is advised in a syndication because of something called "investment security." Selling unregistered securities is a criminal act under federal law, punishable by a fine of up to $10,000, imprisonment for five years, or both. A syndication is an excellent example of a situation needing legal counsel.

This chapter has briefly introduced the four main forms of business in the horse industry. As mentioned, always obtain competent legal and other professional help when selecting the best structure for your equine business. Every case is different and requires individual analysis and treatment. Remember, the best law is preventive law. Obtain the necessary legal, accounting or other professional advice before finally selecting the business form or making any commitments. Plan carefully and plan ahead.

THE BUSINESS PLAN DEFINED

The business plan has been called everything from a road map to success to an essential part of a loan application. Many people in the horse industry only have a formal business plan if they have gone through the loan application process; and many of these individuals do not review their plans on a regular basis.

Alice in Wonderland once asked the Cat, "Would you tell me, please, which way I ought to go from here?" To which the Cat replied, "That depends a good deal on where you want to go." "I don't much care where." said Alice. "Then it doesn't matter which way you go," said the Cat.

If you don't have a plan or an idea of where you want to go, your chances of finding success become nearly impossible. A certain amount of paperwork and planning is essential for any business to reach financially and emotionally satisfying goals.

A business plan outlines everything about the business. Because it has to be a custom fit, the following suggested areas should be personalized:

Purpose Statement
Each plan should begin with a Purpose Statement. This should clearly and specifically define what your company intends to do. This statement need only be a line or a paragraph that describes the intent of the business in the opening section of the business plan, outline the company name, address or location and philosophy. Define why you want to be in business and what you hope to achieve. Having a professionally prepared logo will reinforce the seriousness of your endeavor.

Executive Summary
The executive summary outlines the top management and their expertise. More than a resume, it outlines each person's qualifications, experience and accomplishments. It also highlights the leader's ability to manage money, profit mindedness and shows evidence of stability and direction. List both professional and personal references.

"I ride horses because it's the only sport where I can exercise while sitting down."

Joan Hansen

In the Executive Summary, or under a section for other personnel needs, all employee or contractual labor should be outlined. Each business needs to hire professionals from time to time. An attorney may help develop business guidelines, set up the legal structure and help with licenses, permits, zoning laws and other legal requirements. A tax accountant may help set up the books and do the annual tax preparation. Even a consultant may be hired.

In the horse industry, employees who are willing to clean stalls and groom horses can be the most difficult to hire, train and retain. What incentives will your company offer to insure the retainment of entry level employees? How will the organizational chart look? What salary ranges are normal for this type of business? Your business plan should be able to answer all of these questions.

Business Information
Business information may include history of the industry, information regarding competition and potential clientele base. Selection of the business location could be one of the most important decisions you make. Most horse facilities need to be easily accessible, like near a highway, yet out of the city and away from unfavorable zoning laws and regulations that would inhibit an agriculturally based business. Operating procedures will describe how the business will be conducted on a daily basis. If a breeding business is being planned, examine specific information regarding mare care, foaling assistance, acquisition of feed, bedding, etc. and the final sale of the product. What type of facilities need to be acquired or built to house such an operation? Examine everything from who will be responsible for building the foaling barn, to what personnel will handle the foaling.

Marketing
Marketing is the total offering made to consumers in exchange for something of value. Marketing encompasses researching current competitors' pricing and outlets, learning the purchasing choices made by prospective clients, advertising, customer service and public relations. While advertising is the most common aspect of marketing, it is by no means the only source of getting the message out. Trainers invest time working with youth programs to gain more students and breeders donate foals to equine science

programs to gain name recognition. Brainstorming any and all possibilities is the best way to open the creative process of the marketing plan. Identify different markets and outline your business plan accordingly.

Financial

The financial section is considered by any bank or loan officer, the meat of the business plan. Each business has start-up costs, including capital expenses like buildings, vehicles, tractors, tack, feed, supplies and animal inventory. What it will take to keep this business operating determines the operating budget? Overhead costs may include electricity, building maintenance, painting, fence repair and more. In your financial statement include a break-even analysis, pro-forma income projections, personal balance sheet, long term debt statements and cash-flow projections.

When developing your business plan remember to include all of the professionals you will be working with, like your veterinarian.

Almost as many businesses fail because they do not plan for success as those who do not plan for the lack of sales. A projection of both extremes could defray any unexpected surprises. After all these budgets and tables are completed, you will be more in line with the size, scope and reality of your project.

Supporting documentation for the financial section may include: personal tax returns, personal financial statement, a copy of any lease or purchase agreements for land and/or buildings, copies of letters of intent from people who have agreed to support your business as a customer or supplier and more. Be prepared to show a great deal of private information to acquire a loan. In the horse industry a supplier may be a hay producer, owners of broodmares to be purchased or leased, insurance company, waste removal company, resident trainers or vets, an agent for buying or selling horses and more.

Loan officers recommend that a loan application be perfect the first time, because if the loan is turned down, the loan cannot just be rewritten and resubmitted. Talk to anyone in the banking industry or from the Small Business Administration (SBA) and make sure all the "t's" are

"Horse sense is
the thing a horse
has which keeps
it from betting
on people."

W.C. Fields

crossed and all the "i's" are dotted before you submit your loan application.

General business resources include:

- The SBA at www.sba.gov. They provide loans, business development workshops, counseling, literature, videotapes, and up-to-the-minute news on laws and regulations that affect small businesses.

- The Internal Revenue Service (IRS) provides a business tax kit with forms and publications for small business owners and self-employed individuals, including publication 334, *"Tax Guide for Small Businesses"*.

- Small Business Tax Education Program (STEP). This program is a partnership between the IRS and local organizations that provide workshops on taxes, starting a business, record keeping and more.

- Tax Tips Calendars for Small Businesses. As reported on the IRS Web site, this publication contains helpful hints, general tax information, a listing of the most common tax filing dates, and more, all in one comprehensive publication. The IRS may be reached at 1-800-829-1040, or visit the IRS web site at www.irs.gov.

A proper business plan should be typeset and presented in a binder or other format that reflects your professionalism. The business plan should be consistent, coherent and realistic. Updating the business plan yearly will help keep your business on track.

Actual financial reports are too diverse and detailed to be covered in detail in this book. There are many resources for financial planning, including: software, books, local chamber of commerce, Small Business Administration and SCORE programs. Information about legal and zoning requirements should be researched not only by experts, but by you. You are ultimately responsible for the end result. Check the facts. Realtors have sold property as horse property, when, in fact, the zoning or other requirements designated otherwise. Finding an attorney or accountant who understands the horse industry can be challenging; ask friends you show with, or acquaintances in your local horse council to make recommendations.

With diligence, your business plan can be successful.

FINANCING AN EQUINE OPERATION

Within a six-month period, I received several requests for financial assistance. All were one-page letters, not business plans or formal prospectuses, and all requested nonrepayable loans or sponsorship or even just information about financing and equine operations. I was delighted to know many people want to begin an equine business; however, it was clear that many of these individuals lacked the information and direction needed to acquire basic funding.

Your heart will lead you to the breed, discipline or interest that you want be involved with as a business owner, but your head must do the research to make the dream become a reality. Many people have great ideas, but lack the business acumen to make it more than a great idea. A frequent example is a young rider who wants to become a professional trainer. The professional trainer's life must seem alluring and glamorous to most young riders. These young people often do not understand the capital investment needed or the actual day-to-day demands of the job.

Before delving into the harsh reality of financing a business, I want to pass along my belief that with hard-work, luck and perseverance anything is possible. Stretch your imagination and consider the many business possibilities within the horse industry. Interview people currently working at similar positions to appraise the number of hours you will need to work for the possible income available. Too many young people believe that being a trainer is the only option within the industry. There are many people who have successfully combined a traditional profession like accountant, police officer, retail owner, photographer, or attorney with their love of horses. Many more individuals are exploring innovative professions like massage therapy, behavioral sciences in research and teaching, service industries including overnight stabling, exercising horses, transportation, counseling, insurance and more. Never limit yourself. Use your natural strengths and abilities to guide your decisions.

Now you are ready to get your dream business financed. Raising capital may come from your personal savings, relatives, friends, banks, private investors, board of directors,

"Riding: The art of keeping a horse between you and the ground."

Anonymous

government and/or private foundations. Investors should not be confused with lenders. Investors take substantial risks in exchange for the potential of a large return.

Let's discuss free money first since it is the most limited subject. To qualify for grant money from the government or a private foundation, you need to be developing a business that will be socially beneficial. These endeavors might include: a handicapped riding program, performing medical research, using horses to rehabilitate troubled youth or employing the disadvantaged and/or minorities. There are also grants for education or redevelopment of agricultural-related interests. More information regarding obtaining grants and guaranteed loans can be obtained from your local library or local Small Business Administration (SBA) office. There is a great deal of competition for these grants and many organizations use professional grant writers to help them get noticed.

Many new businesses fail because they run out of money before they become established. Cash flow is the lifeblood

Financing considerations will include; land, fencing, buildings and the horses of your dreams.

for both new and established businesses. Most business have to borrow money at some time, and they must have a solid application - the first time. Before you can expect a bank to finance your operation, you have to learn how to complete a loan application with information that will show you have planned a successful business venture. Just as it takes time and knowledge to prepare a winning horse, you have to research your business and prepare the application so the possibility of your success shines.

Financing a new business is more difficult than obtaining a loan for an existing business. Bankers realize there is a high rate of failure for new businesses, and they are not in the business of losing their investments. Be prepared to overcome doubts by demonstrating that you have the skills to manage your venture successfully. You must know everything about your business, including: zoning requirements, insurance, licenses, taxes and sales tax issues, the professional services you will need, cash flow forecasts and pricing strategies; and you will be expected to provide a resumé of your skills, along with any other people involved in management.

In preparation of requesting a loan, first research similar businesses in order to obtain pertinent details. Do this by talking with comparable business owners. (They most likely will give you more information if you are in a separate geographical market or a drastically different breed or discipline.) Study demographics provided by trade journals and professional organizations. Learn what your local customers pay for similar products and services. Read as much as possible. And attend clinics and college courses when available. Many general courses - from accounting to managing employees to marketing are beneficial and will show lenders how devoted you are to running a successful business. Talk with a bank employee about the loan application before filling it out, visit your local library or SBA office, even research web sites dedicated to business development. Continuing education can also come from subscribing to publications like *Stable Management.*

Loan officers expect a business owner to raise at least 50% of the capital needed before they will consider a loan. You are expected to provide collateral to secure the loan in case you are unable to make the loan payments. This collateral is usually some personal assets with resale value. You may have to pledge your home, truck, land, trailer, savings accounts, certificates of deposit or inventory.

Lenders with catchy titles like "Business Development Bank Officer" will be looking at your loan application and are trained to find specific information. You can expect that your local bank representative has never seen a business like yours before, because horse-related businesses are a very small minority. If your banker wants to make site inspections, this is to your advantage as early as possible in the loan application process. This is your opportunity to explain why people are involved in the horse industry and why it is a sound business investment.

The seven criteria that bankers use to evaluate loans are: Character, Competence, Continuity, Cash Flow, Collateral, Condition and Conformity.

Character is determined by researching your credit history, personal history and references. They are looking for a person who is capable of leading a disciplined life and who has paid previous debts in a timely manner.

Competence measures your capability to operate this type of business successfully. Personal history of employment in a similar capacity is necessary to prove that you understand the market and profitability of your chosen field. Demonstrating your willingness to hire competent professionals when needed is also important; this means hiring lawyers, accountants, even a head trainer or resident vet to insure that you have the advantages of their professional knowledge. This section will include your resumé, plus any additional information you will need to show your determination to operate a financially sound business.

Continuity is the time an existing business has been in operation. It also measures the time each member of the staff, especially the management team, has worked for this organization or in a similar position.

Cash Flow, or in the case of a new business, projected cash flow - measures the ability to generate enough cash to repay the loan. This is a large obstacle for breeding operations because it takes some time and investment to create inventory. Many larger farms sell horses as yearlings at public auctions to create a more predictable cash-flow situation. As a new trainer you may want to have signed "letters of intent" from owners who will send

their horses to you for a specified period of time.
Too many people just hang out a shingle and expect
customers to walk through the doors asking for products
and services.

Collateral is assets you pledge to secure the loan. In
general, after your loan officer has figured the discounted
book value of your assets, they are worth much less than
you thought they would be worth.

Condition or what is the financial condition of your
business will be thoroughly evaluated. This will be
assessed by looking at all financial statements and
projected earnings.

Conformity measures how your business loan fits with
the other types of loans carried by this institution. A
bank specializing in agricultural businesses may have a
better understanding of your business. Banks feel more
comfortable loaning money to endeavors they can
understand.

Part of your loan application consists of your ability to
sell the loan officer on your potential to operate this type of
business successfully. It is your responsibility to provide all
the financial data and information needed to prove that
your business will succeed with the help of their money.
Don't assume that your banker will understand anything
about the horse industry. You have to educate that person,
and when appropriate, show him/her your facility or one
just like it that you hope to build. A business plan is an
important aspect of your loan application and is a subject
unto itself.

Do your homework and present the best loan application -
the first time. In most cases, after a loan application has
been turned down, you can't just rewrite it and resubmit.

🐎 BUYING HORSE PROPERTY

One of the most common areas of legal problems for horse owners involves purchasing horse property. An ideal goal of horse owners is to have a place where they can live, keep their horses, ride and enjoy a "country lifestyle." Prospective purchasers spend a great deal of time locating what appears to be suitable property. Often, real estate agents are consulted to assist in the search for that "perfect piece of ground." As various properties are seen, the excitement can grow and people are consumed by their plans and dreams. This is often wonderful but, unless the enthusiasm is tempered with reason and judgment, great trouble can lie ahead.

"One man's wrong lead is another man's counter-canter."

Steven D. Price

It is important to know that in the last few years the western, southwestern and other sections of the country have experienced substantial growth. With this influx of new residents, formerly rural land is becoming developed as residential areas, schools, shopping areas and facilities to support an enlarged population. This pattern of growth and development has threatened the way of life of horse owners since agricultural land is becoming more urbanized with resulting social, political, and economic changes. Land that is both available and suitable for the keeping of horses is becoming much scarcer. In many locales it is harder to find property that is reasonably near urban areas (where jobs and clients may be), is a desirable location for a home and where horses are allowed by proper zoning regulations.

After what appears to be the perfect property is found a great deal of research and investigation is necessary by any prospective buyer. There are many physical, legal, practical, and political factors that must be investigated before buying any horse property. Too often prospective purchasers think that a parcel of real estate that appears to be rural or agricultural would be suitable for maintaining horses and used accordingly. Wrong! We all know that looks can be deceiving. This is certainly true with real estate. Many factors must be thoroughly investigated before buying the ground.

Ask About Zoning

The first question to ask is "What is the ZONING of the real estate in question?" How property is zoned determines how it can be used. Zoning classifications are now quite common in rural areas. Often, entire counties are zoned to enable planned uses and to control growth and development. Many components are included in zoning, including whether horses or livestock may be kept, maintained and used on a particular property. In addition, there are often restrictions on the number of horses per acre or on each lot, as well as requirements for barns, corrals, pastures, weed controls, water, and other restrictions or requirements. Numerous and sometimes rather unreasonable requirements on the keeping of horses, especially in areas that are near residential development, makes even the most attractive property unsuitable for having horses.

How do you find out about the zoning on a specific piece of property? The most reliable method of determining the zone classification of a property is to go directly to the county or city zoning department or authority. Usually the county department will be very helpful, not only in giving accurate information on the zoning, but can also tell you of restrictions or prohibitions you could face under the applicable zoning ordinance for the planned horse facility. Copies of the zoning laws containing the requirements and restrictions are also available from the department of zoning. Armed with this information, you can be a more informed buyer, or non-buyer, as the case may be.

Real estate agents are also a good source of information on zoning. However, the better practice is to go to the zoning department yourself and get the information directly from the people who enforce the zoning laws. While a real estate agent might know the zoning classification of a piece of land, the technical requirements and restrictions that could adversely affect keeping of horses, might be out of the agent's knowledge or understanding. Get the information on zoning from "the horse's mouth."

In addition to zoning, a prospective purchaser must determine if there are any covenants or rules that affect the property: "restrictive" or "protective" covenants that affect the property, which must be met for its proper use. If an owner of the land does not follow the covenants, legal action and other penalties can follow. Accurate copies of restrictive covenants are available from title insurance companies. Often, it is wise to obtain legal counsel to review and interpret the covenants and advise on their effect. Generally, only subdivided and platted subdivisions contain protective covenants; however, all property should be checked to see if it is affected.

Title insurance companies can be used to determine what encumbrances, if any, are against a property. Also, title commitments can reveal other problems with a property, such as tax liens, *lis pendens* (notification that the title to the property is disputed), judgment liens, and other similar matters. Title commitments from title insurance companies are relatively inexpensive but a very important resource for a buyer of property to know about the legal status and title to the real estate.

Suitability for Horses

The next question that requires investigation involves whether the property is suitable for horses. The idea of "suitability" is very broad and includes area, pasture, environmental concerns, water, weeds, latent dangerous conditions or defects, and political concerns. The question must be asked whether the land is suitable and safe for horses? Are unsafe, toxic trees, weeds or

When buying horse property, remember to imagine how your buildings and equipment will fit into the picture.

grasses growing on or adjacent to the property? Can the land be fenced to ensure the safety of the horses by keeping them confined? Are there places reasonably close to the property where horses can be ridden? What is the nature of the area surrounding the land both in density of population and in the character of the neighborhood? Are services necessary for keeping of horses available (e.g., large animal veterinarians, feed stores, hay crops etc.?) Do local ordinances and regulations allow construction and use of facilities necessary for the proper use of horses? These and similar questions contain both legal and practical

"Judging from

the main portions

of the history of

the world, so far,

justice is always

in jeopardy."

Walt Whitman

concerns and often require obtaining professional help to gather the data necessary for a proper evaluation.

Horse owners often underestimate the amount of ground necessary to properly maintain horses. At least in the western United States, very few tracts of land can provide adequate feed for horses without supplement. New horse owners usually have problems in properly determining the size of land necessary for a horse. Expert advice is often necessary to determine the proper size and location for a horse operation even for experienced horse people. This information can be obtained from local extension offices and special books written for horsemen regarding land planning and barn building. Never be afraid to ask others what they have done, or what they would do differently.

Environmental Concerns

Environmental concerns present a virtual mine field for landowners. If a person buys a parcel of ground that contains toxic waste or substances deemed unsafe by the Environmental Protection Agency (EPA), under federal law the purchaser can be liable for cleanup costs. This liability attaches to the owner of the land, regardless of whether the owner had anything to do with creating the environmental problem.

Also, even if the property does not contain toxic or dangerous substances, the land can be of a type that qualifies it as a "wetland" and makes it subject to the strict regulations contained in the various federal laws that authorize the EPA and Army Corps of Engineers to promulgate regulations regarding the use of wetlands. If the land in question fits the government's definition of "wetland," the landowner must get a permit from the federal government before engaging in virtually any movement of soil on the property. This includes removing trees, clearing vegetation, digging drainage ditches, digging wells, land leveling, road grading and excavating for building foundations. Before beginning any excavation or movement of land, the landowner must go to the local EPA office and look at the regional wetland maps. If the land is included in a designated "wetland" area, a permit for the project must be obtained from the Army Corps of Engineers. The average time for obtaining a permit is in excess of one year.

We hear of environmental problems in urban areas where land is bought that formerly was the site of an industrial business. Why would this be of any concern to a horse owner looking for a nice piece of rural property? The answer is simply that, due to formerly common practices that were followed in the country, serious environmental problems are all too common. For example, in the past many farmers disposed of oil, commercial fertilizer residue, pesticide leftovers, etc., simply by pouring them on what they considered to be less valuable ground. These substances do not simply vanish; they saturate into the ground, leech into groundwater, and contaminate all that they contact. This is how some "Super Fund Sites" have been created that will cost millions of dollars to clean up. Also, most rural areas have had an area for dumping trash. These too often contain toxic materials that have been abandoned for years and require large sums of money to clean up.

In some areas and under certain laws, a defense of being an "innocent purchaser" might be of some help. However, the cost and trouble involved in these environmental matters can be considerable even though the buyer is "innocent." Investigation in this area requires expert assistance. In some instances, a complete "environmental audit" of the real estate is necessary in order to determine whether it is free from these concerns. The best course available to a prospective purchaser is to obtain expert advice and assistance before signing a contract. Professionals will discover and verify the former use(s) of the land. Abstracts and other public records will be searched to determine prior ownership. Investigating whether or not the land is in a designated "wetland" area can be determined at the local office of the EPA. An effort will usually be made to discover what is referred to as "local knowledge" about the particular tract of land—to find out about the "skeletons in the closet." In short, experts, whether attorneys or engineers, will attempt to discover the problems present on the land. The advice of these professionals should be strictly followed in order to prevent the nightmare of environmental problems.

Another area of concern and investigation, especially in the western United States, is that of water. In semi-arid locales, water use and consumption are strictly regulated. There are many rural or rural-appearing properties that are wholly unsuitable for horses because of either the unavailability of water or because water on the property cannot be used for livestock. In many states, household use of water does not allow watering horses or other large animals. Obviously, a property without usable water is totally unsuitable for use as a horse property. The water question can easily be determined by contacting local authorities (e.g. zoning, county agents, utilities, etc.). Water quality also must be investigated well in advance of purchasing property.

Closely associated with water are questions of pollution and groundwater contamination. Equine manure cannot contribute to or cause either groundwater contamination or surface runoff pollution. Also, manure must not cause air pollution or noxious conditions, such as flies or other insects that adversely affect the surrounding area. Other concerns include parasite and rodent control, together with control of dust, odors and pesticide drift. If septic systems are either in place or to be constructed, a potential purchaser must be aware of what tests and inspections are required by local health and/or building authorities.

Horse owners must be sensitive to these problems and take appropriate precautions to comply with all applicable state and local health regulations. Again, a potential purchaser should check with local authorities to find out about all regulations that affect the use, stabling and maintenance of horses in the area. Prior knowledge can prevent costly and serious mistakes.

As discussed, your "dream place in the country" can be a nightmare. Even the most desirable-appearing property can be wholly unsuitable as a horse property. Research, professional assistance, and common sense can go a long way in preventing possible problems. Plan ahead, investigate, research, and get the necessary professional help before you purchase the property. Your dreams and goals can be realized if you know what you are getting into.

🐎 EMPLOYER REQUIREMENTS

s with any growing business, at some point you may find yourself hiring employees. Employees are a major concern and the specifics of the horse industry will only complicate things.

The question becomes, do you hire full- or part-time employees, or do you hire subcontractors to perform specific jobs on an as-needed basis? If you hire contract labor, your paperwork life is much easier. But just calling someone contract labor doesn't make it so. And, if you incorrectly classify people working for you, you may end up paying some big dollars to the IRS and to the state.

It is important to recognize the traits of a typical employee/employer relationship. The following guidelines will help you determine whether you have a typical employee/employer relationship as defined by the laws of most states.

All of the items do not have to apply:
- Job training is necessary.
- Supervision and payroll responsibilities are the employer's responsibility.
- Employer sets the work hours.
- All work time must be devoted to the employer.
- Workplace is restricted (e.g. must work on the site).
- Prioritization of the work is done by the employer.
- Payment is made by the hour or some type of salary arrangement.
- Employer pays the expenses incurred on the job.
- Employee will not incur any financial losses.
- The same job cannot be performed for another employer.
- The worker can quit without recourse from the employer.

The above traits may commonly apply to a stable-cleaner, groom or handyman as a typical employer/employee relationship. A trainer or horseshoer is usually classified as a contractor because he/she performs the job using more of the guidelines mentioned below:
- Work is done by the project.

"Want to end up with a million bucks in the horse business? Start out with five million."

Anonymous

Is your trainer an employee or a contract laborer? Is the judge a contract laborer or employee of show management? Read on to determine the requirements of each category.

- The contractor determines the tasks to be accomplished and the order in which they are to be accomplished.
- Establishes his/her own working hours
- Works for others at the same time.
- Uses own equipment and tools.

If you have any questions, call someone at an appropriate government agency found in the telephone book, the local chamber of commerce or the Small Business Administration. This is why we pay taxes for government agencies like, the Department of Labor and Employment.

For both employees and contract labor, there are federal and state forms to contend with. For a contract laborer, you must keep track of the exact amount paid. At the end of the year, fill out a 1099 form for each individual paid over $600 during the year.

Employees require the following forms:

Federal Forms

Form SS-4
The federal form SS-4 is the application for a federal employer identification number (FEIN) used to set up income tax withholding, FICA and FUTA, through the IRS. For immediate in help obtaining a FEIN call (801) 625-7645 during regular business hours. This is a toll call and you will read your completed SS-4 form over the phone.

A FEIN will be assigned to you and your completed SS-4 form must be mailed within five days.

Form W-4

Each employee must sign a completed and dated W-4. This form should be included in the employee's personnel file. The W-4 tells the employer how many exemptions to consider when withholding federal income tax from payroll checks. Having this form on file is required by the government, and is also the employer's insurance policy against disputes that could arise later with the IRS or the employee. The W-4 is required to be filed with the IRS only in special circumstances.

INS Form I-9

Another item for the personnel file is the Immigration and Naturalization Service's (INS) form I-9. This form was devised to ensure that employers do not hire illegal aliens. The paperwork is not difficult, but is required. This form must be completed within three working days after employment begins. If the documents cannot be presented, call the state INS office regarding the 90 day extension.

The requirements explain that the employer must make a photocopy of the INS form and the support documents (U.S. Passport and a State Driver's License), and keep them in the employee's file. The employee must present identification and proof of employability within the United States. The items in list A, establish both identity and employment eligibility. The items in list B prove only identity. The items in list C verify only employment eligibility.

INS Support Documents

List A:
1. U.S. Passport (unexpired or expired)
2. Certificate of U.S. Citizenship (INS Form N-560 or N-561)
3. Certificate of Naturalization (INS Form N-550 or N-570)
4. Unexpired foreign passport, with I-551 stamp or attached INS Form I-94 indicating unexpired employment authorization
5. Alien Registration Receipt Card with photograph (INS Form I-151 or I-551)

"The best use of

good laws is to

teach men to

trample bad laws

under their feet."

Wendell

Phillips

6. Unexpired Temporary Resident Card (INS Form I-688)
7. Unexpired Employment Authorization Card (INS Form I-688-A)
8. Unexpired Reentry Permit (INS Form I-327)
9. Unexpired Refugee Travel Document (INS Form I-571)
10. Unexpired Employment Authorization Document issued by the INS which contains a photograph (INS Form I-688B)

List B:
1. State or Canadian driver's license or ID card with photo
2. Voter's registration
3. School I.D. card with photo
4. U.S. Military card or draft record or Military dependent's ID card
5. Native American tribal document

List C:
1. Social Security card
2. Certified copy of birth certificate
3. Native American tribal document
4. INS Form I-197

The penalties for failing to comply with this requirement begin at $250 for each unauthorized employee and can quickly reach $10,000 per violation. The possibility of incurring thousands of dollars in fines certainly justifies the extra trouble of compliance. For further information, contact the local INS office.

Quarterly Payroll Reports
Two quarterly payroll reports must be filed each calendar quarter. When filing employee forms, information regarding the payment schedule (usually forms and envelopes) for quarterly Payroll Reports will be mailed to the business address. The employer is required to understand the forms and to file the reports on or before the stated due date.

There are many accounting or bookkeeping services that offer to prepare payroll and to file the necessary forms. The exact extent of each bookkeeping service and fees charged can be obtained by calling businesses that specialize in bookkeeping services. (More information regarding book-keeping services and requirements is covered in Chapter 8, Bookkeeping Procedures.)

Form 941

The purpose of form 941 is to report to the IRS the amount of wages, federal income tax, and Social Security tax applicable to your business. This form tells the IRS what your payroll tax liability was for the quarter and when it was due for payment.

Note: Your payroll deposits should be made payable to your bank using Form 8109. On the back of Form 941, you will find a schedule showing how often the deposits need to be made.

Form 940

This report gives the year's total federal unemployment tax (FUTA) liability for the company's payroll. If you pay wages of $1,500 or more, or have at least one employee for part of a week in 20 different weeks, you are subject to file. All wages are subject to FUTA. If you owe more than $100 FUTA tax at the end of the calendar quarter, you must deposit the tax with an authorized bank by using the federal tax deposit coupon that will be sent to you by the IRS. The annual return, Federal Form 940, must be filed by January 31of the next year.

Form W-2

Employers are responsible for reporting payroll information to the Social Security Administration and to employees with W-2 forms.

Note: Owners of sole-proprietorships and partnerships cannot be classified as employees. Owners of corporations, however, can. These forms are to be sent to the Social Security Administration, not the IRS at the end of the year.

State Requirements

Each state has different reporting requirements. Check with your state government offices, along with city and county offices, for specific requirements. Ignorance is not considered an excuse.

Unemployment Insurance

Unemployment Insurance is a fund established by law to pay benefits to employees who lose their jobs though no fault of their own. All unemployment insurance funds are paid by employers in the form of unemployment insurance taxes.

Your company is liable for unemployment as soon as you hire an employee. Some non-profit, agricultural and domestic employers have slightly different standards. Check your state's requirements.

If an employee files for unemployment, an employer may contest, stating that the employee is not entitled to unemployment insurance.

If the employee is at fault for the termination, he/she may be refused unemployment payments, thus saving the company a claim. The burden of proof is on the employer based on documentation of performance and the reason for termination. All of this should be in writing and in the file of the employee prior to letting the employee go.

Worker's Compensation
Worker's Compensation is insurance that employers must obtain to provide coverage for employee medical costs and compensation for time missed from work due to a job-related injury or occupational disease. All premium costs are paid by the employer.

Employers are responsible for the coverage of both full-time and part-time employees, as well as in contract laborers in some cases. Before a contract laborer begins working for you, it is important to discuss the subject of insurance coverage, especially worker's compensation coverage. For example, if you hire a painter to paint your home and barn, and he falls off a ladder and is injured, you could be responsible for the medical bills and lost income due to his inability to earn a living. That is, unless his company (e.g. Joe's Paint and Repair) has insurance coverage including worker's compensation. It is in your best interest to ask to see a copy of the insurance binder before you hire an independent contractor.

Many state horse associations and councils are working to bring insurance rates for worker's compensation down for the horse industry. The American Horse Council, along with associated state councils, is working with legislators on government policies that will affect the horse industry.

Check your state's requirements for worker's compensation and filing dates. Check with your state horsemen's association for equine-specific information regarding worker's compensation.

There are other responsibilities that you as an employer need to be concerned with. If you are large enough to have 20 employees or more, you have to comply with "COBRA" (the Consolidated Budget Reconciliation Act of 1985). This new requirement concerns employer-provided group health plans. There are also employer posting requirements. The posters range from Anti-Discrimination, Safety, to Equal Opportunity.

Managing employees is very different from riding and enjoying horses. The decision to hire full- or part-time employees is a large step for some equine businesses and all options should be considered carefully.

WHEN, WHY AND HOW TO COMPUTERIZE YOUR HORSE RECORDS

If it seems like everything is being computerized these days, you're right. Computers can actually make life easier, when we choose the right equipment and learn to use it properly. The horse industry is no exception and computers are used more now than ever.

Computer magazines report that approximately 49% of all homes in the United States now have a computer. Computer sales are brisk. As of the year 2000 an estimated 26 million homes have computers and many children will have their own Barbie® or Hot Wheels® logo computers. Having a computer is a necessity of life for many people, and many of them are horse-owners.

Computers can be entertaining, time-saving and frustrating. Many of the newer computers are fast enough and have ample memory to handle your demanding needs. Information about purchasing your first computer can be obtained from magazines, buying guides and talking with friends. Many people watch the local newspapers for computers advertised with special discounts or coupons with the options they want on their computer. A good rule of thumb is that the extra hardware you purchase may be a good investment, but the added software is usually not specific to your needs. Since most software programs are built to run on the "Windows®" operating system you will want Windows® specific software, everything else may or may not be of use to you, so know your version of Windows®, plus memory and speed capabilities. Buy only those software packages the fit your system and needs.

Business owners have to keep meticulous records; horse-owners need to keep accurate records too. Keeping good records is a necessary part of horse ownership. Besides keeping accurate health records, shoeing schedules, feeding notes, show or race data and a training log, there are expenses and major equipment investments. These records can be a great resource to any training program or breeding ventures. A good program will help track time invested for recreational riding programs or provide added

"A horse cannot gain weight if not fed with extra fodder during the night; a man cannot become wealthy without earnings apart from his regular salaries."

Chinese

Proverb

information to insert into the buyers' packets when horses are sold.

Much of the cost of software is directly related to the limited-use license and the honesty of the people who buy and use the software. Computer software designers make it difficult to generate unauthorized copies of the software, but it is still possible. Honesty is still the best policy to keep the price of all software down. The cost of the software should be seen as an investment. It is a tool that may be used for several hours each week for years to come.

One of the most important features to look for in a software provider of horse-related software is the length of time they have been in business – the computer software business. You wouldn't send your favorite colt to a trainer who just hung out his shingle, would you? The length of time a software company has been servicing customers acts as a guide to how they will be able to serve you. It takes time to listen to what people need in the horse industry, learn how they want to keep records and yes, even to work out the bugs. Because of the abundant combinations of hardware, monitors, peripherals, printers and software, it takes time to ensure compatibility.

Customer service is a very important asset when purchasing any computer or software. It is important to understand the availability and limitations of the service provided before purchasing software. It is reasonable to assume that most customer service representatives are competent, however, the consumer still has to take the responsibility to read the documentation and ask appropriate questions.

In addition to customer service, you want to ensure that the software is "user friendly." That means it is easy for you to use. Some softwares offer on-screen prompts, easy pull-down menus and lots of written documentation in a ".doc" file included in the software or a complete User's Guide in the form of a book. Some people learn better by reading information and others learn best by jumping in and using the product. Knowing what type of learner you are, combined with your computer experience, will help you make the best software decisions.

If "the check is in the mail" is the most common lie in our society, then "one size fits all" is the second most common lie. Look for the size of software that best fits your needs. If you are afraid of making an error, err on the side of purchasing a little more computer or programming than you think you need. To do otherwise would be like buying a pair of jeans that are too small, with the intention of losing weight to get into them.

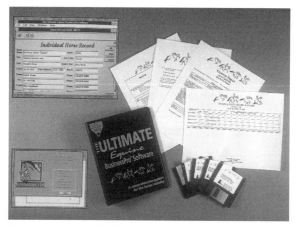

Most people who own horse-related businesses tend to develop their own manner of doing business and keep-

Computers are helping some equine operations become more profitable. Learn how to pick the most efficient system for your business.

ing records. Unlike other industries, there are no set business formulas. When a business owner is operating two separate types of businesses (like a sale barn and a training facility), or are managing their business in an otherwise atypical manner, they may have to consider purchasing additional programming. Having a program that is highly productive will save time and is worth the additional expense.

Software Features to Consider

1. Horse records should include: basic ownership and contact information, feed and exercise schedule, vet records, farrier records, show records and training records. Additional records may include: daily vet or training records, race, trail or endurance records, pedigree, stallion reports or breeding reports.

2. Financial records vary widely. Choices include: checkbook with basic accounting expense and income, profit and loss records. Business accounting should include: invoicing by customer and/or by horse for percentage billing of syndicated horses, profit and loss reports, and track mileage or travel expenses, a way to track continuing education, manage fixed asset and depreciation, and the ability to track time spent with a client.

3. Only a few horse-related software programs have integrated word-processing and address book or database capabilities. Wordprocessing allows the user to type letters, contracts or other documents. A good program is one that allows you to print lists, labels and merge with the wordprocessor. A software program which contains wordprocessing and some form of data management will save you time because you will not have to keep switching back and forth between different programs.

4. In the horse industry, it is vital to keep track of events, horse shows, farrier appointments and more. It is important to keep information in one handy place, like a calendar section. It should be printable and be referred to often.

5. Employee records are important to business owners. This should include hire and review dates, current pay schedules and a running record of vacation times and absences.

Flexibility is key to good software because all horse operations are managed differently. Computers should enhance productivity and give you more time to enjoy your horses. However, computers are not magic. The old adage is also true of computers, "garbage in results in garbage out." It takes time to input information before the computer and software can work for you. Also, make sure you make back-up copies of your information and save your work often in case of electrical or mechanical failures. Computers do not "crash" and lose information very often, but it is devastating when it happens.

When researching computer software, look into the availability of demos or limited use sample products. Each software company has their own theories and practices on demos.

Recently someone told me she downloaded a demo version from the Internet. The software demo needed more memory than her computer had available. She downloaded the demo and it locked-up her whole system.

Know the software specifications and make sure it matches your computer. Also, downloaded software can contain viruses. Your best bet is to understand the demo program completely. Read software product reviews and product brochures, then ask a lot of questions.

It helps to compare computer software features. Don't just look for a product with the most bells and whistles check that the software you choose has the options that will help you be more productive. Make sure the reports you are interested in keeping or putting in each horse's files are printable. These reports should contain all the information you desire and also be easy to read. Many programs provide extra options that allow you to input pictures or your own logo.

Software ownership is a lot like a marriage. Easy to get into and difficult to get out of because once you register your software - it's yours and returns are almost unheard of in the software industry. Software can be a valuable asset to a large equine business or an enjoyable way to keep records for a back-yard horseman. When you find yourself in the market for computer software, it pays to do your home-work. Select a program that is easy to use and best serves your needs.

EQUINE BUSINESSES AND TAXES

The form of horse businesses is very important; however, from a tax standpoint, the EXISTENCE of the business is probably the most important aspect of its business standing. Owning and keeping horses is very expensive. It is natural that horse owners would want to deduct as many of the expenses as possible. In years past (prior to the 1986 Tax Reform Act), the horse industry was notorious for its tax shelters. The business was also appealing to many wealthy horse lovers who benefited from the deductions. The Internal Revenue Service (IRS) targeted the horse industry for review and established unique standards and regulations to prevent abuses. The question became whether the horse enterprise was a business or a hobby?

Section 183 of the Internal Revenue Code provides that an individual or a Subchapter S corporation cannot deduct expenses that are greater than the income from an activity, if that activity is "not engaged in for profit." This provision is referred to as the "hobby loss" provision. It means that losses from a horse activity cannot be deducted against income from other sources unless that horse activity is a "business" and not a "hobby."

It is very common for horse owners to begin as hobbyists. They enjoy riding, buy a horse and then become addicted. Initially, their interest in horses is financed by their other income. As the new owner's activities multiply and expand, expenses increase. The point is reached when the horse owner asks, "When can I deduct these expenses?" The answer under the tax law is, "When your horse activities become a business and not a hobby."

Under the law, hobby losses are deductible only to the extent of income from a hobby activity, and are thus, very limited. The ultimate question in business versus hobby cases is whether the taxpayer entered into and continued the activity with the OBJECTIVE OF MAKING A PROFIT. Of course, it is easy to say that any horse activity had a profit-making objective. The Internal Revenue Service has established tests, other than the mere statement of the horse owner, to establish whether an activity had a valid objective of making a profit.

"Those who look down eventually get there."

Kip Rosenthal

The Two of Seven Presumption

The two of seven presumption was formulated by the Internal Revenue Service for exclusive application to horse activities. The Tax Code provides that if an activity shows two profit years within a seven-year period (starting with the first profit year), the activity will be presumed to be a business venture. This "two of seven" rule only creates a presumption that the horse activity is a business, and the IRS can attempt to rebut the presumption by taking the position that the activity was really a hobby. If this occurs, the burden is on the IRS to show that the facts and circumstances still indicate that there was "no profit motive" despite the fact that the horse person made a profit two years out of seven in the activity. Other tests and factors are used by the IRS and the Courts to determine whether a profit motive is truly present in the horse activity so the applicability of the "two of seven" can be determined. There are nine (9) factors in the Internal Revenue Service's regulations, used to determine if a horse activity is engaged in "for profit".

These factors are as follows:

1. The manner in which the activity is conducted. It is essential to keep good books and records and use businesslike methods.
2. The horse person's expertise, or that of his/her advisors, is examined. Research and study into the economics of the horse activity by the horse person or the advisors, and the utilization of this information in the conduct of the activity are evidence of a profit motive.
3. The time and effort expended in the activity are important. Devoting considerable personal time to the horse activity, especially if the activity does not have substantial personal or recreational aspects, can indicate the horse person's intent to make a profit. Partial or total withdrawal from another occupation to devote time to the horse operation, may be evidence that it is engaged in for profit.
4. The expectation that the assets used in the horse activity may appreciate in value. The IRS regulations provide that the term "profit" includes appreciation in the value of assets, including land, used in the activity.

Thus, even if no profit is derived from the current operations, an overall profit may result if the appreciation in value of the horses, the land, or other assets used in the horse activity is taken into account, along with the current income from the activity.

5. The taxpayer's success in similar operations is a factor to consider. If the taxpayer has made similar unprofitable horse activities profitable in the past, a profit motive could be present in the current operation.

6. The taxpayer's history of income or losses from the activity, including the two of seven year test, is another important factor. Internal Revenue Service regulations provide that a SERIES OF PROFIT YEARS is strong evidence that the horse activity is engaged in for profit. It is acknowledged that a series of loss years during the starting stages of a horse operation is not unusual. However, if losses continue beyond the period normally required to make similar operations profitable, this can lead to a conclusion that the activity is not engaged in for profit. Unforeseen circumstances, such as disease, natural disaster, or a depressed market, can be taken into account under this factor.

7. The amount of occasional profit, if any, earned by the horse operation is also examined. The ratio of profits to losses is an important element in this factor. It is quite easy to lose money and quite difficult to make money in the horse business. The IRS regulations provide that an occasional small profit from the activity which generates large losses will not be determinative that the activity is a business. However, the regulation also provides that "an opportunity to earn a substantial ultimate profit in a highly speculative venture is ordinarily sufficient to indicate that the activity is engaged in for profit, even though losses or occasional small profits are actually generated." This statement seems to apply directly to the horse business.

8. The financial status of the taxpayer is another factor. If the taxpayer does not have substantial income from other sources, this could indicate that his horse operation is engaged in for profit.

"God forbid that I

should go to any

heaven in which

there are no

horses."

R.B.

Cunningname

-Graham,

in a letter to

President

Theodore

Roosevelt

9. The elements of personal pleasure or recreation are the final factor. IRS regulations provide that personal motives in carrying on an activity may indicate that the activity is not engaged in for profit, especially when recreational or personal elements are involved. However, an activity will not be treated as a hobby merely because the taxpayer has purposes in addition to making a profit. In other words, it is fine to enjoy the horses, provided other factors indicate the presence of a profit-motive.

According to the Internal Revenue Service, any one of these factors is not more important than another. All of the factors are considered in determining whether the activity qualifies as a "business" for tax purposes or whether it is a "hobby."

Cases interpreting and deciding whether particular operations are businesses or hobby activities are often decided by the United States Tax Court. The following cases show how the nine factors given above weigh in the analysis of horse operations that involve the business versus hobby issue.

Mills v. Commissioner (T.C. Memo 1990-432) This case involved a physician who initially bought an Arabian horse for his daughter, became interested in breeding Arabians and ultimately owned 69 horses over a ten-year period. The Tax Court held against the taxpayer's contention that this breeding operation was a business. The Court reviewed the nine factors and found that they were not present in the doctor's favor. It found that he did not carry on the activity in a business-like manner, he made poor breeding decisions, did not keep good records, made no attempt to cut expenses or maximize income. His large income from his medical practice allowed him to operate at a loss, and his personal contact with the operation was in connection with its more pleasurable aspects.

Abbene v. Commissioner (T.C. Memo 1998-330) In this recent case the taxpayer was unsuccessful. In this case the taxpayer and his daughter ran a thoroughbred sport horse operation that had losses of $180,000 over three years. Although the taxpayer spent a substantial amount of time in the operation, the facts that he and his daughter were inexperienced, had no formal business plan and the father's large income influenced the Tax Court's decision that this operation was a hobby and not a business.

Haun v. Commissioner (T.C. Memo 1998-349) This case involved an employee of a telephone company who trained and sold roping horses. The taxpayer lost approximately $80,000 in two years during which he only earned $150,000 in outside earnings. Although the evidence showed that Mr. Haun was a life-long horseman who had consulted accountants and other experts, the Tax Court ruled that he failed to prove that it was his intent to make the roping horse activity profitable. The court found that the operation was a hobby and thus the taxpayer was liable for the income tax deficiency claimed by the IRS.

Stephens v. Commissioner (T.C. Memo 1990-376) In this case the taxpayer won. The Tax Court found that the taxpayer's operation was a business. Stephens was a full-time employee of the Ford Motor Company who decided to raise Quarter Horses. He had previously studied vocational agriculture and had worked with horses on his family's farm when he was young. When Stephens started his breeding operation, he consulted professionals who helped him formulate a business plan. He concentrated his efforts in establishing a small, quality broodmare operation. The taxpayer kept excellent records of every event of significance to his business. Mr. Stephens devoted substantial time and effort to the operation, both before and after work and on weekends. The Court was impressed that not all of Mr. Stephen's participation was pleasurable when it stated in its opinion that, "on those occasions when he had to sleep in the barn in order to be near a foaling mare, he must have concluded that the enjoyment was completely eliminated."

Perry and Hofer v. Commissioner (T.C. Memo 1997-417) This is an example of a case where the taxpayers' business-like conduct of their boarding and breeding operation, their meticulous record keeping, and their experience in the industry successfully won the case for them. Although in this case the taxpayers had full-time outside employment, the Court found that their other income ($100,000 annually) was not enough to shelter the losses from the horse operation. In addition to the taxpayers' meticulous record-keeping, the Tax Court was impressed by the fact that they also performed all of the daily chores in caring for the horses. The Court found that the taxpayer's engaged in their horse operation with an "actual and honest objective of making a profit."

Morley v. Commissioner (T.C. Memo 1998-312) In this case the question before the Tax Court was whether a dentist who earned $128,000 per year could properly deduct the losses sustained in his Arabian horse-breeding operation. The Court held that the dentist had properly deducted the expenses since the horse-breeding operation was a business and not a hobby. In its decision, the Court discussed several factors that influenced its decision: first, that the dentist conducted the operation in a business-like manner, keeping extensive records, maintaining current business plans, marketing the operation, and keeping separate bank accounts on the horse business; second, the taxpayer had made up for his inexperience by consulting experts in the horse-breeding business; third, that the dentist devoted substantial personal time to the operation and performed much of the necessary, and somewhat unpleasant labor

Raising and training horses comes under special limitations by the IRS and every horseowner should know the rules.

connected therewith; and finally, that the dentist was intending that his horse-breeding operation would provide for his retirement.

Seebold v. Commissioner (T.C. Memo 1988-183) In this case the Tax Court found that the taxpayers' operation was a business operated with the intention of making a profit even though it had shown no profit. The Seebolds became interested in Appaloosa horses, first for pleasure, then later as a business. The taxpayers consulted with several knowledgeable horse people when starting their activity. The Tax Court reviewed the nine factors in the regulations and found in favor of the taxpayers. The Court found that the operation was conducted in a business-like manner, the Seebolds had worked hard to develop their expertise in the horse business more than 40 hours a week devoted to the horse activity. There was the potential for one of the taxpayer's horses to appreciate in value through extensive training, thus ultimately increasing the amount of stud fee that could be charged and the value of the offspring; the Seebold's losses were predictable start-up losses and, although no profit had been made, they were projecting a modest profit in 1987. The taxpayer's income from other sources was modest when compared with the losses generated by the horse operation. This fact coupled with the Seebold's intention to make their Appaloosa activity a source of income in later years, suggested that a profit motive existed. Finally, the Court was influenced by the facts that the taxpayers did not operate the activity for pleasure or recreation, by the way they conducted the operation, a great deal of effort, devotion, and hard work was necessary.

From these cases, it is very apparent that there is no easy test for determining whether a horse operation will qualify as a business. Each case is judged on its individual facts and circumstances, applying the nine factors found in the IRS regulations. In all cases where an operation is challenged by the IRS as being a "hobby" rather than a "business" a key element seems to be how the taxpayer actually conducts the operation. If basic business principals including complete records, proper and current business plans, marketing, and other similar factors are present, the taxpayer's chance of success is greatly improved. The Tax Court also looks at the taxpayer's experience or, if the person is inexperienced, at his/her attempts at becoming educated in the conduct of the particular horse operation. In fact, in the recent case of Drummond v. Commissioner, the United States Court of Appeals, Fourth Circuit, reversed the Tax Court's decision that the taxpayer, whose horse operation was found to be a hobby, could not defend his case based on his reliance on the professional advice of his tax advisor. The U.S. Court of Appeals ruled that the Tax Court's decision was wrong and that since the taxpayer's advisor had been fully informed about the conduct of the horse operation in question, that the taxpayer could rely in good faith on the advisor's opinion. Again, obtaining expert professional assistance is not only necessary but can pay great dividends if challenged by the IRS.

Passive Activity Losses

Probably the implementation of the limits on passive activity losses in the Tax Reform Act of 1986 has had the most direct impact on the horse industry. For a number of years, the horse business has benefited from the investment capital in it by people who, because of their high tax brackets, needed to shelter large sums of income. The substantial deductions from horse operations afforded these individuals the opportunity to avoid significant tax liability. The horse business benefited from the infusion of capital and, in many cases, from the lack of concern over the amount of losses and deductions generated by the business. Obviously, in these cases, profit was not a motive.

In Section 469 of the Act, Congress virtually eliminated these tax shelter benefits. This section provided that deductions from passive business activities may not be deducted from other income. The large investment in horse operations as a tax shelter became unattractive to high-bracket taxpayers, and the horse industry lost a major source of capital investment.

The Internal Revenue Code now provides that a taxpayer must "materially participate" in the activity for the activity to be "nonpassive" and to exclude it from the passive activity limitations. "Material participation" is defined as regular, continuous and substantial involvement in the operation of the activity. This concept is relatively new and has not yet been fully clarified and defined by court decisions or regulations.

The Internal Revenue Service has adopted some regulations that serve as guidelines to aid in determining when a horse person's participation in an activity will be deemed "material." Among the standards is testing the number of hours the taxpayer devotes to the activity. For example, at least 100 hours of participation in the activity is required during the tax year. Very recently, the IRS proposed regulations that attempt to explain whether various equine activities will be treated as one activity for the purpose of computing the 100-hour test. These proposed regulations address the problems of taxpayers whose equine activities include a breeding business and a separate training or boarding enterprise and who seek to combine their hours spent at each to satisfy the test. The regulations provide that whether activities can be combined or must be treated as separate activities depends on the relevant facts and circumstances, including: (1) similarities of the types of the activities, (2) control, (3) common ownership, (4) geographical locations of the activities, and (5) the interdependencies of the activities. The new regulations and their applicability require current expert analysis and advice. Other standards require the taxpayer to be active at least five years or material participation by the owner out of the last ten years.

Recently, amendments to the passive loss rules have been proposed, making them more readily available. One proposal still requires that the taxpayer participate materially in the horse business, the new law would allow a more reasonable calculation of the time requirement necessary to satisfy the passive-loss rules. The activities of other participants in the horse business, such as partners or other shareholders, can be combined to meet the requirements. Also, the proposed law would allow the taxpayer to include all management time in the horse business, such as supervising employees, trainers or farm managers in the time calculation.

The Internal Revenue Code requires a significant commitment of time by the taxpayer in some substantial activity in order to avoid the passive activity limitation. This area, like most other areas of the horse business, requires expert consultation. The regulations and interpretations are complex and technical. The counsel of professionals is necessary if the taxpayer is going to pursue avoidance of Section 469. While it may not be necessary for the taxpayer to have "dirt under his fingernails and manure on his boots," it certainly wouldn't hurt.

"Any farmer can rope, but it takes a real cowboy to pull his slack."

Jack Kyle

BOOKKEEPING PROCEDURES

Since business people and "hobby" horse-owners are under the watchful eye of the Internal Revenue Service, it is imperative that individuals who wish to be successful in the horse industry keep good records. It is important to develop an accurate, functional, easy system of record-keeping prior to starting up a horse business.

All equine businesses should have the following items in their bookkeeping system:
- Detailed operating statements
- Comparison of current results to budgets and prior periods
- Financial statements
- Information for tax returns and reports to regulatory agencies
- Sufficient control to protect assets and detect errors.

The prospective equine business owner needs to review the following items:
- Form of business chosen: Sole Proprietorship, Partnership, Corporation or LLC
- Industry standards
- Number of employees, now and in the future
- Requirements of the location, if the location would ever move or have a second location.

Experts recommend that the first step in setting up a book-keeping system is selecting of the tax year or year-end system. The term tax year refers to the annual accounting period. The selection of a year-end is sometimes dictated by form of ownership. For instance, a regular corporation has no specific restriction, while an S corporation or part-nership usually must follow a calendar year. Be sure to consult with an expert before making a decision, because tax laws tend to change.

The second step is to select a method of accounting. The two most common are the cash method and accrual method. The cash method recognizes income and expens-es based on when cash is received or disbursed; it provides the most flexible means of deferring taxable income into future tax years. The accrual method recognizes income

"Horses change lives. They give our young people confidence and self esteem. They provide peace and tranquility to troubled souls — they give us hope."

Toni Robinson

and expenses based on when income is earned or an obligation to pay a debt is incurred; it generally provides better
matching of revenue and expenditures.

The green ledgers or accounting journals found at office
supply stores can provide an inexpensive organized format
to begin keeping records. Some of these ledgers even have
suggested column headings to remind you to keep track
of the date the money came in, who it is from, the amount
received and if there is any sales tax to be collected. The
cash paid out side of the ledger has more columns which
track not only the amount paid out, but to whom, even suggestions for tracking where the money is being spent, (e.g.
salaries and wages, telephone and rent, office supplies,
advertising, taxes and more.)

During the start-up stage of your business you want to
contact various consultants including: an accountant, the
Small Business Administration (or Service Corps of Retired
Executives, SCORE), and your local community college
or continuing education programs. Make sure that your
accounting method fits your needs. You may want to add
special entries into your ledger for the equine-related
publications you subscribe to, memberships including:
American Quarter Horse Association (AQHA), International
Arabian Horse Association (IAHA), USA Equestrian,
American Horse Council (AHC), etc. and remember to
allow for special promotional expenses, such as showing
horses.

Once a method of accounting is adopted, it can be
changed only with IRS permission. Permission is usually
granted in the case of switching from the cash method
to the accrual, and routinely denied in the reverse.

In the horse industry the most common mistake made when
setting up a bookkeeping system happens when the owner
doesn't understand the importance of a bookkeeping system and ignores the need. Such business owners tend to
use the shoebox method, allowing receipts and invoices to
build up in piles or shoved into boxes. The second mistake
is overkill. Although not nearly as frequent, overkill occurs
when the owner invests a fortune in complicated hardware
and software, then realizes it is too complicated to utilize
effectively or it doesn't meet the needs of the business owner.

Today's business world offers more options with respect to who will keep the books. The three most prominent options are:

Keep them yourself: This should be the choice if the business is extremely simple, has few employees, a single location and if it requires a small amount of time. If this method is chosen, accountants recommend using a calendar year and a cash-accounting method. This simplifies the use of the "Schedule C" form used in tax preparation.

Bookkeeping services: These services usually compile receipts, canceled checks and check stubs, then process the data and prepare financial statements. If the system is simple and outside reports are infrequent, a bookkeeper may be all that is needed. When choosing any type of bookkeeping service, make sure they understand the horse business, tax regulations that apply to this business and that you are knowledgeable enough to check their work.

Record keeping is a vital part of building a firm foundation for your business and will make a business successful over the long haul.

Bookkeeper/Accountant: More complex systems generally require an accountant. In today's economy, it is possible to find someone willing to work evenings or part-time to help with the costs of starting a business. Again, make sure the accountant you hire understands the horse business and the tax regulations that apply to this industry. Then you need to be willing to become knowledgeable enough to check their work.

COLLECTION OF DEBTS

People involved in the horse business, just like those involved in other businesses, often have trouble collecting debts owed to them. Whether it is bills for boarding or training horses, shoeing, veterinary services, feed bills, or other facets of the horse business, getting paid can be a problem. Collection of debts is more laborious in difficult economic times. Unlike other businesses the horse industry often does not allow many discretionary purchases. Horses must be fed, cared for and treated by veterinarians. These necessary services, even in hard times, require that the provider be paid.

There are a number of methods available in attempting to collect debts. These range from hiring an attorney or collection agency to writing letters or making the calls on your own. As expected, the more expensive way of debt collection is by utilizing the services of a professional. Attorneys will charge either, an hourly fee or a percentage of the amount collected, plus costs in either case. Hourly rates for lawyers can range from a lower range of $70 to $120 per hour to higher amounts of $150 to $200 per hour. Regarding the selection of an attorney, a client should always know and agree to the lawyer's fees prior to actually retaining the attorney. Percentage fees by attorneys can also range from lows of ten percent (10%) to twenty-five percent (25%), to a high of forty percent (40%). The client must know and agree to, preferably in writing, any percentage fee to avoid later difficulties.

Collection agencies generally use a fee structure based on a percentage of what is collected. It is quite common to see a graduated scale of fee arrangement used by these agencies.

Whether you use an attorney or a collection agency, you - the client, will be responsible for the payment of all costs. These will vary depending on whether or not a suit is filed or if there is difficulty in serving the debtor with legal process.

In cases where the person decides to use professional collectors, a number of things must still be done by the client.

> "Stable thinking is the ability to say, 'neigh.'"
>
> *Source*
>
> *unknown*

1. First, the creditor must provide the necessary evidence to prove the case. This can be done by furnishing bills, contracts, purchase orders and other documents common in business transactions to show that there was a sale or that services were performed and the debtor was notified of the amount that was due for the goods or services. Copies of any correspondence, or telephone memorandums, should also be organized and furnished to the professional collector for later use in preparing the case.

2. Second, the client should make himself available to meet with the agency, or the lawyer, to assist in preparing and organizing the case against the debtor. This can also mean appearing in court and testifying at the trial, if necessary.

3. Third, the creditor should keep an open mind in listening to the professional's suggestions on settlement or resolution of the claim. Although most business people want to have every penny due them, this is not always possible. The old adage, "A bird in the hand is worth two in the bush," has wisdom and merit in many cases. Professional collectors can often evaluate chances of recovery and negotiate settlements better than amateurs. In many cases, a professional is best able to gain maximum dollars from the debtors. These are some of the main reasons for considering professional assistance in collecting larger debts.

In contracting any debtor, all creditors must be aware of the existence and effect of both Fair Debt Collection Acts that have been enacted by Congress and the various states. These acts are designed to ensure fair debt collection practices. Although they principally apply to collection agencies, they also apply to creditors who attempt to collect the debt in any other name other than their own. Some of the state acts expand the definition of a "debt collector" to include any creditor who is attempting to collect a debt. The laws set forth very strict definitions for creditors and debt collectors and provide both civil and criminal penalties for violation.

The basic proposes of these laws is to eliminate abusive debt collection practices, and protect consumers against debt collection abuses. The laws require that notice of the debt be given the debtor, and sets forth restrictions against threatening or abusive behavior by creditors in attempting to collect. Also, communications with third parties by creditors is subject to strict regulations. Any creditor who attempts to collect his or her own debts must be aware of the existence of the laws stemming from the Fair Debt Collection Acts and avoid any prohibited conduct.

Of course, the business person has other options available to him to collect debts. The most common collection attempt is to contact the debtor and remind them of the bill and try to discover why the bill has not been paid. If the reason for non-payment is dissatisfaction with the service or merchandise, perhaps some adjustment or minor accommodation will lead to payment. If financial difficulty is the reason for failure to pay the debt, a method of payment over a period of time or receiving a promissory note can lead to satisfaction of the debt. (A promissory note would have to include when the

Every horse breeder knows that it's selling the horses and receiving complete payment for each that takes time and effort.

payment would be made along with interest and attorney's fees if a collection suit is necessary.) Obviously, these methods are successful only if the parties are dealing in good faith and are not trying to ignore or avoid paying the obligation.

Even when it becomes apparent that the debtor is simply trying to avoid paying, the creditor still has some options available to try to collect the debt short of hiring professionals. The most common is the Small Claims Court. This court has limited jurisdictions ranging from $1,000 to $5,000. Local laws should be consulted when considering the filing of a case.

Small Claims Courts have many advantages to the general public including the modest cost in filing a suit, and the

"The most important principle is to want to do it, to be committed before you start off to getting to the other side of every fence every time... If you are not certain about whether you want to go or not, do yourself and your horse a favor — don't start."

Capt. Mark Phillips, The Horse and Hound Book of Eventing.

prompt hearing of cases. A big advantage to these courts is that usually attorneys are not allowed to represent parties in the court. People represent themselves and present their own cases and defenses. This option can represent a considerable savings for a simple case with adequate documentation. The Small Claims Courts aims to present a fair and impartial verdict, without unnecessary delay and expense. The court proceeding or trial is less formal than the usual trial, with each side presenting his or her case. At the close of the presentation the court makes its ruling. Unlike more formal trials, when the parities leave the courtroom they know who won and who lost. The rulings are usually clear and understandable, and the parties have "had their day in court."

However, in all collection proceedings, whether professionally done or through the use of a small claims procedure, additional steps are often necessary for the winning party to collect the judgment. People are often surprised that the Court does not go out and collect what it ordered the creditor to pay. The court's job is to hear the evidence presented by both sides and, based on that evidence, make a decision. If a party sues a debtor and the courts rules that the debt is due and owing, it will grant the creditor a judgment in the amount of the debt, plus court costs. Attorney fees, in certain limited cases, especially where there was a contract between the parties or a promissory note that was the basis for the suit and which allowed for the court to assess the losing party with the winner's attorney fees are also awarded. Once this judgment is entered by the court, it is up to the winning party to collect. The judgment only gives the prevailing party the right to collect the amount of the judgment.

Common Collection Procedures
This chapter is not intended to be an exhaustive course on how to collect a debt, just to help you know how to get started and where to look for help. The laws of the states vary, and local laws must always be consulted. Also, it is recommended that professional advice be obtained before deciding on or attempting any legal proceedings or procedures. However, the following is a brief description of some of the common procedures available in collecting after obtaining a judgment:

1. **Levying on Property** – in most states, the real and personal property is subject to execution to apply to a judgment. However, the law provides certain exemptions on parts of the debtor's property, limiting the effect of this procedure to some extent. For example, there are exemptions and limitations on levying on a debtor's residence, on real estate that is subject to a homestead exemption (which in theory preserves a home for the debtor), and on personal property necessary for the debtor to support himself and his family. Also, a debtor's clothing, tools of the trade or profession, family mementos, and vehicles used for gainful employment are usually exempt from execution. Most state laws also exempt household goods up to a specific value from levy. State and federal law should always be consulted to determine limitations on levying on the property of a judgment debtor. Of course, property that is pledged or mortgaged prior to obtaining the judgment is taken subject to the mortgage. In other words, the security interest of the bank or other lender in a debtor's property is protected from execution in most cases. All non-exempt property that has not been previously pledged is subject to execution, including corporate stock, bank accounts, cash and bonds.

   The process for turning property which has been levied upon into cash to apply to satisfaction of the judgment is governed by law. Usually the sale is conducted by a sheriff or other official (or court appointed officer) and, after deducting the expenses of the sale, the proceeds are turned over to the judgment creditor to apply to the judgment. Again, state and federal laws must be consulted in determining both the method of execution and sale of seized property.

2. **Attachment** – is a legal process which allows a defendant's non-exempt property to be taken into custody to obtain jurisdiction over the property or to give security to satisfy a plaintiff's claim if he recovers a judgment.

   Attachment procedures are created by statute which must be strictly followed. It is a procedure that is used by attorneys and other professionals mainly to obtain jurisdiction over out-of-state party or to create security for a future judgment. Attachment is most commonly done prior to filing suit.

3. **Garnishment** – is a proceeding where a judgment creditor obtains property or money of the judgment debtor which is held by a third party. Most commonly, the "property or money" are wages or payments due, and the "third party" is the debtor's employer or one who owes him money for goods or services. Garnishment is a method of collecting to satisfy a judgment and requires strict compliance with the appropriate statutes.

As in the case of Attachment or Levy on Property, certain exemptions apply under both state and federal law to garnishment. These exemptions principally apply to wages and earnings of a debtor. The law seeks to avoid making a debtor completely destitute. Therefore, a certain percentage of his earnings are exempt from execution or garnishment. However, as to non-exempt earnings, garnishment can be a very effective method of collecting a judgment.

Briefly, a garnishment is accomplished by serving a legal document (sometimes call a "Writ of Garnishment") on the employer or other party who holds the money or property of the debtor. The employer or other party must respond to the court and the creditor within a certain period of time, stating how much of the debtor's money or property they are holding. After this response, the third party then must pay either into the court or to the debtor, depending on the state law, the non-exempt property of the debtor to be applied to the amount of the judgment. The law of some states provides that these Writs of Garnishment are continuing. This means that until the judgment is satisfied, the employer or third person must pay the non-exempt amount each payday or each time they possess any money or property of the debtor. Again, the laws of the states vary on the subject of garnishment, and a lawyer should be consulted. However, this is on of the most effective and common ways of collecting judgments.

In all collection proceedings there is one overriding matter that brings everything to a stop – bankruptcy. If a debtor files any form of bankruptcy during the state of collection proceedings, no further action can be taken. Exclusive jurisdiction over the debtor's financial affairs is taken over by the United States Bankruptcy Court, and its designated Trustee. All attempts to collect take the form of filing claims against the bankrupt estate. Secured claims, such as mortgages or deeds of trust, are given priority and are paid first. All other unsecured claims are paid out of the remaining assets, if any. In cases of bankruptcy, unsecured creditors are lucky to receive anything.

4. **The Agistor's Lien** – in the livestock business, including horses, there exists a legal right and procedure known as the AGISTOR'S LIEN. This is a statutory lien for the amount due to those who feed, herd, pasture, keep, board, or provide veterinary care to horses and other livestock. Agistor's liens are created by and interpreted under the laws of the various states. The laws of the particular state must be consulted to determine the existence and scope of its agistor's lien laws.The law of Colorado and most other states has long provided that an "agistor" has a lien against the livestock for the cost of the care provided to it. Included in this lien are costs of feeding, herding, pasturing, keeping, ranching, boarding of livestock, or for medical care provided to such livestock. If these costs are not paid by the animal's owner, the agistor can after following proper statutory procedure, sell the animal and apply the proceedings against the debt. The basic requirements to perfect an agistor's lien are:

   • Exclusive physical possession of the animal(s) on which the lien is claimed.
   • The animals is not stolen.
   • The agistor has no ownership interest in the animal(s) such as being a partner.

   Usually state law requires that the agistor's lien be filed with designated county or state officials, such as the Clerk and Recorder or the Secretary of State. After filing, the lien does not automatically force the debtor/owner to pay the amount of the lien. To enforce the lien and collect the amount due, the agistor generally must foreclose the lien. This means a lawsuit must be filed in a designated court, seeking an order of court that authorizes the agistor to sell the horse at a public sale within a certain period of time. For example, the Colorado statute gives the agistor no more than 45 days from the date of the court order to sell the animal. The law also requires the agistor to give the owner of the livestock to be sold, notice of the time and place of the sale. The procedure is not simple and its steps must be strictly followed. The costs of foreclosure by the agistor can be recovered against the horseowner. Anyone who owns horses, or is in the horse business, should know about agistor's liens and their effect. The agistor's lien can be a powerful tool for stablekeepers, veterinarians, and others.

Another method by which horses can be removed from the owner, by operation of law, is pursuant to a court order for cruelty and/or neglect. For horses to be removed from the owner action must be filed against the owner for cruelty. (Please see Chapter 14 Animal Abuse and Neglect Laws.)

Each state's law may have variations regarding the process, scope and use of the agistor's lien. The provisions of the law of each state must be reviewed when considering using the agistor's lien procedure. Since there are many strict procedures to follow, using an experienced attorney is recommended.

Collection of debts in all businesses and ventures can be very difficult and discouraging. Horseowners and business people like to think that those they do business with are as honest as the horses they love. This is not always the case. A basic understanding of available collection procedures, and the problems that can be encountered, is helpful. Remember, in most cases, get professional help and advice BEFORE problems arise.

BRAND INSPECTION LAWS AND HORSE OWNERSHIP

Many states, especially in the west, have brand inspection laws that govern the ownership and transfer of livestock, including horses. In Colorado, and in states with similar laws, ownership of livestock cannot be properly transferred without a brand inspection conducted by a state brand inspector. The purpose of these inspections is to verify the identity and ownership of the horse(s) being sold or transported.

The name "brand inspection" is somewhat confusing because even unbranded horses must be inspected when sold or transported over a certain distance from their home stable. The "brand inspection" includes both an inspection of the horse to see what, if any, brands it is marked with, but also includes a detailed physical description of the horse. Such as the horse's breed, color, gender, age, date of birth, approximate weight and markings.

A horse owner must contact the state brand board under three circumstances.
1. Whenever horses (cattle, mules or donkeys) are transported over 75 miles within the state
2. Any time horses (cattle, mules or donkeys) are transported across state lines
3. Any time there is a change of ownership! Any change of title at all. Both the buyer and the seller are equally liable for obtaining the brand inspection.

It is possible to get a permanent transportation card on a horse that is good for the duration of ownership. This permit is good anywhere in the continental United States. Exceptions are when transporting a horse to Alaska through Canada or to Hawaii. In those cases, it is necessary to get another permit the week of transport.

Items to Remember
1. Inspection is required regardless of whether or not the animal is branded.
2. Inspection is required on all classes of livestock (horses, cattle, mules or donkeys). Registration papers or lack of registry does not exempt inspection.

"Books are the quietest and most constant of friends; they are the most accessible and wisest of counselors, and the most patient of teachers."

Charles W. Eliot, The Happy Life

3. The definition of a brand for, the purpose of description, is a permanent mark on the hide of an animal registered with any state as a livestock brand. Tattoos are not brands.
4. Inspection is required at the point of origin, unless released by the local inspector.

Brand inspections are required when horses travel to more than a local show or are sold

Regulations

1. An inspection is required *every time* an animal is sold or purchased, or when any change of ownership occurs, regardless of whether or not the animal is transported after or prior to the sale.
2. An inspection is required when livestock is to be transported over 75 miles totally within the boundaries of the state, the exception being the permanent brand card.
3. Except in cases when the owner has a permanent brand card, an inspection is required every time livestock leaves the state regardless of the circumstances.
4. The owner of the horse obtaining a "PERMANENT TRAVEL CARD" may accomplish items 2 and 3, above. These cards are good for the entire time the horse is owned and are available at a slight additional cost from the state brand board. Brand inspectors welcome the opportunity to attend club/organization meetings to discuss brand inspection requirements and how permanent travel cards can be obtained.
5. Any time livestock is to be transported on a public road, proof of ownership should be available for

inspection by the State Patrol, law enforcement or a brand inspector.

6. Animals being transported by commercial haulers must have a "Bill of Lading" showing the point of origin, destination, number of head, color, gender, and the hot iron brands signed by the owner or agent of the stock.
7. Animals being transported by anyone other than the legal owner should have a letter or note from the owner authorizing that transport in conjunction with the inspection certificate.
8. Livestock crossing a state line must be accompanied by a current health certificate showing current vaccinations and a negative Coggins test. Contact your local veterinarian or the state veterinarian office for specific information.

Out-of-State Livestock Purchases

Several states do not have a livestock inspection law, and therefore a certificate of inspection cannot be obtained. Contact the local livestock market to inquire about state regulations.

Always get a valid bill of sale and a health certificate when purchasing animals in non-inspection states.

The requirements of a legal bill of sale are:
- Seller's name,
- Buyer's name,
- Complete description of the animal(s) being purchased. Color, gender, breed, markings, registration numbers, and/or brands
- Signature of the seller
- Signature of the buyer
- Signature of a witness residing in the county where the transaction takes place.
- Having a bill of sale notarized is not required, but probably a good idea in case a dispute arises.

The State Brand Board also has some jurisdiction over livestock after an Agistor's Lien has been filed. (Please refer to Chapter 9, *Collection of Debts*, in the section regarding Agistor's Liens.)

Inspection Fees Help Support the Horse Industry in Some States

Recent legislation in Colorado, patterned after laws in some other states, earmarks a portion of each brand inspection fee for support and promotion for the horse industry in the state. This modest amount provides an excellent source of funds to a board comprised of representatives of the various facets of the horse industry who use the money to support the industry.

The individuals at the Brand Board stress that they are not in the business of prosecuting violators, but are there to help. However, they will prosecute owners who knowingly do not comply with the state's rules. Jail time and fines are listed among the penalties.

Source: **Gary Shoun,** Commissioner, State Brand Board of Colorado.

CONTRACTS

The universal rule to which there can be no reasonable exception is to get all agreements *in writing*. In the horse business, or in any other business for that matter, agreements that are not in writing - oral contracts - are virtually impossible to enforce. In many instances, by statute, contracts that are not in writing are not enforceable. Examples of this include contracts for the sale of personal property over a certain sum of money (usually $500) and contracts for the sale of real estate.

This chapter examines the elements of a proper contract, the need for contracts, and how to analyze and understand common contracts. Other than for the sake of example and instruction, no forms of contracts are included here. Although some books on the market do report to contain examples of "do-it-yourself" contracts, this book is an exception. I firmly believe that any business person should have competent professional assistance before entering into a binding contract that could affect his or her business. Thus, no "cure-all" or universal forms are in this book.

We all know that we no longer live in a simple and straightforward time when "a person's word is his bond." Our world is both complex and legalistic, requiring formality and comprehensive contracts and agreements. The day of the handshake to seal a deal is gone. It has been replaced with reducing all agreements into writing which contain the rights and obligations of all parties and any other provisions that are agreeable to and part of the transaction. Today, expert assistance is necessary in formulating, crafting, and interpreting many of the complex business transactions in the horse industry.

Even in a situation that involves a less complex agreement or transaction, a written contract is vital. In the sale of a horse, boarding agreement, training contract or breeding transaction, written documentation is necessary for the protection of all parties.

Elements of a Contract

In law, there is much discussion concerning the elements of a contract. Elements means those terms that make up a

> "We have a choice: to plow new ground or let the weeds grow."
>
> *Virginia Department of Agriculture in a report in the late 1950s*

proper and legally enforceable contract. The "elements" also called "requirements," are:

FIRST: All contracts require an offer by one party who has the legal capacity and authority to make the contract.

SECOND: The offer is accepted by the other party.

THIRD: A "consideration" is something you give (e.g., money) or do (e.g., provide a service) in return for something else.

FOURTH: A meeting of the minds of the parties to the contract.

FIFTH: Reasonable certainty.

These five elements seem quite simple to understand and enforce, but they have been the subject of interpretation, controversy, dispute, and litigation for over 200 years. Since these elements are not as simple as they first appear, a more detailed discussion and analysis is appropriate.

An *offer* is legally defined as a proposal that, by its terms, is intended to become binding if the party to whom it is made accepts the offer. An offer can be to buy or sell a horse for a certain sum of money, to trade a horse for another horse or something else of value, to board a horse for a certain sum of money per month, to train a horse for a specific purpose, or to breed the other party's mare to a particular stallion for a fee. There are many other examples of "offers" in connection with horses.

"Legal capacity and authority to make a contract" refers mainly to age and mental state. In many states a minor (person under 18) is legally incapable of making a binding contract. A person who is insane, mentally retarded, or suffers the rages of a form of senile dementia, such as Alzheimer's disease, ordinarily lacks the mental ability to enter into a contract. This can also apply to an individual who is drunk, high on drugs, or very ill at the time the contract is made, or who doesn't understand the implications of the contract. This is known as "mental incompetence."

Legal authority to make a contract is important when a person is representing another. For example, if a trainer is asked to sell a horse while the owner is away on business and gives the trainer the necessary papers to transfer the horse, the trainer obtains the legal authority to make the sales contract on behalf of the owner. This creates a "principal" (the owner) and "agent" (the trainer) relationship.

When dealing with an owner's representative, a person is well-advised to get the specifics of the agent's authority in writing. Often this authority is expressed in a "Power of Attorney" which identifies the parties, sets out the agent's authority, and contains any limitations set by the owner. This paper may state the lowest price to be accepted and the terms to be considered. This document should also be notarized to make it more solid.

Acceptance is the next required element in a proper contract. This is simply saying "yes" to the offer. Agreeing to do, take, perform or act on what has been offered is "acceptance." The law requires that acceptance of an offer must be of identical terms of any other previously agreed upon offer before the agreement can be bound by the party who is accepting.

Consideration as a vital and necessary element of a contract can be defined as a promise to do something, not to do something, or anything in-between. It can be a promise to pay a certain sum of money, a promise to trade a certain item, forgiveness of an existing debt, or a promise not to sue or make a claim. In other words, almost any type or form of promise can satisfy the legal requirements of "consideration" in a contract.

Meeting of the minds simply means that all parties to the contract must understand and agree to the terms. The law requires that the parties know what they are getting into by entering into the contract. The rights, obligations, duties, and requirements of the contract must be known to and agreed upon by all parties.

Certainty is the fifth element of a proper contract. A contract must be sufficiently definitive and complete in its terms so that the parties know and understand their respective rights and obligations. These "rights and obligations" cannot be estimates or guesses on what the parties are agreeing to do. The terms must be such that all parties know the material elements of the contract; for example, how much money will be paid, when it will be paid, where it will be paid, to whom it will be given, when the object of the

"If you have built

castles in the air,

your work need

not be lost; that

is where they

should be.

Now put the

foundations

under them."

Henry David

Thoreau

contract will be delivered, where the delivery will occur, who will pay the transportation, etc. These are some examples of the requirement of "certainty" in a contract.

Without these five elements, preferably written on a dated sheet of paper and signed by the parties or their duly authorized representatives, there is no contract. There is no specific requirement as to the form of a contract; However, the elements must be properly included in the writing to make it an enforceable document.

With the passage of equine liability laws in the majority of states, these statutes now require contracts and agreements regarding equine activities to include specific language giving **notice** of the statute and the legal standards for which liability is, or is not, imposed on equine professionals. These laws are designed to place people on notice that equine professionals and others are not liable for the injury or death of participants in equine activities resulting from the inherent risks of equine activities (see Chapter 12 *Liability of Horsemen*). Although this statutory NOTICE would seem to be more appropriately included on a Release, Training Agreement, or similar document, the statutes direct that the language be included in all equine agreements.

Again, one should get professional advice before entering into any contract. The money spent on attorney's fees can be the greatest bargain any horse owner can receive. Not only can proper legal draftsmanship be obtained by using a qualified lawyer, but also many of the statutory pitfalls and traps can be avoided.

Points to remember when writing a contract

1. Every contract should have the date of creation or when it was signed. It should also have the dates that events are to happen or when specifics of the will contract take affect.
2. The body of the contract should include details that are to be understood by all parties: terms of payments, warranties, descriptions of the services to be rendered or animal being sold, and default statement (what happens if the terms of the agreement are not met.)
3. Signature(s) of the parties involved. This should reinforce that all parties have read and understand the

agreement. This may include contract information, phone numbers and addresses.

4. Include any required NOTICE provision required by state law for inclusion in contracts and agreements that involve equine activities.

Bills of Sale and Sales Contracts

Probably the most universal use of contracts or written agreements for a horse owner is in the area of horse sales. Most states require written bills of sale for horses. By statute, for the transaction to be legal, most states require that the seller give the buyer a written Bill of Sale containing specific information about the animal being sold, including the horse's age, color, sex, markings, brands or tattoos. The buyer's and seller's respective addresses are required, and some states require a statement from a state brand inspector that the information in the Bill of Sale is accurate. In all cases, the prospective buyer of a horse should be aware of the particular state's requirements before purchasing the horse.

In addition to a Bill of Sale, most horse sales involve a written sales agreement between the buyer and seller. This document contains the five elements of a contract (legal capacity, acceptance, consideration, meeting of the minds and reasonable certainty) and serves as the agreement that controls the transaction. Since these written sales agreements are so common and important in horse transactions, a review of the areas covered by this contract is important. Also, see the special section regarding auctions.

The first item to cover in the sales agreement is the identity of the parties. The full and correct address of the seller, together with information concerning registration of the horse, where appropriate, should be included. The registration certificate, if any, should show the registered owner to be the same person as the seller; and the agreement, or Bill of Sale, should provide for the execution and delivery of the certificate to the purchaser.

The full and correct name and address of the buyer should also be included in the sales agreement. If the horse will be financed or pledged as security for a debt (commonly, a portion of the purchase price of the animal), the exact name of the buyer, together with any trade names, should be included. For example, if the buyer does business as "Blackmore Farm," the proper designation of the purchaser in the contract and any security agreements covering the horse would be: John Doe, dba Blackmore Farm. Of course, if the buyer is a partnership or a corporation, the name of the entity would be included as the buyer.

The sales agreement should also contain a full and complete description of the horse, including the horse's name, year of birth, sex, color, sire, dam, and any appropriate breeding information. In the case of a broodmare, the stallion's name, date of last breeding, payment of stud fee, and any other appropriate data should be included.

Most sales contracts contain provisions concerning the health of the particular horse. Pre-purchase physical examinations by a veterinarian of the buyer's choosing are quite common. Veterinarians are able to examine the horse for physical soundness and, in most cases, for physical fitness for particular purposes. In general, the following categories are covered in equine pre-purchase examinations:

- Description of the horse (including name, age, color, brand or tattoo, markings, height, weight, and rectal temperature)
- Symmetry of the horse (head, neck, body, legs, and hoofs)
- Eyes (reflexes, lids, mucous membranes, cornea, ophthalmoscopic examination, etc.)
- Nasal and paranasal (air flow, odor, noise, mucous membranes, percussion, and exudate [any abnormal fluid oozing from tissue])
- Pharynx, larynx, and trachea (palpation, cough induction, noise, auscultation [listening with a stethoscope for sounds produced in the body, especially in the heart and lungs] at rest, auscultation after exercise, and auscultation after recovery)
- Cardiovascular (pulse, both rate and quality, jugular vein, auscultation at rest, after exercise and after recovery)
- Pulmonary (respiratory rate, quality, auscultation at rest and after exercise)
- Musculoskeletal (examination of legs, palpation, flexion and response to hoof testers)
- Mouth (lips, gums, tongue, teeth, mucous membranes,

odor, bite and age by teeth)
- Digestive (auscultation or stomach sounds, rectal exam and inspection of feces)
- Urogenital (external inspection/palpation and rectal examination)
- Vices (observed)
- Blood sample (if deemed necessary or requested)
- Radiographs or X-rays (if indicated or requested).

Other pre-purchase tests can be performed if either desired by the prospective purchaser or advised by the veterinarian. The obvious purpose of these examinations is to determine the soundness of the horse and its suitability for the proposed use. However if the buyer wants the horse to be given a pre-purchase examination by a veterinarian prior to buying, this provision must be included in the sales contract. Most experienced horse people insist that a pre-purchase examination clause be included in the contract when buying a horse.

Other important items to be covered in the sales agreement are the price of the horse and the terms of payment. The terms of the sale, whether cash or on installments, must be fully covered by the contract. If the sale is for cash, the amount to be paid and when the payment is to be made must be clearly stated in the agreement. If the sale is on an installment basis, a number of subjects must be clearly spelled out in the contract including who will keep the horse until it is paid for.

The sales price must be stated, together with the amount of any down payment. The terms of the installment sale must be clearly stated; for example, the amount to be paid, whether payments will be monthly, quarterly or annually, when each installment payment will be due, where the payments are to be made, to whom they are to be paid whether there is to be any security on the installment portion of the transaction, whether interest will be charged and, if so, how much, and any other similar matters should be included.

The sales agreement should also contain a clear and accurate statement of all liens and encumbrances on the horse being sold. This is a very important provision to a buyer, for obvious reasons; the purchaser wants to accurately know the purchase price being paid for the horse. The buyer does not want to be surprised later, to discover that, in addition to the price paid to the seller, there is an additional amount owed to a secured creditor on the animal. If there is a lien or encumbrance on the horse, it must be disclosed to the buyer and dealt with in the sales agreement. In some cases, the buyer is assuming the debt on the animal; if this is so, the contract should so state. If the amount of the debt on the horse is to be paid from the sales proceeds, this too should be addressed in the sales agreement, together with provisions ensuring that the buyer will receive the horse free of any encumbrance.

If the sale involves a granted or retained security interest in the horse, a number of issues must be addressed in the sales agreement and other necessary documents to protect the security interest. In the situation where there is a retained security interest in the horse, the Uniform Commercial Code governs how the security interest will be perfected to protect the seller (secured party) and the buyer (debtor). This is done by means of a Security Agreement and Financing Statement form (UCC Form 1) which includes the following information: description of the collateral (horse), full names and addresses of both the debtor and the secured party, description of the horse, and location of the horse until payment is completed. UCC Form 1 is filed and/or recorded with a designated state officer or agency to complete the security arrangement. Of course, if the debt is paid, the lien is released by written notification to the designated agency as provided by the law of the state of the transaction.

In addition to the sales agreement and UCC Form 1, in a case where there is a retained or granted security interest, the debtor also signs a promissory note containing the terms of the loan. All promissory notes must comply with the requirements of applicable negotiable instrument laws to be valid and enforceable. This simply means that the promissory note must be in writing, be signed by the maker/debtor, and be for a certain sum of money; the debt must be paid on a certain date or within a certain time and, if interest is charged, it must be set forth. Any other conditions such as penalties for late payments, interest increases, or payment of attorney's fees on default - must also be stated in the Note. If the promissory note is secured by a security agreement as previously discussed, this too must be stated in the Note. It is important to know that a horse cannot be repossessed unless there has been a security interest retained or granted in the Bill of Sale or in the Security Agreement. Without provisions authorizing repossession, trying to take the horse back can involve trespassing, confrontations, and other problems. Obviously, to avoid difficulties, proper legal steps should be taken to ensure the validity and enforceability of the promissory note and Security Agreement.

If the parties have agreed that mortality insurance on the horse will be required, the contract should so provide. The amount of insurance, payment of premium, conditions of insurance, and any other mutually agreed upon matters, should be included.

Although many people are, by nature, optimistic and feel that an agreement will be fulfilled, reality shows that defaults are frequent. Therefore, the sales agreement should provide for remedies in the event of a default. Examples of defaults include: a breach or failure to perform one or more terms of the agreement, failure to pay as provided, removal of the horse from the state without the consent of the creditor, bankruptcy of the debtor, an attempt to sell the horse before payment has been completed or allowing the horse to be seized for the failure of the creditor to pay other debts. The parties to a sales agreement should be aware of the possibility of default and address appropriate remedies.

For instance, in the case of a default caused by a breach of one of the terms of the agreement, the parties might include a provision in the contract that the breaching party has a certain period of time to cure the breach. Of course, in the case of a more serious default, the contract should contain protection for the innocent party and penalty provisions for the one breaching the agreement. These penalty provisions, which are principally financial in nature, if discussed early and included in the provisions of the sales agreement can certainly be deterrents to a party considering not performing his or her obligation. Anticipation of problems can go a very long way in preventing or, at least, minimizing the effect.

"Imagination is more important than knowledge."

Albert Einstein

Included in most complete sales agreements are provisions for attorney fees and costs to be paid by parties who breach the terms of the contract. This can be one of the most effective deterrents to nonperformance since attorney fees and costs can be very expensive and, in many cases, can be greater than the original amount in controversy.

In addition to provisions in a sales agreement that provides for attorney fees and costs, arbitration clauses are becoming quite common. An arbitration provision simply means that the parties agree to have any disputes or disagreements involving the contract settled by arbitration rather than by lawsuit court. Arbitration is usually quicker and much less expensive than litigation and is rapidly becoming the preferred method of dispute resolution.

Auctions contain the elements of a sales contract. When a person makes a bid at an auction, he/she is offering to buy the horse or tack for a certain price. The auction may contain a sealed bid called "with reserve," meaning the person selling the horse has set a limit on the minimum bid that will be accepted. Many auctions have rules requiring that the horse must sell to the highest bidder. This is legally called "without reserve." Again, understand the requirements of the auction and those of the buyer and seller.

Express and Implied Warranties in Sales Contracts
In horse transactions, a variety of disputes can arise, leading to either litigation, arbitration or some other form of dispute resolution. The most common disputes involve breach of warranties under Article II of the Uniform Commercial Code. Since these controversies are so common, they are reviewed here in some detail.

The first of the two types of warranties is the "Express Warranty." This is a statement, description, or promise made by the seller to the buyer, relating to the horse or its uses, becoming a part of the basis for the transaction, creating an express warranty that the horse shall conform to the statement, description or promise. Common examples of express warranties include: representations of the fitness of the animal for a particular purpose; for example "this horse would be a perfect hunter/ jumper," or "this horse is a great race horse," or "your breeding program will be well served by this excellent broodmare."

An express warranty by a seller to a prospective buyer clearly becomes a basis for the transaction, because the seller, in making the promise or statement, obviously knows of the buyer's plans or expectations for the horse and is saying to the buyer expressly: this horse will meet your plans and expectations. If, after the transaction is completed, the horse does not live up to the promise or do as represented, controversy will surely result.

Another type of express warranty that can result in litigation involves representations concerning the health of the

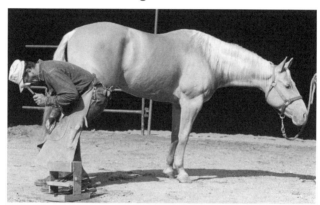

When you tell your farrier how you want your horse shod, you are creating a verbal contract in exchange for payment.

horse. Most individuals in the horse industry are sophisticated enough to substitute contract provisions placing the duty on the buyer to obtain an examination by a veterinarian of the buyer's choosing, in place of an express warranty by the seller.

An "Implied warranty" is also a promise, statement, or description, not expressly included in the written agreement, but made a part of the transaction merely by operation of law. An implied warranty includes: a warranty that the horse is fit for the ordinary purpose for which horses are used, the seller has the right to sell the horse, and fitness for a particular purpose. The buyer is relying on the seller's judgment or skill in selecting the horse when the seller answers questions about the horse.

Since an implied warranty is not specifically set out in a sales contract, it can become a source of controversy because of diverse interpretation. The saying "There are two sides to every story" can take on a whole new meaning in trying to resolve a case involving a claim of breach of implied warranty. Again, fully and completely setting out the expectations of the parties in the written agreement can avoid many of these controversies. However, since an implied warranty arises by operation of law, it is present in every transaction; thus, the buyer and seller alike should be aware of its existence and effect.

In addition to the sales agreement, other common written contracts in the horse industry include the breeding contract, training agreement, and boarding agreement. Regardless of the type of contract or its subject matter, to be enforceable it must contain the elements of a contract as previously discussed. However, specific types of contracts have their own unique areas that must be addressed.

Breeding Contract

A breeding contract should contain the following specific items:

- Identity of the mare and stallion
- Location of the service
- Rebreeding rights, if any
- Statement of all charges incurred in the breeding and who will be responsible
- Veterinary services required, emergency treatment, physical examination, and certification of whether or not the mare is pregnant
- Provisions regarding a guarantee of live birth.

The term "live foal" should clearly be defined, for example, as a foal that stands and nurses after foaling.

A breeding agreement becomes even more complex when the mare is to be bred using artificial insemination. The use of specific language regarding a live birth should cover proper collection of semen, amount to be delivered, transportation, payment of both customary and unexpected costs, and other logistical complications. Additions to the contract may cover the presence of a veterinarian during insemination, as well as certification that only the designated mare was bred during the procedure.

Problems generally arise in breeding contracts regarding payment, such as how and when the stud fee will be paid. It should be understood by both parties that the owner of the stallion has the right to assert a Breeder's Lien if the fee is not paid. Having this written into the contract helps avoid surprises and fewer bad debts will be incurred. Also, if there is to be any foal sharing, a separate agreement containing this arrangement should be made and signed by all parties.

Other common developments that must be addressed in Breeding Agreements are what happens if the mare does not become pregnant or if she does not carry the foal to term. If no pregnancy occurs or if the mare aborts, is there a full or partial refund of the breeding fee? Will there be another breeding attempted without any additional fee? The answers to these questions must be addressed in the Breeding Agreement since there is no such thing as 100% success or guarantee that every mare will become pregnant. Since semen is often shipped between states or even countries, enforcement of a "live foal guarantees" can be difficult. If the parties have not provided a method for resolving these problems, expensive and prolonged litigation can result. It is far better to provide in the Breeding Agreement a specific provision as to how these potential problems will be resolved. Provisions containing a "choice of jurisdiction" clause designating where controversies must be resolved (which state) are helpful. Whether controversies or questions will be resolved by arbitration or other forms of alternate dispute resolution are to be utilized, and any other necessary details thereof should be addressed. Probably the most effective clause could be providing a form of "security" that ensures performance of the terms of the Breeding Contract. Escrowing a certain amount of money until the event occurs, such as the live birth of a foal, or, if the parties have agreed, to be refunded to the mare's owner if the mare is unable to become pregnant.

Often, under the general category of "breeders contracts" are agreements whereby mares are leased for the purpose of breeding. As with all leases, the agreement should be in writing and contain clear statements of the agreed-upon terms and conditions. The lease should cover expenses, including veterinary services, transportation, risk of loss, responsibility for the mare's general health and mortality insurance. The agreement should contain a warranty of the person leasing the mare to the other party, that he/she owns the horse or has the right to enter into the lease; if the broodmare is secured, that he/she has a written release from the secured party authorizing the lease, and that any foals born be free and clear of any liens or encumbrances.

It is obvious that professional help is often needed in preparing a comprehensive breeding contract. There are many pitfalls to be avoided and an experienced attorney's service is often required to reach the desired result. A breeding contract is not for the inexperienced horse person, nor is it to be casually entered into.

Training Agreement

A training agreement, properly drawn, can avoid many dis-agreements and controversies that can lead to tremendous expense. It is critical that the purpose and scope of the training is clearly understood by both parties, and that the contract reflects this. An agreement with a trainer of race-horses is completely different than with a trainer of show horses. What the owner expects from the trainer must be set out in the agreement. Since training can be a very sub-jective matter, fairness to all parties (including the horse to be trained) requires a clear understanding of the abilities of the trainer and the expectations of the owner. Also, questions of costs, boarding fees, expenses, veterinary expenses, insurance and other similar issues should be addressed in the agreement.

If showing the horse is part of the training, the costs involved in showing should be discussed and resolved ahead of time. The owner should be aware that the costs of showing vary greatly; and he/she should know what is being undertaken. Also, tack and associated materials should be inventoried; if left in the trainer's possession, the parties should agree who is responsible in case of theft or loss.

If the agreement is for training a racehorse, very special and unique matters must be addressed. The contract must clearly state who has the right to make decisions concern-ing the training and racing of the horse. Usually, these decisions belong to the trainer, but the owner may want the right to either make these decisions or, at least materially participate in the decision-making process. If this is not clearly understood and agreed in the contract between the owner and trainer, severe controversy is almost assured.

Another critical area in race-training contracts is whether or not the trainer may run the horse in claiming races. If the owner would not approve of running the horse in a claiming race and the trainer goes ahead and runs the horse in a claiming race, problems can result. Obviously, any Training Agreement must define the rights and duties of the parties so controversies and misunderstandings are avoided.

Boarding Contract

The boarding of horses is a very common area where a written agreement is important. A Boarding Contract should include a statement of the costs, whether they are to be paid weekly or monthly, where the payments are to be made, what kind of facilities will be provided for the horse (e.g., box stall, paddock, pasture), and whether veterinary services will be provided. All requirements of the boarding facility as to health certificates of incoming horses should be included (e.g., Coggins tests, inoculations, wormings). Also, provisions concerning what to do if the horse becomes ill or injured, any requirements of the owner's health or mortality insurance company as to notice of illness, injury and related matters should be contained in the contract's terms. These requirements are discussed in detail in Chapter 17, *Insurance Considerations*.

Just as with all other contracts, the Boarding Contract should be in writing, signed by all parties, and contain the rights and obligations of the signers. The owner of the boarding facility normally will present his/her Boarding Contract to the horse owner prior to the animal moving in. Sometimes the agreement is a printed or copied form regularly used by the stable for all boarders. On occasion, the contract will be negotiated by the parties covering specific concerns and conditions that are present. In all cases, the agreement should clearly state what is being provided, how much money will be required, what will be furnished, what is not included, what will happen if payments are late or not made, and what will be done in the event of an emergency. Also, the document will probably discuss the question of any restrictions on access to the facilities (including time restrictions, forbidden areas for riding, use of facility for training). In short, all rules and regulations should be set out in the agreement or in a written attachment thereto, signed by the parties.

The principal goal of contracts is to describe, in writing, the understandings and agreements of the parties. A properly drafted contract attempts to avoid misunderstandings and controversies by clearly stating the respective rights and obligations of those who have entered into the transaction. A contract is an important business tool and has many applications, including evidence in a trial or arbitration hearing, documentation for tax reasons, and for normal record-keeping purposes. Too often, people involved with horses forget that a contract is just as important in this business as in any other enterprise. This is a mistake that can be very costly. Conduct your horse activities as you would any other business. **GET IT IN WRITING!**

CASE STUDIES

Bills of Sales and Sales Contracts

Chuck Cutter is in the market for a younger and more competitive cutting horse. After attending many sales, talking to trainers and owners of potentially acceptable horses, he finds a four-year-old gelding that seems to be exactly what he wants. The horse is owned by Owen Owner who lives in Illinois, is trained by Tom Trainer who lives in Texas, and is competitively shown by Rita Rider who lives in Oklahoma. The horse is kept at Rita's when it is being shown and at Tom Trainer's facility in Texas, between competitions and when being further trained.

When Chuck Cutter sees the horse in Arizona at a cutting competition. He talks to Rita about purchasing the horse. Rita says the horse is for sale but says that Chuck should talk to Tom Trainer about the details of the sale. Tom is also at the cutting, so he and Chuck talk about the horse and reach a possible agreement about the sale. Tom says that he is authorized to handle the sale and that Chuck should write the check to him for the $20,000 purchase price. Tom says he will give Chuck a Bill of Sale in exchange for the check and that no further agreements are necessary or needed. Chuck wants a pre-purchase veterinary examination of the horse, a Coggins test and the worming and inoculation record of the gelding. Tom Trainer says he has been a well-respected cutting horse trainer for over thirty years and his word is his bond. He says that the horse is sound, the six-month-old Coggins test is still okay and the horse is current on his wormings and inoculations.

Tom Trainer tells Chuck he has bought and sold hundreds of horses and all that is needed is a Bill of Sale.

Discussion:

1. Since Tom Trainer is such a well-known and respected trainer, should Chuck Cutter rely on his statements regarding:

   a. His authority to sell the horse for $20,000?

   b. The physical condition and medical record of the horse?

   c. That a Bill of Sale is the only document necessary for the transaction?

2. Is the fact that the horse is owned by Owen Owner, who lives in Illinois is significant for Tom Trainer to have authorization to sell the horse? Is it necessary for Chuck Cutter to get anything from Owen to complete the sale? Could this include notification to a breed association of the sale of the horse to Chuck? Would a power of attorney from Owen to Tom Trainer giving the latter the complete authority to sell the horse and receive the sales proceeds make Chuck Cutter's position more secure? Also, the law of what state must be followed regarding the validity of the Bill of Sale, Illinois where the owner lives? Arizona where the horse is being shown when the agreement for his sale is reached? The State of Texas where Tom Trainer lives? Or the state of Rita's residence, Oklahoma, because the horse is being shown by Rita at the time of the sale?

3. If Tom Trainer's representations that the horse is "sound" prove to be false, does this create problems for him, or the horse's owner, or for Chuck the purchaser?

   a. Is Tom Trainer the duly authorized agent of Owen Owner when he makes the representations of soundness to Chuck Cutter? If so, both Tom and Owen could be liable for the false statements if they are known to be false.

   b. If Tom makes the statement that the horse is sound, not knowing whether or not that is true, could he be accurately called "negligent" for

> "Never approach a bull from the front, a horse from the rear or a fool from any direction."
>
> Cowboy saying

making the statement without knowing its accuracy?

   c. If Chuck Cutter decides to go ahead with the deal without a pre-purchase veterinary examination, could he complain if a medical problem becomes apparent after the purchase is complete?

4. Could the various problems with this transaction be minimized or avoided by a properly drawn Sales Contract, setting out the exact terms of the sale, including the following:

   a. The authority of Tom Trainer to act on behalf of Owen Owner

   b. All conditions of the sale, including the pre-purchase veterinary examination

   c. A provision of which state's law will govern the transaction

   d. An inventory of what documents are necessary to complete the sale, including:

      (1) Bill of Sale

      (2) Current Coggins test

      (3) Any assignments required by breed associations

      (4) Written results of the pre-purchase veterinary examination

      (5) Medical record including worming and inoculations.

      (6) Brand inspection.

In summary, this case study illustrates some of the problems that can be present in a horse sale. Although sometimes experienced horse people get offended by insisting on written contracts containing the conditions that must be satisfied before the sale can be concluded, the universal rule of **GET IT IN WRITING** must be followed.

Express and Implied Warranties in Sales Contracts

During Chuck Cutter's search for a suitable cutting horse he hears about the four-year-old gelding being shown by Rita. Chuck does not have a chance to watch the horse in action but hears that Tom Trainer, a famous cutting horse trainer, has worked with the horse. Chuck Cutter contacts Trainer and asks about the horse. During the conversation, Tom Trainer says this gelding has the potential of "going all the way." He says the horse is already well trained at cutting and after Tom tells him of his plans for competing on the horse, Tom recommends the horse to Chuck, saying, "This sounds like the right horse for you."

Discussion

Assuming Chuck Cutter relies on the statements made by Tom Trainer, has either an express or implied warranty been created? If the horse fails to prove to be suitable for cutting horse competitions, would Chuck have a claim against Tom for breach of warranty?

Based upon the facts of this case study, Chuck Cutter as a potential buyer of the horse has made his expectations and plans for the use of the horse as a competitive cutting horse known to Tom Trainer. If Tom has the authority to sell the horse for its owner, Tom's statements about the level of the horse's training as a cutting horse, and that is the right for Chuck could be considered an express warranty. However, the statement that the horse has the potential of "going all the way" would not be considered an express warranty but more of a "sales pitch" that might not come true.

If Chuck as buyer, and Tom as agent, for the owner reach an agreement and reduce its terms to writing, without mentioning that the horse is to be used as a cutting horse, would Tom's statements about the horse's training and potential be considered warranties? In this case, these representations fall into the category of implied warranties. Since the anticipated use of the horse is made known to the seller's agent who makes representations as to the status of the horse's training and fitness for use as a cutting horse, which statements were relied upon by the buyer, the law would find that these are implied warranties. This is especially true since a well-known cutting horse trainer made the representations. Thus, Chuck Cutter would probably have a successful claim against Tom Trainer if these warranties as to the training and fitness of the horse as a cutting horse are false.

Training Agreements

If there are no problems with the transaction and Chuck Cutter is the proud and happy owner of the cutting horse, let's assume he wants the horse's training to continue. He is very impressed with Tom Trainer and wants Tom to work with the horse to bring it to a more refined level of cutting. What, if anything, should Chuck and Tom do to finalize their agreement regarding further training of the horse?

Discussion

It is very important for Chuck and Tom to have a written agreement. The Training Agreement should include a statement of the type of training, the cost, the period of time covered by the agreement, whether board of the horse is included, responsibility for any veterinary or farrier services, provisions for showing the horse at cutting competitions, insurance requirements, and other similar provisions should be included. The test of whether an agreement is complete is the answer to the question, "are the goals and responsibilities covered along with all the costs?" If the answer to this question is "yes," the agreement is probably complete.

Boarding Contracts

Chuck Cutter decides the horse should be turned over to Rita Rider to be boarded at her Oklahoma ranch. Rita is to ride the horse at cutting competitions and take full care of the horse during the time of these contests.

Discussion

Of course, Rita and Chuck should have an agreement relative to Rita's competing on the horse. However, as a part of that agreement or as a separate contract, there should be a Boarding Contract between Rita and Chuck covering the board and general care of the horse. This agreement should cover the items covered in this chapter regarding cost, type of care, extra services, etc. The contract should make very clear the rights and responsibilities of both Rita and Chuck. Rita should know exactly what is expected of her in caring for the horse, and Chuck must know his financial and other responsibilities. If both parties know "where they stand," problems and controversies can be avoided or at least minimized.

🐎 LIABILITY OF HORSEMEN

The horse industry and horse people have felt the effects of a large number of claims and lawsuits by injured parties. In our society, it now appears that whenever a person is injured (including all horse-related activities), the first thing to do is try to place blame on someone else. We do not take the blame ourselves—it's always the "other guy's fault." As the frequency of lawsuits has increased, so has the novelty of theories advanced to place the blame on others. This is certainly true in horse-related cases, and has led to vast increases in liability insurance premiums or, in some cases, total unavailability of insurance coverage.

The threat of lawsuits and the high cost of liability insurance has had the effect of creating a shortage of good facilities for training horses and riders. The horse industry has lost potential owners, riders and participants in the business. Due to this fear of economic disaster caused by successful lawsuits. If people are unable to follow their interest in horses and riding, the industry will be the loser.

This chapter discusses the traditional theories of liability that apply in the horse world and concentrates on common situations where horse owners or keepers have been sued for harm allegedly done by a horse. The term "keepers" refers to individuals who have control and/or custody of a horse or horses. This term includes trainers, breeders, livery stables and outfitters.

Ways of taking precautions to avoid or limit liability are also discussed. The latter part of this chapter covers legislation that has been enacted in over 40 states, which limits the liability of the sponsors of all horse activities. These laws have created a great deal of interest in horse circles and have been in effect long enough for them to be interpreted by the courts of several states. These decisions and their effect are discussed. Finally, the question of the sufficiency and effect of releases and waivers will be outlined.

Traditional Theories of Liability

For the last 200 years, horses have been classified by the law as domestic animals that are usually gentle creatures. They have long served the needs of man, at first as the pri-

"Always remember that when you are kicked from the rear, it means you are in front."

Fulton J. Sheen

mary method of travel, and in more recent times, as a great source of pleasure and recreation. However, when harm and injury caused by a horse occurs, under two legal theories, strict liability and negligence, the law holds the owner or keeper liable for the harm.

STRICT LIABILITY is a legal theory that imposes liability on the owner or keeper of a horse who knows the animal has DANGEROUS PROPENSITIES and the person fails to take necessary or reasonable care to prevent injuries that could be caused by the horse. Dangerous propensities are characteristics or actions by a horse that are dangerous. The knowledge of the keeper or owner of the horse of its habits and tendencies and how this knowledge is used or communicated by the owner or keeper is key in determining liability. This rule of law is analogous to the old adage that "each dog is entitled to one bite." After that bite, the owner of the dog is on notice that his dog has a tendency to bite and might be vicious. If the dog bites again, the owner is responsible. To understand the concept of "knowing a horse's dangerous propensities," it is helpful to examine how various courts have treated the question.

Recently, the Arizona Supreme Court held that a horse owner who has no prior knowledge of a horse's dangerous propensities is not liable for the injuries suffered by the plaintiff. A Florida Appellate Court held that horses are not presumed to be dangerous. Ownership of a horse alone cannot be the basis of a liability. There must be evidence showing that the owner has had knowledge of a dangerous propensity before he or she can be held liable.

Courts in New York, Colorado and Indiana have followed the basic rule of law that actual knowledge of a horse's dangerous propensity is necessary to hold the owner liable. The New York case involved a claim by a woman who was injured when she fell from one of the defendant's horses at a riding stable. The court held that the plaintiff had failed to present sufficient evidence of notice of the horse's vicious propensity and that the plaintiff could not rely on the implication of vicious propensity merely because the horse was a Thoroughbred stallion.

In a case prior to the Colorado statute limiting liability for equine activities, the United States District Court for

Colorado held that a horse known to bite or kick may have dangerous propensities, but a that horse with a tendency of expanding its chest (blowing up) while being saddled does not have an actionable dangerous propensity.

The Indiana Court of Appeals stated in a recent decision that the owner or keeper's act or omission, not the horse's, is what may lead to liability. However, the owner or keeper of the horse can breach his/her duty of care to the injured party only if he/she knew that the horse had a dangerous propensity.

The "dangerous or vicious propensity" rule is of only limited effect in some cases since there has been a reluctance to follow the rule when the injured person is a child. The common involvement of children in horse-related accident cases has led to some interesting decisions. The North Carolina Supreme Court considered a case involving an injured nine-year-old child who had been kicked in the head by a horse after the child had crawled under a fence to enter the paddock. The court held that the vicious propensity rule did not apply in this or any other case where the injury is not caused by the viciousness of the animal. The North Carolina court ruled that the determinative issue of liability was not whether the owners knew of any vicious propensity, but instead whether they should have allowed the child to play with the horse when they knew he was inexperienced around horses.

The Supreme Court of New York recently had before it a case involving a four-year-old child who was kicked in the head by a gentle horse with no known viscous propensity. In this case, the child had crawled under the corral fence to pet the horse. The court held in favor of the claimant and against the owner of the horse and stated that the presence of a horse on property creates a particular danger to young children, which requires a further duty to provide protection for children. The court further said that providing additional fencing or eliminating easy access to the horse by children could satisfy this duty of additional protection.

A decision of the Court of Appeals in Kentucky also involved a young child crawling under a fence and being kicked in the head by a horse. In the court's opinion, the location of this incident made the dangerous propensity

"Knowledge may
give weight, but
accomplishments
give us luster,
and more people
see than weigh."

Lord

Chesterfield

rule inapplicable. The horse in question had been kept in a fenced pasture in a residential neighborhood. The court stated that normally the keeper of a horse is not subject to liability unless the horse has known vicious propensities; however, the introduction of a herd of horses into a neighborhood populated by many young children presented a different situation under the law. The court held that the doctrine of "attractive nuisance" made the keeper of the horses liable. Under this legal doctrine, anyone who maintains upon his/her property any condition or thing that is dangerous to young children because they are too young and inexperienced to recognize the danger, and which may reasonably be expected to attract young children to the property, is under a duty to exercise reasonable care to protect the children against the dangers of the attraction. This case could, at least in Kentucky, cause difficulties for horse owners and keepers whose horses are kept near residential neighborhoods. In all states, it should be remembered that the law attempts to especially protect young children from all perils. Horse owners and keepers must be very careful to protect young children, even if they trespass, from danger.

The doctrine of dangerous or vicious propensities is alive and well and is somewhat protective to horse owners and keepers. However, it does not protect and apply to all situations. There is no substitute for taking reasonable precautions and having adequate liability insurance.

The other traditional theory of liability under which horse owners and keepers have been held liable is the theory of NEGLIGENCE. This theory means "a failure to do an act which a reasonably careful person would do, or the doing of any act which a reasonable person would not do, under the same or similar circumstances to protect others from injury, death or damage." If an owner or keeper of a horse has knowledge of its dangerous propensities and fails to warn another person of them, this is negligent and liability results for injury or damage. This failure to warn, or failure to take measures or precautions to prevent injury by a horse, is "negligence."

The theory of negligence is broad and requires an analysis of the facts and circumstances of each case, to which is applied the definition of "negligence" to determine fault and the resulting liability. Of course "liability" means responsibility for harm to another. As previously discussed, the courts of North Carolina, New York and Kentucky applied negligence theories rather than the vicious propensity rule in finding that the horsemen are liable to the injured children.

The traditional theory of "negligence" is an ever-present factor to be aware of in any horse operation. Vigilance, awareness, and proper risk management are precautions necessary to avoid liability, or at least to minimize its effect.

Other Forms of Liability
When a horse owner thinks of the term "liability," he/she thinks of the various types of liability that can attach to claims by persons injured or otherwise harmed by riding or being near horses. However, there are many other forms of "liability" to which horse owners and keepers are vulnerable. This includes a keeper being liable for failing to provide a safe place for horses in his/her care, liability for failing to keep horses in adequate and secure pastures or corrals, and being legally responsible for damages caused while riding.

It is becoming more common to see claims by horse owners against persons with whom they board their horses based on negligent care. These cases are generally based on the legal theory of "bailment" or breach of the bailment contract. Bailments or bailment contracts obligate the keeper of another person's horse to protect and care for the horse, and then return the animal to the owner in good condition when the contract is over.

Often bailments are for a specific purpose, such as boarding or training. If a horse dies or is injured in the care of the keeper (the "bailee"), a breach of the bailment contract can be claimed and a lawsuit or claim can be made against the bailee. The success of these claims depends on whether the owner ("bailor") can show that the bailee was negligent in his/her care or treatment of the horse, and that this negligence was the cause of the injury to, or death of the horse. Obviously, these cases can be as personally and financially devastating to the losing party as those involving claims made by parties who were injured while riding. The reputation and business of keepers or trainers can be ruined by adverse results in cases by boarders or customers.

It is important that those who keep and care for other people's horses know that their duty goes far beyond providing proper food and water; it includes providing a safe facility, free of hidden and apparent dangers, as well as a secure environment for the horses.

Considering the number of accidents that happen at horse facilities, all but a very few could have been prevented. It is extremely important that the keepers of horses carefully assess their facilities for dangers and hazards that could kill or hurt the horses in their care. This practice is known as "risk management" and should be done regularly.

Examples of the universal hazards and dangers that exist at horse facilities are fire, electric shock, escape, injury caused by sharp objects and trash, theft, motor vehicle traffic, vandalism, and drowning. With some inspection, thought, analysis and preventive measures, the dangers of these and other hazards can be minimized.

Fire
There exists in most stables and boarding facilities, a tremendous potential for fire. Hay, sawdust, straw, wood shavings and other combustible materials are everywhere. Many horse facilities are constructed of wood, contain electric wiring, and might house gas-powered tractors or other implements. All of these are disasters waiting to happen. Even in barns or stables constructed of aluminum or steel, the presence of many hazardous and combustible materials amplify the fire danger. Fire is one of the principal fears of horsemen. However, many fire hazards can be eliminated or minimized by taking simple precautions, such as:
- posting NO SMOKING signs
- having fire extinguishes charged and handy
- keeping aisles, stalls and storage areas clean
- storing hay, straw, wood shavings, and sawdust outside of barns stables in separate facilities
- having barn wiring professionally checked and enclosed in metal conduit
- removing flammable liquids and gas or diesel implements from the barn
- installing an acceptable smoke detector system designed for a barn

Electric Shock

Electrocution is a very serious problem that has created both tragedy and substantial liability. Both horses and people are at risk. Having the wiring and electrical system inspected by a professional electrician can avoid these problems. Low hanging overhead wires can be raised to a safe height. Electrical connection to waterers and pumps and be checked and made safe. Wire can be enclosed in conduit. Fixtures, fuse boxes, and electrical connections can be inspected and repaired if necessary. In short, most risks of electrocution and many fire hazards can be avoided by taking reasonable precautions.

Escape

Another very preventable hazard is loose horses. Latches and hinges on stable doors and corral gates should be regularly checked and maintained. All gates, fences, corrals and other containing structures should be periodically inspected and necessary repairs made. Whenever feasible, closing springs or devices should be installed on doors. Thought should be given to establishing a procedure to insure gates and doors are closed and secured at night. In summary, the liability both to the owners of horses and any member of the general public can be avoided by preventing the escape of horses in one's care.

Injuries to Horses

Doing the simple tasks of removing sharp objects, barbed wire, trash and equipment from areas where horses are kept lessens the chance of injury to horses. Historically, farms and ranches have had areas where trash is dumped. With the passage of time, and drifting of dirt, these trash piles often become buried and invisible. The contents of these piles— including metal, glass, wire, etc.—can be lethal to horses.

Inspect and become familiar with the areas where your horses are kept to minimize the risk of harm. When hazards are found, they should be removed. Pastures and other areas should be checked for old cisterns, wells or anything else that might cave under the weight of horses.

These simple precautions can minimize liability for failing to provide a safe place for horses, and can negate one of the stated exceptions to the protection of many of the equine liability statutes now in effect.

Theft

Unfortunately, horse thieves are still around and plying their evil trade. People who care for horses have a duty, both legal and moral, to provide reasonable security for the horses in their care. The theft of horses is a very real problem because horses are relatively easy to steal, especially if they are in pastures. Horses can easily be lured into a trailer with a bit of grain and be many miles away before their loss is discovered.

Check on pastured horses periodically. Inspect gates and fences with security in mind. Even horses that are not kept in pastures but are in stables, paddocks or corrals are very vulnerable to theft because of their accessibility. Security precautions should be taken for all horses to avoid difficulty.

Motor Vehicle Traffic

Most horse people are aware of the hazards of horses being exposed to motor vehicle traffic. The needs for care to keep horses off roads and to ride carefully around traffic are well-known. However, motor vehicle traffic around barns and stables is often ignored. Facility owners take it for granted that people driving into a horse facility will be careful. Experience has shown that this is not always true, and facility owners can find themselves in lawsuits for failing to make reasonable efforts to warn or control traffic on their property.

It is important to pay attention to motor vehicle traffic at your place. Warning signs and other devices are inexpensive and can avert trouble. Vehicles and trailers should be parked in areas where they will not be hazardous to either horses or people. Signs directing visitors where to park and to drive slowly can help avoid accidents. Watching traffic on the property and policing traffic can also be helpful in meeting the responsibility of providing a safe facility.

Vandalism

Unfortunately, in our society there are people who take pleasure in vandalizing and damaging the property of others. Horses and horse facilities can be targets for these sick, perverted people. We hear of cases where horses have been killed and maimed, fences cut to allow horses to escape, the poisoning of animals, and many other heinous acts of vandalism.

Most acts occur at night or in remote areas where apprehension is unlikely, so it is hard to prevent. If you know or
suspect that your horses or facility might be a target of
vandalism, you have a duty to take reasonable security precautions. What precautions are "reasonable" depends on
many factors including cost, chance of deterring vandals,
and logistics. Sophisticated and expensive security systems
are not required. However, installation of lights, locked
gates, well-placed television cameras, and regular security
checks might be required.

Being aware of what is happening in the area of your horse
facility is important; know whether vandalism is or may
be a threat. Keep tabs on the horses. Be aware where the
horse property might be vulnerable. Remember to take the
required precautions.

"A horse never
runs so fast as
when he has
other horses to
catch up and
out race."

Ovid

Drowning

The risk of a horse drowning at a horse facility might seem
unlikely and remote; however, it has happened. Drowning is
a very real hazard in some instances. If the property contains ponds, tanks, lakes, or other bodies of water in areas
where horses are kept, precautions are necessary. This is
especially true where new horses are turned into pastures
that contain water areas. In the winter, an inexperienced
or new horse can wander onto a frozen pond, fall through
the ice, and drown. Horses of any age can get into trouble
around water. If the property contains a lake or pond, precautions are necessary to avoid liability. Fencing off bodies
of water is the best way to prevent drowning. It is obviously
not wise to assume that a horse will stay out of and away
from the water nor to rely on the conception that all horses
can swim.

Summary

Experienced horse people know that if there is a way,
horses can get into trouble, they will find it. There are
undoubtedly many additional risks and hazards to the ones
covered in this chapter. Liability is not limited to riding or
being near horses. Conditions that horse caretakers allow to
exist through their own carelessness or inattentiveness can
be fatal to horses. All horse owners and caretakers should
inspect the property often and look for hazards. If necessary, obtain professional help to make the property as safe

and secure as reasonably possible. In reality, it takes very little effort to make most horse facilities safer. Think ahead to avoid liability for failing to provide for the safety of horses in your care.

Liability Incurred While Riding

Many people are surprised to discover that riding a horse can make a rider liable to others. Liability can attach to riders on a number of legal theories. It should be noted that this is a liability against the rider of a horse, not necessarily involving the horse other than as the method by which the rider is transported.

A common form of liability encountered by riders is that of trespassing onto private property. Many riders innocently stray onto the property of others. Some riders unfortunately have very little regard for private property rights and feel that the owner of the property will never know they are there. In either event, trespassing on the property of another can create both civil and criminal liability. It is very important for a rider to know where he/she is riding and to have permission from the proper party to be on the property.

Another area in which horseback riders can be liable to a landowner is for damaging the owner's property. An unattended or improperly extinguished fire can lead to massive trouble. Cutting down trees, collecting arrowheads or other souvenirs, and defacing property also lead to liability. In general, not respecting the property of others usually gets a rider into legal trouble.

Failing to protect animals on the property of another is a common source of liability imposed on a horse rider. The usual problem arises when the rider fails to close gates or removes barriers such as panels used to restrain livestock. The losses that can result from this carelessness are very substantial. Simply closing any gate opened prevents this problem.

Riding over planted crops is another liability. Many areas where people ride are located adjacent to private property that contain cultivated areas. Horses passing over growing crops are more than a source of irritation; it can impose liability on the rider for the resulting crop losses.

Another potential area of liability is driving and parking a vehicle in an unauthorized area. Most publicly owned trailheads have designated parking areas for vehicles and trailers. However, on weekends and busy times, these areas can be full and riders often park on any available ground. Often this alternate parking is on private property, and trouble can result.

The above examples are of the types of liability horse riders can encounter and are by no means all inclusive. Using common sense and courtesy can prevent these problems, though, all too often, both of these virtues are in short supply.

- Know where you are riding and get the consent of the property owner if you are going to ride on private land.
- Don't build fires unless this is done in a safe area, and be sure the fire is out before you leave.
- Shut gates and replace panels or other barriers encountered.
- Park your vehicle only in designated and proper areas.

Horseback riding is very enjoyable, but it certainly requires common sense and courtesy to avoid trouble. Whether you call it "horse sense" or an application of the "Golden Rule" riders must be aware of and respect the rights of property owners.

Statutes That Limit Liability for Horse Activities

Recognizing the damage to the horse industry, horse-ownership and enjoyment caused by lawsuits, verdicts and high insurance premiums, over the past ten years a majority of state legislatures have passed statutes that limit liability for horse activities. The first state to enact this legislation was Washington, followed by Colorado. At the present time 43 states have passed legislation which, in some form, limits the liability of equine professionals and sponsors from claims for injury's or death resulting from the inherent risks of equine activities. The following states have enacted these laws:

Alabama, Arizona, Arkansas, Colorado, Connecticut, Delaware, Florida, Georgia, Hawaii, Idaho, Illinois, Indiana, Iowa, Kansas, Kentucky, Louisiana, Maine, Massachusetts, Michigan, Minnesota, Mississippi, Missouri, Montana, Nebraska, New Hampshire, New

"Whatever is

good to know

is difficult to

learn."

Greek proverb

Jersey, New Mexico, North Carolina, North Dakota, Ohio, Oregon, Rhode Island, South Carolina, Tennessee, Texas, Utah, Vermont, Virginia, Washington, West Virginia, Wisconsin, and Wyoming.

The Colorado statute is very typical and was a model for many of the laws that limit liability for horse activities. On July 1, 1990, a law entitled "Equine activities—legislative declaration—exemption from civil liability" became effective in Colorado. This statute exempts "equine activity sponsors, equine professionals, or any other person (including corporations and partnerships) from liability for injury to or death of a participant resulting from the inherent risks of equine activities." The Colorado legislature stated in the bill that persons who participate in equine activities are exposed to some risk. However, the lawmakers found that the state and its citizens "derive numerous economic benefits" from such activities. The legislature stated that its interest in passing the law was to limit the civil liability of persons involved in equine activities.

The statute defines "engaging in equine activity" to mean "riding, training, assisting in medical treatment of, driving, or being a passenger upon an equine, whether mounted or unmounted, or any person assisting a participant or show-management."

The term "equine activity" covers six categories and includes:

First. "Equine shows, fairs, competitions, performances, or parades" that involve horses (including, "dressage, hunter/jumper shows and grand prix jumping, 3-day events, combined training, rodeos, driving, pulling, cutting, polo, steeplechasing, English and western performance riding, endurance, trail riding, western games, and hunting")

Second. Equine training or teaching activities are included as "equine activities."

Third. Is the boarding category.

Fourth. Riding, inspecting, or evaluating a horse belonging to another for the purpose of possibly purchasing the equine is included.

Fifth. Rides, trips, hunts, or any equine activity of any type that is sponsored by an equine activity sponsor.

Sixth. Horse shoeing.

"Equine activity sponsors" are defined as anyone or any group that sponsors, organizes or provides facilities for an equine activity such as pony clubs, 4-H clubs, hunt clubs, riding clubs, schools, therapeutic riding programs and more. "Operators, instructors, and promoters of equine facilities" including stables, clubhouses, pony rides, arenas, and fairs are also included under the category of "equine activity sponsors."

Under the statute, "equine professionals" are defined as persons engaged for compensation in instructing a participant or renting an equine to a participant for the purpose of riding, driving, or being a passenger upon the equine; or rental of equipment or fees to a participant.

"Inherent risks of equine activities" means "those dangers or conditions which are an integral part of equine activities, including but not limited to:
(I)   The propensity of an equine to behave in ways that may result in injury, harm or death to persons around them.
(II) The unpredictability of an equine's reaction to such things as sounds, sudden movement, and unfamiliar objects, persons, or animals.
(III) Certain hazards such as surface and subsurface conditions.
(IV) Collisions with other equine or objects.
(V) The potential of a participant to act in a negligent manner that may contribute to injury to the participant or others, such as failing to maintain control over the animal or not acting within his or her ability."

The statute defines "participant" as any person or professional who engages in an equine activity, regardless of whether a fee is paid for the participation. This is as broad a definition as one can imagine.

After making the definition of terms set forth above, the law provides that except for certain specific exceptions, equine activity sponsors, equine professionals, and any other person shall not be liable for an injury to or the death of a participant "resulting from the inherent risks of equine activity." Except for the specific situations in the statute, no participant or their representative shall make a claim against the equine activity sponsor, professional, or other person for injury, loss, damage or death.

The six specific situations in which an equine professional, activity sponsor, or other person would be liable for a participant's injury or death are:

1. The statute does not apply to horse racing.
2. Knowingly providing faulty equipment or tack that causes injury or death.
3. It does not apply when the equine provider fails to make reasonable and prudent efforts to determine the participant's ability to safely manage the particular horse, based on the participant's representation of his/her ability.
4. The statute does not apply to dangerous conditions on the equine provider's property for which warning signs were not posted.
5. It does not apply if the equine provider commits an act or omission that constitutes willful and wanton disregard for the participant's safety, and the act or omission causes injury.
6. The law does not apply if the participant is intentionally injured.

To take advantage of the statute's protection, the law requires equine professionals to post and maintain notice signs in clearly visible locations where the equine professional or sponsor conducts the horse activity. The statute requires the following warning language on the sign:

WARNING

UNDER COLORADO LAW, AN EQUINE PROFESSIONAL IS NOT LIABLE FOR AN INJURY TO OR THE DEATH OF A PARTICIPANT IN EQUINE ACTIVITIES, RESULTING FROM THE INHERENT RISKS OF EQUINE ACTIVITIES PURSUANT TO SECTION 13-21-119, COLORADO REVISED STATUTES.

The law requires that the warning notice be in black letters a minimum of one inch in height. The statute also requires that every written contract or document entered into by an equine professional for the "providing of professional services, instruction, or the rental of equipment or tack to an equine participant, whether or not the contract involves equine activities on or off the location or site of the equine professional's business, shall contain in clearly readable print the warning notice."

A review of the statute's provisions makes it clear that the Colorado General Assembly intended to limit liability, suits and claims in horse activities. In general, its goal was met without damaging the legal rights of the public. Equine providers are still required to use prudence and care in the conduct of their activities. What the legislature has added is accountability for one's own actions. Accountability has almost been forgotten in American law.

Not all of the statutes enacted in the various states are identical to the one passed in Colorado. The statutes vary in scope and wording to some degree. Most protect equine activity sponsors, equine professionals, and providers of horses from liability for injury or death of participants in equine activity that result from the inherent risks of such activity. Most statutes contain exceptions to the protection of the statute in cases involving intentional wrongdoing, willful and wanton misconduct, providing faulty equipment or tack, or other similar exceptions. These acts are intended to make participants in equine activities responsible for their own actions and to protect people who provide the horses or sponsor the activity.

The principal purpose of these statutes was to stem the flood of lawsuits and claims against equine professionals and providers which was forcing many out of business. By 1990, liability insurance premiums were so high that many in the horse business could not afford the premiums. Also, many insurance companies, fearing the inordinate exposure and risk of large losses from horse-related claims, stopped writing insurance to cover equine businesses. There was certainly a real danger that the horse industry would suffer serious economic harm unless some protective measure in the form of legislation was taken. Thus, the legislatures of the majority of states, following the lead of the states of Washington and Colorado, passed equine liability legislation.

Now that most states have equine liability statutes as part of their law, has the situation improved and the economic damage to the horse industry been eased? The answer to this question cannot be in the form of a simple "yes" or "no." There have been many positive results. Insurance premiums for horse businesses have become more affordable. Insurance policies covering equine operations and horse owners are now readily available. Some policies written on houses and real estate (e.g., "homeowners" policies) include coverage on liability for horses owned by the policyholder. Most farm and ranch insurance policies now cover liability protection for horses on the property.

The courts of a number of states have interpreted the effect and application of the provisions of their respective equine liability statutes. Probably it would be safe to say that in this area, the effect of the statutes receive something of a "mixed review." Initially, it was the goal of proponents of the equine liability statutes that they would sharply decrease the number and frequency of civil lawsuits brought by injured or damaged parties against horse providers and equine professionals. Although cases of this nature are somewhat less frequent, a sharp decrease has not been seen. The principal reason for this less-than-expected result is probably the "exceptions" to the effect of the law stated in each version of the statute. Lawyers are very clever at molding cases to fit one or more of these exceptions. They undoubtedly feel that if they can get the case to fall under the exception, sympathy for their injured client, or a jury's unfamiliarity with or fear of horses, will help them win or force a settlement. To some degree, this tactic has worked.

Another area of the various statutes that has been troublesome to many courts is defining exactly what is meant by "inherent risks of equine activities." Courts in Wyoming, Illinois, Colorado, Washington, and other states have been troubled with questions of whether a particular accident or occurrence resulting in injury or death was an "inherent risk" of the particular equine activity. Examples of these cases include whether falling from a horse is an inherent risk, whether a horse spooking or shying is a normal risk, and cases involving run-away horses have given some courts trouble.

A common problem experienced by attorneys who defend horse owners and equine professionals in cases of equine liability statutes is the reluctance of trial courts to grant either motions to dismiss or motions for summary judgment based on these laws. This reluctance of trial courts is very costly to defendants, because they are forced to go through trial preparation and, in some cases, a complete trial before the equine liability law is found to be applicable and the defendant wins. This defeats the benefit of the statutes, because the defendant is forced to go through very expensive trial preparation and pay defense costs, even though they ultimately win based on the statute.

As a point of information, in lawsuits, it is very common after a case is filed and the defendant served for the defendant's attorney to file a motion to dismiss the case based on some legal or factual basis. In equine liability cases, the ground for requesting the court to dismiss the case is the equine liability statute in effect in that state. If the court agrees that the statute bars the lawsuit, the case is over and the cost is minimal to the equine provider or professional, compared to costs incurred when fully preparing and trying a case.

A summary judgment is something like a motion to dismiss; however, at its basis there is no material issue of fact upon which a court or jury can reasonably find against the defendant. As a matter of law, the defendant who asks for the summary judgment receives this relief and the case is over.

In virtually all cases brought against equine professionals, providers or sponsors, motions for summary judgment based on the fact that the state has an equine liability statute are submitted to the court. At this point, in determining whether a summary judgment should be granted the court looks to see if there is any unresolved or unanswered question of fact. Unfortunately, trial courts have a reluctance to grant summary judgments or dismiss cases based on equine liability statutes. Courts are often hung up on either the applicability of one or more of the exceptions in the statute, or, quite commonly, on the question of whether the particular injury was the result of an inherent risk of equine activity.

"Cats seem to go on the principle that it never does any harm to ask for what you want."

Joseph Wood

Krutch

Courts traditionally try to see that parties to lawsuits have their day in court. There is an understandable reluctance to deprive litigants of their right to a trial before one is even held. Both dismissals of actions and summary judgments do stop proceedings prior to a trial. Thus, a problem common to cases that involve equine liability statutes is this judicial reluctance unless there is clear evidence that the claimant's injury was undeniably one of the known inherent risks of equine activities and that none of the statutory exceptions could apply.

The purpose of the equine liability statutes is to discourage suits against equine professionals and providers. It is impossible to statistically know if this goal has been met. The number of suits against equine providers and professionals seems to be fewer. However, since courts have been reluctant to dismiss cases or grant motions for summary judgments, the costs have not been reduced. Court costs and attorney fees in defending lawsuits can be very costly and can exceed $50,000. If the equine professional or provider carries insurance, the insurance company is obligated to provide an attorney and pay the fees and costs. However, if the party who is sued is not insured, he or she must pay his/her own attorney fees and court costs. Under American law, attorney fees cannot be recovered by the winning party from the losing party except in very limited instances; probably not in suits that involve personal injury claims against equine professionals and providers.

In view of the reluctance of courts to dismiss cases based on the equine liability statutes, horse owners and providers who are sued cannot rely on the statute for economic or legal protection. If a suit is filed, the horseman can expect a prolonged procedure that could include a full trial prior to the court determining whether the claim is barred by the applicable equine liability statute. This is very expensive.

Remember, keep your liability insurance in effect to protect you from liability to an injured party, and possibly more importantly, to pay the costs and attorney fees incurred in defending the lawsuit. You cannot rely on any equine liability statute to protect you from financial damage. **The equine liability statutes are not substitutes for carrying adequate liability insurance.**

Constitutionality of the Equine Statutes

An important consideration for the viability of the equine liability statutes is whether they can withstand attacks on their constitutionality. Obviously, the statutes have opponents, principally claimant's trial lawyers and groups that allegedly protect the public interest. The opposition claims that these laws favor a special interest—horse owners and keepers—and violate the equal protection clause of the United States Constitution and various state constitutions. The answer to this criticism is found in the statement of legislative intention in the Colorado statute as follows:

"The general assembly recognizes that persons who participate in equine activities may incur injuries as a result of the risks involved in such activities. The general assembly also finds that the state and its citizens derive numerous economic and personal benefits from such activities. It is, therefore, the intent of the general assembly to encourage equine activities by limiting the civil liability of those involved in such activities."

The first constitutional challenge to the statutes reached the appellate court in the State of Louisiana. In that case, arguments were made that the Louisiana statute favored a limited class of people, and violated the equal protection clause of the state and U.S. Constitution. In upholding the constitutionality of the statute, the court said the statute promoted the legitimate state interest of promoting the horse industry. The court stated that the statute does encourage the ownership of horses by limiting an owner's liability except in certain instances. Eliminating a considerable risk of liability from the equine professional or sponsor, the court said the law encouraged participation of persons in supplying equine activities to the benefit of the entire horse industry. The court found that the law relates to a legitimate state interest of promoting the equine industry, and the statute does not violate the equal protection clause of the Constitution.

This case was welcomed by the horse industry. Although it did not settle every question concerning the constitutionality of all equine liability statutes, it is a very good authority for addressing the propriety and constitutionality of the equine liability statutes.

Releases

Much has been written and discussed about the effects and desirability of releases, or waivers, in the horse business. In our society, we all have been asked to sign waivers or releases—at a hospital, when renting an automobile, by our dentist, at ski slopes, and before engaging in any activity where there is an element or risk of danger. A release is viewed as being akin to an insurance policy; if a person signs a release, he/she is barred from pursing a claim against the released party. However, in many cases, this is simply not true.

To be binding and enforceable, the law requires that a person who signs a release fully know the actual facts, including the risks, and in knowing these risks and facts, voluntarily elects to assume the risks in return for being allowed to participate in the activity. In the usual case when a potential rider is asked to sign a release before riding a horse, for the release to be effective the prospective rider either must know or be advised of all the potential risks and misfortunes that could be encountered when riding the horse.

If after knowing all of the facts and risks and after fully reading the language of the release, the rider goes ahead and signs it, it would be less likely to be contested. Releases are often thrown in front of the rider immediately before the group mounts for the ride, so it is easy to see how difficult relying on releases can be in the horse industry.

While some releases are useless, well-drafted releases properly used and executed may protect a horse business from negligence liability. The courts of a number of states have considered the effect of various releases. Decisions have universally examined the language of particular releases, the age of the signers, and the circumstances of the signings.

Recently, courts in California upheld a release signed as a condition to taking a riding lesson by a riding student who was also a lawyer . The lawyer-student was subsequently injured during the lesson and claimed the release violated public policy. The court disagreed stating it could find no constitutional or statutory authority that put horseback riding in the public interest. A similar result was reached by an

Illinois court that found there was no public policy against enforcing riding stable releases; the court specifically found that the release was a binding contract in which the plaintiff had given up the riding student's right to sue.

A Michigan court held that a release signed by a guest at a resort ranch was valid and enforceable. The court noted that the language of the release clearly called the issue of liability to the signer's attention by stressing the dangerous aspects of horseback riding. Yet, a release signed by a fourteen-year-old riding student was voidable according to a Georgia court. This is why a well-written release requests that a parent or guardian sign for anyone under 18 years of age.

In 1998, a Colorado Supreme Court case (*B&B Livery, Inc. v. Riehl*, 960 P.2d 134) captured the attention of the horse industry when it upheld the validity of a release signed by a claimant immediately prior to participating in a trail ride. What makes this case especially significant is the court's discussion of what is necessary to make a release valid and enforceable. The decision of the court stated that the question must be whether the intent of the parties was to extinguish liability and whether this intent was clearly and unambiguously expressed in the release; further, that the release agreement should be written in simple and clear terms, not be too long or complicated, and the signer must understand that he/she is, in fact, granting the horse provider a release.

The use of "form releases" obtained from legal form stores or "do it yourself books" is very dangerous. Often these forms are too broad, complicated or vague to be enforceable. Horse businesses that are properly run should be aware that a matter as important as the avoidance of liability claims, should not be left to amateurs. Competent professional legal help, in properly drafting valid and enforceable release agreements, is a prudent investment. In all of the cases above in which releases were upheld, they had been signed by competent adults and were drafted by or with the assistance of attorneys.

CASE STUDIES

Traditional Theories of Liability

Case I

Olive Owner is the proud owner of a three-year-old filly named *Star*. Although Star has been in training for the past year, she has a tendency to kick objects or people who approach her from the rear. Olive has been kicked once by Star, and the horse's trainer has also been kicked and has avoided several attempts by Star to give her a "boot." The trainer tells Olive about these incidents and warns her to be aware of this problem.

It is our responsibility to protect our most precious resources and avoid liability cases.

Frannie Friend and her six-year old daughter, Judy, are invited by Olive to come to the stable and see Star. Judy is very excited because she loves horses. Her mother, Frannie, is concerned because, even though she wants Judy to see the horse, she is afraid of horses. Frannie asks Olive if it is safe for Judy to see and pet Star. Being very proud of Star, Olive says that as long as she is holding Star's lead rope, Judy will be perfectly safe. There is no mention of Star's tendency to kick. Unfortunately, even though Olive is holding Star's lead rope, Judy's excitement in seeing and being near the horse bothers Star. Frannie is there, but Judy breaks away from her mother and runs up behind Star. Judy is kicked and injured.

Assuming that the state in which this incident occurs does not have an equine liability statute, is Olive liable under traditional theories of liability for Judy's injuries? Certainly Olive knew of the propensity of Star to kick since she herself had been kicked and also was warned of this problem by the trainer. Did Olive have a duty to warn Judy's mother,

Frannie, that Star kicks? Should six-year-old Judy have been warned? Was Frannie partially responsible for Judy's injury for not restraining her daughter to prevent her from running to the horse? Did Olive take reasonable precaution by holding Star's lead rope?

Discussion:

In the above case study, it is very clear that Olive knew of her horse's vicious propensity to kick. The fact that she had personally been kicked and was warned about the problem by a professional trainer charges Olive with actual knowledge. To allow anyone, especially a six-year-old child near the horse, makes Olive responsible for the resulting injuries and damages. In this scenario, the obvious best and most careful course of action would have been to not allow either the child or her mother in any close proximity to the horse. Olive should have warned Frannie that the horse has a tendency to kick, and should have suggested the horse be seen from a distance and not petted.

Case II

Assume that, rather than go to the stable where Star is kept, the horse is boarded in a pasture near the house occupied by Frannie and her daughter, Judy. The pasture is secured by a three-rail wooden fence and is adjacent to a residential street. Olive places NO TRESPASSING signs in several places on the fence. Judy is but one of several children who lives in the neighborhood. The horse comes up to see Judy and appears to Judy to be quite friendly. She wants to pet the horse, and is kicked after crawling through the fence.

Discussion:

Is Olive responsible for Judy's injuries? Certainly Olive has warned people not to trespass by posting the signs. The child would not have been injured if she had not trespassed onto the land and climbed through the fence. Don't parents have a duty to warn their children about danger and prevent them from going into areas where they can be hurt?

The legal doctrine of ATTRACTIVE NUISANCE is clearly applicable here. The owner of the horse, knowing children are in the area and that they will be foreseeably attracted to the horse, had a duty to adequately protect these young children from harm. The law presumes that young children, such as six-year-old Judy, cannot appreciate or recognize danger. Thus, the owner of the attraction, such as a horse, had a duty to reasonably protect the children against the dangers of the attraction. The fact that young children trespass at the time of an injury does not relieve the owner of the attraction from liability.

Also, failure of a young child's parent to control or supervise the child is not a defense to an injury under these circumstances. When young children are at risk, the law requires horse owners to exercise reasonable care to prevent harm. What constitutes "reasonable care" depends on the facts and circumstances of each case. Although a three-rail fence might be adequate to keep horses in the pasture, it might be wholly inadequate to keep young children from crawling through or under a fence to get near the horses. An electric fence also might restrain horses in an enclosure, but can be harmful to children in the area. In fact, installing and maintaining an electric fence might, in itself be considered negligent where children could come it contact with it. The facts and circumstances of each case must be examined to determine what is "reasonable."

Other Forms of Liability

Case III

Olive Owner decides to move her horse from her home to a boarding facility. She hears that the Mediocre Stables has space available at a reasonable price. Olive goes to the stable and meets with the owner, Stella Slob. In walking around the facility, Olive notices that the wooden barn houses a stack of hay bales, a pile of wood shavings, a tractor, several gas cans, and a pile of old rags and trash. Power wires leading into the barn are sagging and latches on the doors don't work properly. Olive asks Stella about these problems. Stella replies, they are working on the place but haven't yet been able to complete the necessary repairs. Stella assures Olive that her horse will be well-cared for and, as an act of good faith, agrees to reduce the monthly board bill by $25 if Olive places her horse at Mediocre Stables. Since Olive is desperate for a place to board her horse, and since Stella has made her such a "good deal," she places her horse at the stable. A week after the horse is at the stable, a fire destroys the facility including Olive's horse.

Discussion:

1. Is Stella Slob as owner of Mediocre Stables liable to Olive for the loss of her horse in the fire? Did Stella have a legal duty to protect Olive's horse while it was boarded at her stable?

   a. From the description of the condition of Mediocre Stables it was clearly a disaster waiting to happen. The unsafe conditions described made the occurrence of a fire or other catastrophe very foreseeable; to ignore them imposed liability on the owner of the stable.

   b. Was Olive partially at fault for placing her horse in a facility that was clearly substandard? It could be argued that Olive should have realized that Mediocre Stables was dangerous and that she contributed to the loss of her horse. However, since Olive's horse was placed in the care of Stella, a special responsibility was imposed on Stella as a "bailee." This means Stella had a duty to care for Olive's horse, and to keep it safe and secure while in her possession. The fire that destroyed the horse was clearly caused by the faulty condition of Mediocre Stables, thus imposing liability on Stella for the loss of the horse. Olive as the "bailor" in this situation had no responsibility and could not be legally blamed for the loss.

   c. It is obvious that the dangerous conditions that existed at Mediocre Stables could have been easily corrected. If the hazards had been removed or corrected, the fire would probably not have occurred and there would have been no loss. Thus, the stable owner would not have been liable.

Liability Incurred While Riding

Case IV

Bob Blowhard is a horseman who likes to ride and explore new trails on weekends. Usually, he rides with friends on public trails. However, the usual trails are crowded on weekends with other horseback riders, hikers, bicyclists and

"When you peel back the layers of racing, you are left with the horse and the groom."

Trainer and TB commentator Charlsie Canty, The Backstretch Magazine joggers. Also, it is hard to find places to park vehicles with trailers and is a general hassle. In driving around, Bob notices some rather large farms near where he keeps his horse. Some of these farms contain cattle in fields and some of the other fields are very neat with straight rows of small, green plants growing. On weekends, nobody seems to be around and these farm fields are vacant except for a few cattle. Bob and his friends see no harm in riding in these fields since they do not see any "No Trespassing" signs. There is a barbwire gate that is unlocked and easy to open. So the horses' feet do not get caught in the wire, they open the gates wide and lay the gate back along the fence. Herding the cattle and "playing cowboy" adds excitement and pleasure to Bob's riding experience. It is also fun to ride across and among the straight furrows in the other fields. In short, Bob and his friends have found a great new place to ride, free from the bother of crowds, traffic and other hassles. However, at the end of their ride, Bob and his friends forget to close the gate.

Discussion:

1. Have Bob Blowhard and his friends done anything that could subject them to criminal and civil liability during their ride on the farm?

   a. Criminal and civil liability could be imposed on the riders for trespassing on the farm property. "Trespassing" is entering upon the private property of another without the consent of the owner.

   b. Any damage done by Bob and his friends while riding on the farm to either the livestock or growing crops could result in civil liability for damages and criminal charges for vandalism.

   c. Whether or not the owner or occupant of the land had posted "No Trespassing" signs makes no difference. A trespasser is still liable for going onto property without proper permission regardless of whether signs have been posted.

2. Leaving the gate open and allowing the cattle to escape imposes additional liability on Bob and the other riders. If the cattle wander onto a public road and are struck by a car, liability will be imposed on the riders. Any damage or loss both to the cattle

and any motorist or member of the public, is the responsibility of careless riders who failed to close the gate.

Statutes Limiting the Liability for Horse Activities

The following cases occurred in states that enacted Equine Liability Activity Statutes. In each case, the injured party pleaded the statute as a defense to the claim. Each case will be designated by its state of occurrence.

Michigan   Case V

A claimant's right arm and left shoulder were injured when a horse at a stable bit her. The horse was owned by a boarder at the stable; the claimant alleged she was bitten when she walked by the door of the horse's stall. The claimant was at the stable to help her daughter groom her own horse. The court found that the Michigan statute was properly applied by the lower court in granting a summary judgment to the stable.

Massachusetts   Case VI

The injured party sustained his injuries when the horse he was riding during lessons fell over backward with him. Suit was brought against the stable and the riding instructor. The court granted the defendant's motion for summary judgment based on the Massachusetts equine statute.

Illinois   Case VII

A person was kicked by a livery stable horse on a public trail in this case. The claimant was riding her own horse on the trail when she came upon two friends who were riding horses rented from a livery stable. The two friends were stopped on the trail and were talking. The claimant joined their conversation. One of the rented horses became agitated, turned its body toward the claimant's horse, and kicked both the horse and rider. The rider sustained an injury to her leg. The court held that the claimant's injury was the result of the inherent risks of equine activities and thus was barred by the Illinois statute.

South Dakota   Case VIII

A man was injured when he was struck in the face by a gate while working at a rodeo. The rodeo was sued on the theory that it was negligent in allowing the person to be in a position where he could sustain an injury. The rodeo defended on the grounds that the South Dakota equine statute applies to rodeos as equine activities and that the man's claim was, thus, barred. Surprisingly, the lower court held the statute unconstitutional. However, the state Supreme Court reversed, holding the statute constitutional, and the injured party's claim was barred.

Colorado   Case IX

The claimant was injured while riding a rented horse. Prior to riding, the claimant signed a release containing the statutory warning about the effect of the Colorado statute as barring injuries resulting from the inherent risks of equine activities. The Supreme Court upheld the validity of the Release and found that its language was unambiguous even though the release contained language that expanded the release to include all forms of liability. The effect was to bar any recovery by the claimant from the stable.

Wyoming   Case X

This case involved a claim for injuries when the claimant was thrown from a horse owned by a riding club. The injured party alleged he was injured because of the negligent selection of the horse by a representatives of the club. The claimant also alleged that the club had warranted that the horse that was selected for him would be safe. The court held that the Wyoming Recreation Safety Act precluded recovery.

🐎 PRODUCT LIABILITY

A horse owner buys a 50 pound bag of horse feed. Within hours of feeding it to his horse, the animal is either very sick or dead. Another horseman purchases medicine for his horse, which is designed for preventing of a specific disease or condition. After administering it to the animal, the horse either dies or becomes violently ill. Another horse owner buys new tack for her horse, including a new cinch. After installing the cinch on her saddle, while riding, it breaks and she is injured.

All of these incidents involve the products liability law, which attempts, in proper cases, to compensate the victim for his/her losses by assessing damages against the company that produced the defective product. Common product defects include: faulty packaging, inadequate warnings of possible dangers from the product, design flaws, and manufacturing defects. In most personal injury cases or matters involving damage to property, the claimant must show that the injuries occurred because of someone else's negligence. However, in a product liability case, the law of most states imposes "strict liability" on the manufacturer and, sometimes on the seller, of the defective product. This means it is not necessary for the injured party to show negligence, but only that the injury was caused by the product that was in some way defective.

Common Defenses

Manufacturers are given several defenses to product liability suits and claims, including:

1. That the person bringing the suit or claim was not really injured by the product.
2. The statute of limitations has expired. In all matters, victims have a limited time in which to bring suit for damages, usually one or two years from the time the injury occurred, was discovered, or when the product was sold to the first purchaser (not necessarily the injured party). After this time-period expires, no suit can be brought against the manufacturer.
3. The product was altered in some unforeseeable way after it left the manufacturer's factory. If a customer, seller or shipper alters the product, and the alteration

> "Nothing is as hard to do gracefully as getting down off your high horse."
>
> *Franklin P. Jones*

causes or contributes to the injury, the manufacturer may not be liable.

4. The injured party assumed the risk of using the dangerous product. Some products are inherently dangerous and a person can be hurt if careless.

5. The danger of the product was so obvious that special warnings were not needed. This defense is not as successful as some of the others under the product liability law. Generally manufacturers give warnings with almost all products, even the most obviously dangerous.

6. The product was used, or more accurately "misused," in an unforeseeable way by the victim. An example of this defense is trying to use a cinch as a towrope.

7. The "state of the art" defense means the product was the best available one, using the knowledge available at the time of its manufacture.

Duties of the Manufacturer of a Product

To understand product liability law, it is important to know the three basic duties imposed on manufacturers of products:

1. The product must be made so that it conforms to the manufacturer's plans and specifications.

2. The manufacturer has a duty to identify every possible hazard that could be reasonably anticipated to arise from using of the product. Under this duty, a manufacturer must look at both how the product can be used as well as how it might reasonably be misused. Under this "uses and foreseeable misuses" requirement, a manufacturer is required to anticipate the uses to which its product might be put other than that originally intended. For example, the manufacturer of a plastic feed bucket should know that a customer might use it as a stepladder or stool.

3. The manufacturer of the product must use every reasonable effort to eliminate the hazards from the product by designing them out, if possible. If the hazards cannot be designed out, the manufacturer must provide adequate warnings or instructions directed to the person who is going to use the product. The factors that must be considered by the

manufacturer in determining "adequate warnings" include who is going to use the product, where the product will be used, and under what conditions it will be used. The manufacturer must determine if the warning must be attached to or placed on the product. If non-English speaking users are involved, the warnings must be bilingual. Pictures warning of hazards might be necessary. The warning must be in simple and understandable language to be effective. In summary, the warning must reach and be understood by the users of the product.

Protect Your Rights

It is important for the horseowner to know what to do when an injury occurs due to a defective product. Several steps should be taken after an injury, to protect the injured

Making sure that all of your tack is of the best quality, well fitting and in good condition will help in avoiding product failure.

party's rights and preserve a complete factual record for future use.

The most important thing to remember is: KEEP THE EVIDENCE. Gather whatever is left of the product and keep it in a safe place. This is critical to preserving a link in the chain of evidence that goes directly to the question of what caused the injury and why. Often, product liability cases involve later testing of what is left of a product. Remember to keep the evidence.

Consult with a lawyer as soon as possible for advice and counsel. Not all attorneys handle product liability cases; however, consulting with your lawyer will often result in a

"The stable

wears out a

horse more than

the road does."

French

proverb

referral to a specialist in the field. Product liability law is a very specialized and technical area of the law. It is important that an experienced attorney be consulted as soon as possible after the incident.

Gather all the facts. Note the manufacturer's name, the model of the product, and any serial number, keep sales receipts and retain any packing or instructions. Write exactly when and where the incident occurred and under what circumstances. List the names, addresses and telephone numbers of all witnesses to the incident, including all doctors and hospitals or veterinarians who treated the injured party or horses.

Product liability cases usually occur without warning. Although they are not too common, they do happen with serious results. It is always best to be aware of the potential danger of a product and use it properly. You should also know what to do if you are a victim.

🐎 ANIMAL ABUSE AND NEGLECT LAWS

It is true that the overwhelming number of people oppose animal abuse and neglect. Whether intentional or unintentional through ignorance, society seeks to stop cruelty and punish abusers. The media seizes upon stories involving abused or abandoned animals and virtually all states have laws that protect animals from abuse and neglect. These laws have resulted from a growing concern about the mistreatment of animals, including horses. Although there seems to be a universal recognition of the need for such legislation, there is disagreement over how the problem should be handled.

There is a growing battle between groups known as "animal rights" groups and other groups, or individuals who are perceived as harming animals. There is much confrontation and controversy between advocates of "animal rights" and those conducting rodeos, horse shows, endurance rides, hunter/jumper competitions, etc. The more extreme animal rights groups have conducted demonstrations and attempted to disrupt rodeos, horse shows, and other performances they deem to be exploitive of horses and other animals.

These demonstrations and other disruptions have led to the passage of the Animal Enterprise Protection Act of 1992 by Congress, which makes it a federal offense to disrupt activities involving animals, including horse shows, rodeos, and other competitive animal events. This law became effective on August 26, 1992, and is intended to stop the increasing number of violent and unlawful acts by purported "animal rights" extremist groups against people conducting animal activities.

In the opinion of many, the activities of extremists have done serious harm to legitimate efforts to eliminate animal abuse and neglect. In the case of horses, most experts agree that in addition to strong anti-cruelty laws, there is a need for statutes that clearly address the question of what constitutes "proper care." This latter category involves proving a failure to give proper care, which, without definition and standards, can be very difficult. Also, most cases involving horses fall in the area of not properly caring for animals rather than beating or openly abusing the equine.

> "A horse is the projection of people's dreams about themselves - strong, powerful, beautiful - and it has the capability of giving us escape from our mundane existence."
>
> *Pam Brown*

Horse groups and horse owners acknowledge the need for proper laws to avoid abuse and cruelty and are working for logical and enforceable statutes in these areas. However, with increasing urbanization, horse owners and keepers are frequently becoming the target of unfounded accusations of cruelty and abuse because of a lack of knowledge or misinterpretation by uninformed accusers. For example, horse owners have been charged with failing to properly feed their horses because inexperienced people thought the horses looked "skinny." Trainers have been accused of abusing a horse in training by "running the horse around a small pen at the end of a rope." Riders have been viewed as being "cruel" for using spurs, bits, martingales and other controlling devices. When uninformed people see what they consider to be abusive or cruel activities in connection with horses, they often complain to authorities. Unless the investigating officers are knowledgeable or properly trained, horse owners or trainers can be wrongfully charged with violation of animal cruelty laws.

Every sport can be viewed with suspicion, when looked upon by untrained eyes.

An example of positive legislation regarding animal abuse and neglect is the "Animal Protection Act" enacted in Colorado in 1990. In the language of the Act, its policy and intent is stated as follows:

"The general assembly hereby finds and declares that the protection of companion animals and livestock is a matter of statewide concern; and that it is the policy of this state that persons responsible for the care or custody of such animals be persons fit to adequately provide for the health and well-being of such animals."

The purpose of this legislation is to provide for the protection of mistreated, neglected, or abandoned animals, including horses. The Act provides for the seizure of animals and punishment of abusers. The Colorado statute created the Bureau of Animal Protection, which is charged with enforcement of the act. Officers are trained to recognize improper care of horses and other animals. Quite often, symptoms of neglect are not readily apparent to untrained observers. Through the efforts of animal rescue groups, veterinarians and other horse experts, law enforcement officers are trained in what to look for in neglect cases. Officers are educated on what does not constitute abuse, as well as, what actions are abusive. False or frivolous charges have a better chance of recognition by authorities. This makes the job of officers easier and the rate of apprehension and successful prosecution of actual wrongdoers greater. Other states have enacted similar laws, with varying approaches to enforcement.

Enacting and enforcing animal protection laws, and laws protecting those legitimately using animals in competition, are only one part of addressing the problem. The solution, in the opinion of most experts, lies in educating the public in the proper care and use of horses and other animals. This does not mean giving animals human personalities and emotions. What education is attempting to achieve in areas of proper care and use is how horses are constituted, their nutritional and medical needs, their tendencies, reactions, fears, pleasures, and related matters. If people understand the nature and needs of horses, they can better care for them and avoid unintentional abuse.

A graphic and dangerous problem faced by horse owners across the country is the attempt by "animal rights" groups to classify horses as "companion animals." While this might seem harmless, the true ramifications of this movement can be very damaging to horse owners. The state of California was the birthplace of the push for the "horses as companion animals" movement. Using the commonly popular idea of stopping the slaughter of horses for food as their purported goal, animal rightists activists sought to "piggyback" the concept of horses as pets into the state law. Traditionally, in the majority of states, horses were and still are classified as "livestock." To change this classification to "companion animals," a category traditionally used for dogs and cats, creates problems for horse owners.

Some of the problems that would plague horse owners if horses were legally classified as pets are as follows:

- First, horses would lose the protection of applicable and well-established agricultural codes and tax treatment.
- Second, complaints of cruelty or abuse would be handled by local "animal control officers" a.k.a. dog catchers, who probably would have little or no training or knowledge about the proper care and treatment of horses.
- Third, horse owners could be faced with the same "pet population control" measures that relate to dogs and cats, such as requiring spaying and neutering of horses, and obtaining permits from the government to keep and breed un-neutered horses.

People engaged in horse activities and horse ownership need to be aware of laws addressing cruelty and neglect, as well as, efforts to reclassify the horse as companion animals and the ramifications of such action. Certainly it is important to educate the public about proper care and understanding of horses. Anti-cruelty and neglect legislation indicative of a universal concern about animal welfare. Intelligent and rational legislation is the answer, not emotional and destructive laws backed by groups with their own agendas.

This concern about extreme legislation has spurred a variety of organizations to address the questions of animal cruelty. An example is the "Animal Welfare Code of Ethics" enacted and approved by the Colorado Cattlemen's Association in 1990. The Code's "Statement of Duty" contains an illustration of what seems to be happening in the responsible livestock industry, as follows:

"It is a livestock producer's duty to oppose inhumane treatment of livestock at any stage of the animal's life. Persons who willfully mistreat animals will not be tolerated in our business. We will provide any assistance necessary to proper officials during the investigation and prosecution of individuals who abuse livestock under their care."

The American Horse Council assisted in the passage of the "Commercial Transportation of Equine for Slaughter" bill by Congress. This law addressed the concern that horses being transported to facilities for slaughter were being shipped in improper vehicles and under inhumane conditions. To stop this practice, Congress passed the Act in 1996, which requires that vehicles with proper headroom, of adequate size, with interiors free of sharp edges, maintained in sanitary condition, and with proper ventilation, be used. The law also requires that the horses have adequate food and water, be rested off the vehicle after 24 hours, and that horses be determined physically fit by a veterinarian before loading for travel. This legislation directly addresses the abuses of the prior practices in transporting horses to slaughter.

Associations in every facet of the horse industry have developed rules, standards and tests to protect riders, horses and animals in competition. Show horses undergo testing for drug abuse, judges check for humane curb straps and other equipment. Surgical alteration of show horses is forbidden, and other similar restrictions are enforced

The Professional Rodeo Cowboys Association (PRCA) has approved a fine of $100 against any cowboy who "jerks down" a calf during calf roping. A "jerk down" occurs when a calf roper flips a calf on its head or back after it is roped. This fine helps prevent potential injuries to the calves.

Although there has been substantial progress in the area of enacting anti-cruelty legislation, much remains to be done. Laws must define reasonable standards of care for horses. Protective statutes must provide for penalties appropriate to punish wrongdoers and deter others from improper conduct toward horses. Forfeiture of horses must be forced in extreme cases, to prevent recurrence of abuse. Adequate training of law enforcement personnel is necessary for proper enforcement of anti-cruelty laws. Finally, education of the public about the existence of these laws and proper methods of care of animals must be undertaken.

What is more important than just setting rules is that the courts stand behind these organizations when they are taken to court. An example is the case of <u>Higginson v. American Quarter Horse Association</u> involving a quarter horse stallion named Silver Inspiration, found to have had his tail surgically altered, which violated a new rule of the AQHA's tail testing program. The owner, John Higginson of Sunland, California, appeared before the AQHA's Executive Committee, who revoked the horse's show privileges, suspended Higginson from participation in AQHA approved shows for 90 days and fined him $500. Twice Higginson requested reinstatement of show privileges, then filed a case against the AQHA, asking for monetary damages for alleged injury to his reputation as a trainer and loss of income to his breeding program with Silver Inspiration; he also asked for mandatory reinstatement of the stallion's show privileges and attorney fees. On August 25, 1992, the Texas court decided in favor of the American Quarter Horse Association and against Higginson, ruling that he reimburse the AQHA for its attorney's fees in defending the case.

Horsemen and organizations must continue their efforts to ensure that horses receive proper care and are free from abuse and neglect. The answer to the problem lies in the passage of reasonable, enforceable and intelligent laws that are introduced and promoted by horsemen rather than uninformed "animal rights" groups who often have sinister motives.

In summary, horse people have to be "proactive" in the legislative process. They cannot allow uninformed and emotional groups to propose and pass legislation that could be destructive to the horse industry. National and state legislation should be closely monitored to be sure improper and harmful laws are not successfully passed. Horse people can no longer sit on the sidelines. To protect their way of life they must actively participate in the process.

🐎 HORSE TRAILERING

common part of horse ownership and use is trailering a horse to a veterinarian, horse shows, rodeos, trails, polo matches, and similar places. The ownership and use of horse trailers is very common in the equine world. Until recently, a horse owner did not have to have any special license to haul his horses from place to place, unless a great number of horses necessitated the use of a large van or semi-trailer. Effective April 1, 1992, Congress passed the Commercial Motor Vehicle Safety Act. Under this law, it became illegal to hold more than one driver's license, and uniform minimum nationwide testing and license standards were enacted for the drivers of large trucks and buses.

"The air of heaven is that which blows between a horse's ears."

Arabian

Proverb

Goals and History of the Commercial Motor Vehicle Safety Act

The goal of the Act is to improve highway safety by ensuring that drivers of large trucks and buses are qualified to operate those vehicles on highways. The Act provides that each state retain the rights to issue driver's licenses, and establishes minimum national standards that each state must meet when licensing drivers of larger vehicles, known as, Commercial Motor Vehicle (CMV) drivers.

In years past, many of the 50 states did not require the drivers of large buses or vehicles to have any special training, which created inconsistent rules throughout the nation. The Act is an effort to change the inconsistencies and establish uniform standards for testing the skills of drivers of large vehicles, including horse-hauling rigs.

Under these laws, the driver of a rig as small as a six-horse gooseneck trailer pulled by a one-ton pickup (if gross vehicle weight exceeds 26,000 pounds) is now required to obtain a Commercial Driver's License (CDL). The CDL is obtained from the state motor vehicle bureau, and has additional requirements.

- A written test and driving skills test is required.
- The driving test has to be taken in the type of vehicle the applicant expects to use in hauling horses.
- In addition, a detailed background check of each applicant is necessary; with strict reporting of

accidents, traffic convictions, and similar matters required.
- A medical certification verifies that the driver has the physical ability to operate the vehicle is an important new requirement being imposed on drivers. This medical certificate must be carried by the driver along with his commercial driver's license.
- Another new legal requirement is that the driver must carry a logbook to record all trips of over 100 miles from his/her place of residence.
- Finally, the new federal laws have strict inspection requirements and certifications for commercial vehicles.

Each State to Provide Regulations and Exemptions
Federal regulations are only minimum requirements and each state may enact further safety standards. Each state even has the option to "grandfather" drivers with good driving records and skills test. That is, if they meet special criteria set by the federal government. States are able to choose to exempt drivers from having to get a commercial driver's license if they only transport their own horses for nonbusiness purposes. Often the drivers of farm vehicles are exempt from having to get a CDL.

Horsemen are subject to the Federal Motor Carriers Safety Regulations because they often carry hay, straw or shavings, all of which are extremely flammable and considered hazardous. It is the driver's responsibility to understand the safety standards adopted by their state and have appropriate licensing and insurance coverage.

The Federal Motor Carriers Safety Regulations probably affect more horse owners than the CDL requirements. These are not new requirements. They apply to vehicles used in interstate commerce, which have a gross vehicle weight of over 10,000 pounds and the transportation is "in furtherance of a business enterprise."

It is important to distinguish a "hobby" equine activity from a commercial equine enterprise. Obviously, hauling horses for others for hire is a business enterprise that is clearly subject to applicable motor carrier laws and regulations. However, hauling your own horses, or those of another without charging for the service, generally does not make the hauler a commercial carrier.

Because of these requirements and the states' implementation of these laws, smaller truck and trailer rigs may be regulated as well. It could happen that an owner of a two-horse trailer with a 1/2-ton pickup truck is subject to some Federal Motor Carrier Safety Regulations. The driver may not be required to have a commercial driver's license, yet may be required to carry both a health card and a logbook when operating the vehicle.

The federal penalty to a driver who violates this provision is a civil penalty of up to $2,500 or, in aggravated cases, a criminal penalty of up to $5,000 in fines, or up to 90-days in prison, or both. An employer is also subject to these penalties, if he/she uses a driver to operate a commercial motor vehicle (CMV) without a proper license.

It is important for each person who hauls horses to know the specific requirements of the particular state regarding driving vehicles that pull horse trailers. The telephone numbers of various state offices of motor carriers is included in Table A at the end of this chapter.

The American Horse Council provides three brochures entitled: "*How Federal Motor Carrier Safety Regulations Affect Horse Trailers*," "*The Commercial Driver's License Program*" and "*Office of Motor Carriers Division Offices*." All are prepared by the Federal Highway Administration. Send $2 to AHC at 1700 K St. N.W., #300, Washington, DC 20006-3805 to order the brochures.

For most horse owners traveling to your destination in a structurally sound vehicle with a little comfort and style is important.

Considerations When Hauling Horses

Of course, horsemen want to safely and comfortably haul their horses. Even trips that stay within the horse owner's own state have basic requirements for hauling a horse. Included in the documentation necessary for every trip is proof of ownership of the horse. A brand inspection, proper travel card, or other sufficient proof of ownership is necessary to transport horses. With theft of horses being rather common, plus the imposition of quarantines to control infectious equine diseases, law enforcement agencies are vigilant in monitoring the hauling of horses. It can be very embarrassing to be hauling your own horse and be unable to prove ownership if stopped by the highway patrol.

It is very important when hauling a horse that the horse is healthy, has all necessary shots for the areas where the horse is being taken. Be aware that often roadside rest areas have been sprayed for weeds, so grazing in those areas should not be allowed. It is also important to realize that horses need to drink substantial amounts of water. To avoid problems getting horses to drink or at least drink safe water, many experts recommend taking adequate water with you from home. On longer trips, many horsemen exercise their horses every four hours or so. There are many additional habits or procedures that benefit hauled horses and make their journeys safe and comfortable. Such as; proper shipping boots, bran mash pre-flight meals, non-slip rubber footing and wood or paper shavings to absorb moisture.

Commercial Horse Transports

Especially for longer trips, the use of commercial horse transporters is very common. Another term for commercial transportation carriers is "common carriers." These businesses haul horses for a fee and are regulated by both state and federal laws. The carrier who hauls horses has the legal status of a "bailee" (see Liability of Horsemen, Chapter 12). This means that the carrier has a duty to safely haul the horse(s) to the destination and then deliver them to the proper party, in the same condition as when the horse(s) was initially picked up by the carrier.

Common carriers, including commercial horse haulers, travel interstate and are regulated by federal laws, especially the Interstate Commerce Act and the Commercial Motor Vehicle Safety Act and the regulations thereunder. Among the requirements of these laws are limitations on the number of hours horses or other livestock can remain loaded, plus feed and water availability requirements and mandatory periodic unloading provisions.

There have been a number of cases involving injury, death or damage to horses being hauled by common carriers. In cases of the death of a horse, disputes as to the value of the lost animal are common. The carriers often claim that the limitation of liability, found in the "small print" on the bill of lading, limits its liability to $2,000 per horse. In taking this position, shippers are relying on the Carmack Amendment to the Interstate Commerce Act, which permits agreements between shippers and carriers to limit the latter's liability when shippers are offered various rates for the service based on the value of the cargo. In other words, if you ship horses for the cheapest rate, the owner of the horses is agreeing to limit the carrier's liability to $2,000 per horse. Unfortunately, many shippers are unaware of this limitation and, when a carrier claims it after a loss, are very surprised.

Experience shows that most horse owners, trainers, and others involved in shipping horses are unaware of limitations on the liability contained in the transportation company's bills of lading. Unfortunately, many shippers ignore the "fine print" and are surprised to learn that this often semi-microscopic print contains language limiting the carrier's liability for loss or damage to the horses it carries.

READ THE ENTIRE BILL OF LADING. It is very important for the owner of the horse to know exactly what limitations the carrier is imposing. Protective measures are available such as trip or longer term insurance that cover both the risk of loss from death as well as injury to the horse during shipment. Also, the horse transportation company might offer an option to purchase a higher limitation on the value of the horse(s) for a higher transportation charge.

In any event, horse owners who ship horses by common carriers should by aware of these problems and take appropriate measures to protect their investment. The subjects of necessary documentation, health measures, insurance, and possible limitations of carrier's liability should be addressed by horse owners who transport or ship their animals.

Table A

State Motor Vehicle Offices

Also, check for current information and forms on the internet at www.driversmanuals.com or try "your state Department of Motor Vehicle."

Alabama	334-242-2999	North Carolina	919-715-7000
Alaska	907-269-5551	North Dakota	701-328-2500
Arizona		Ohio	614-995-0714
Phoenix	602-255-0072	Oklahoma	405-231-4607
Tucson	520-629-9808	Oregon	503-945-5000
Arkansas	501-324-9057	Pennsylvania	800-932-4600
California	800-777-0133	Rhode Island	401-588-3020
Colorado	303-205-5613	South Carolina	401-588-3020
Connecticut	800-842-8222	South Dakota	800-952-3696
Delaware	302-326-5000	Tennessee	615-251-5216
DC	202-727-5000	Texas	512-424-2600
Florida	866-467-3639	Utah	801-297-7780
Georgia	678-413-8400	Vermont	802-828-2085
Hawaii	808-532-7700	Virginia	800-435-5137
Idaho	208-334-8606	Washington	360-902-3600
Illinois	800-252-8980	West Virginia	800-642-9066
Indiana	317-233-6000	Wisconsin	608-266-2353
Iowa	800-532-1121	Wyoming	307-777-4375
Kansas	785-296-3671		
Kentucky	502-564-4540	Guam	671-475-5000
Louisiana	877-368-5463		
Maine	207-624-9000		
Maryland	800-950-1682		
Massachusetts	866-627-7768		
Michigan	616-754-3275		
Minnesota	651-296-6911		
Mississippi	601-987-1271		
Missouri	573-751-4600		
Montana	406-444-1773		
Nebraska	402-471-2281		
Nevada	877-368-7828		
New Hampshire	603-271-2251		
New Jersey	888-486-3339		
New Mexico	888-683-4636		
New York	800-225-5368		

refer to your area code in NY Directory

ESTATE PLANNING FOR HORSE OWNERS

orse ownership brings with it many responsibilities. Everyone knows about the need to properly care for his or her horses: to feed them, provide adequate water, keep them in safe and secure surroundings, and provide veterinary care. However, many horse owners are unaware of the need to consider their horses when planning their estate.

For most people, estate planning means planning for our death and the distribution of the property we have accumulated. This means who gets the property and in what proportions. Usually, the person's family is the recipient of the major portion; sometimes, charities, schools or organizations important to the maker of the will receive a gift (bequest). The most important tool used in the distribution of one's property is a properly drawn will. "Properly drawn" means that will satisfies the legal requirements of the particular state where it is prepared and signed. Usually, this means the will must be written, dated, signed by the person making the will ("testator" in the case of a man, and "testatrix" in the case of a woman), and witnessed by two or more independent witnesses. Wills are not required to be filed in courts or other official places and are normally kept in a secure place by either the lawyer who draws it or by the person whose will is made.

This chapter is not intended to be a detailed discussion or analysis of estate planning, but is meant to share some information and suggestions to help horse owners properly provide for the care and disposition of any horse(s) that is/are part of the estate.

According to the law, and for the purposes of determining assets, horses are considered personal property. (Please note, however, that animals are living creatures that need care and feeding, making them unlike other personal property.) When a person dies, all of the assets become part of the estate. If the person has made a valid will prior to death, the provisions of the will dictate how his/her personal property shall be divided, distributed and disposed of.

A business including a horse-related business is considered an important part of an estate. Businesses require special

"We have almost forgotten how strange a thing it is that so huge and powerful and intelligent an animal as a horse should allow another, and far more feeble animal, to ride upon its back."

Peter Gray

planning. This is discussed in more detail in Chapter 1, Forms or Equine Businesses.

What Happens if You Don't Plan

If you die without a will or other estate-planning tool (such as a living trust), your property will be distributed according

to the laws of "intestate succession" of the state where you are living at the time of your death. One who dies with a will is legally described as dying "testate." A person who dies without a will dies "intestate."

Rather than directing how the property is distributed and

It is important to plan for the future care of your horse. After all, no one can live forever.

administered in a will, an intestate estate is distributed according to a statutory scheme contained in the laws of the state where the decedent resided at the time of death. The distribution of the decedent's property is determined by the marital and family status of the deceased. If the decedent is married at the time of death, the surviving spouse receives a portion of the estate, depending on whether there are surviving children. If there are both a surviving spouse and children, in the majority of states the spouse receives one-half of the estate and the surviving children divide the remaining half. If there is no spouse and only surviving children, the children divide the decedent's estate. Generally, the statutory scheme of distribution follows bloodlines without regard to in-laws, friends or other possible recipients. In very few cases is this imposed plan of estate asset distribution satisfactory; and in many cases, it can work a severe hardship on the decedent's survivors. As a lawyer, I strongly advise everyone to have a will. It is easy, relatively inexpensive, and can save family and friends a great deal of trouble later.

Advantages of Having a Will

The main advantage of having a will, is in specifying how

your property will be distributed and how that will be accomplished. Having a properly planned estate and a current will are both good business, but, more importantly, an act of love for the family and animals of the deceased person.

Every horse owner should have a will that, in addition to the other necessary provisions concerning the distribution of his/her property, provides for the immediate care of the horses upon the death of the owner. Unlike inanimate objects that are owned by the deceased, horses require uninterrupted care. This obviously includes immediate feed and water, necessary veterinary care, proper boarding, and other similar arrangements. Horses cannot wait for administration of the estate, proper appointment of estate representatives, hiring of attorneys or accountants, or the filing of necessary probate papers. They must be cared for without delay.

One of the most important provisions in every will is the selection of a Personal Representative (also known as "Executor" or "Executrix") who is the person or institution (such as a bank) charged with carrying out the wishes and directions in the will. Horse owners should select a Personal Representative who is both able and willing to carry out the directives related to the horses expressed in the will and who is knowledgeable enough about horse care to see that the directives are properly followed.

Thoughtful consideration should be given to the question of suitable disposition of the horses identified in the will. Who does the horse owner want to receive the horses? Is the recipient able to care for the horses? Does the recipient want the horses? What is in the best interest of the horses? If the recipient cannot receive the horses, what alternative plan would be best for their proper distribution? Obviously, a horse owner should not leave his or her three-year-old Quarter Horse gelding to 75-year-old Great Aunt Maude who lives in a one-bedroom apartment in Brooklyn, New York.

Occasionally, a newspaper article appears in which an eccentric millionaire leaves money or property to a favorite animal. However, this is invalid under the law because animals are unable to hold legal title to a house, car or other personal property, much less open a bank account. To address the problem of people wanting their horses or other animals to be cared for after the person's death, many states authorize the creation of trusts for the care of animals. Usually these trusts appoint a person or a suitable organization such as a humane society or animal rescue group, to have physical possession and custody of the animal. There is a sum of money or a portion (or all) of the estate set aside for the care of the horse or animal for the rest of its life. These trusts are not allowed in all states, and competent legal advice should be obtained if a trust for the care of a horse or other animal is desired.

Some people have asked that, upon their death, their horse or other beloved pet be put to sleep. At one time these provisions were followed without question. However, this practice has been successfully challenged and is no longer common.

In my practice, I advise my horse owning clients to prepare a separate written letter for use by the Personal Representative or custodian of the horses and their care. I suggest that the letter include the current name, address and telephone number, veterinarian contact information; the health record(s); any special instructions concerning the feeding and care of the horse(s); and any other useful information about the horse(s) such as disposition, suitability for particular uses, and other behavior characteristics. These letters have proven to be very helpful to custodians or Personal Representatives who must deal with and, in many cases sell, or donate the horses to comply with the decedent's wishes.

There are many pitfalls involved in failing to properly plan one's estate. Horse owners should consult a competent attorney to prepare their will and should feel comfortable with the guidance this person provides. Horse owners should take extra care in providing as much information as possible to the attorney during this process. Remember, the attorney might not be experienced in providing for the care and disposition of horses in a will. Ask questions, give the attorney as much information as possible, and consider what is in your horse's best interest. Think ahead, and remember to provide for your horses in your estate plan.

🐎 INSURANCE CONSIDERATIONS

Selecting the Right Insurance Agent

A capable insurance agent should be considered as one of the most important people on your team. A good rule of thumb is to select an agent who accounts one-fourth of his/her business to writing horse-related policies. As with any other business partnership, you want to interview this person to ensure that his/her knowledge is up-to-date and that the product fits your individual situation. Ask others in the industry for references. Some good questions to ask include: "Do you have any advanced degrees or training?" "As an agent, how many companies do you represent or policies are you able to offer us for your specific needs?" "How many years of experience do you have writing this type of policy?" When comparison shopping for an agent, remember to tell each agent the same information about your operation. You may want to have your questions written down, and then write down each prospective agent's answers to help you compare. Make sure to compare prices for the same service(s) and coverage. Indications of a good agent will be his ability to ask you specific questions about your operation and offer some helpful options. The best option for you should be affordable and provide excellent protection of your investment(s).

Requiring some type of recertification education is also becoming popular. There are state and national tests insurance brokers and agents must take to sell insurance within each state. It is a growing trend for the state insurance commissions in some states, to require a specified number of hours of higher education in addition to passing the state and federal exams. In addition to these tests, agents can earn special designations or degrees by taking exams provided by universities or organizations interested in promoting the profession. By passing these additional exams, the agent/broker may add initials behind his or her name, like CIC, CPCU, or IIA

Once you have determined the professional expertise of an insurance agent, it is important to discern that the insurance company itself is strong and healthy. Even after the agent tells you the company is in good shape and the

"Gipsy gold does not chink and glitter. It gleams in the sun and neighs in the dark."

Saying of the

Claddagh

Gypsies of

Galway

paperwork looks impressive, check the information for yourself at your local library.

Publications for references include: Best's Insurance Reports, Standard & Poor's, Moody's Investor Services and Duff & Phelps.

Make sure the insurance company is licensed in the state where you reside. The state insurance commissioner, super-intendent, or director can inform you of the company's insurance status in your state. In some states you will want to look under regulatory agencies in the "blue" or govern-ment-blue pages of the telephone book. Making a few calls will protect you, the insured party, in the event the insur-ance company ceases operation.

If you still want to know more about your insurance agent, contact the National Association of Professional Insurance Agents or Independent Insurance Agents of America. Standard & Poor's will send you a list of rated insurance companies. Call Standard & Poor's Insurance Rating Information Department at 212-208-1527 (be prepared to hold while a representative picks up your call.)

It is of the utmost importance that the insurance agent you select has a working knowledge of the horse industry and listens to your specific needs. Determining what types of insurance the agent/broker has experience with is impor-tant, as well as his concentrated experience in insuring similar types of facilities or activities. Quality of coverage, not price, should be the determining factor after all bids are reviewed.

Several forms of insurance coverage apply specifically to the horse industry. The six basic types of coverage are: mortality, loss of use, surgical/major medical, liability, prop-erty (i.e. tack) and auto insurance and coverage for the drivers. Liability can be divided between farm operations liability and competition liability. (Competition liability is covered in depth in Chapter 12 Liability of Horsemen and case studies and product liability is covered in Chapter 13.) Since mortality insurance has many of the elements of all equine insurance, the next section will study the details.

Examining Equine Mortality Insurance

Mortality insurance is another name for the life insurance

for horses. Most mortality policies cover death by sickness or accident. It also covers theft. The average rate may range from 3% to 6%, of the total value of the horse. Avoid "limited morality" forms of coverage; they cover death due to accidents only not due to sickness.

Horsemen often have mortality insurance on their horses, but make the common mistake of applying what they know about human life insurance to the policies on their horses. This can create problems and misunderstanding due to the differences between the two types of policies. Too often horsemen do not understand the terms and limits of their equine mortality insurance.

Insurance policies are contracts. In return for the premium, the company agrees to provide certain coverage. In the case of equine mortality insurance, it covers for the death of the horse during the policy period (usually one year).

The policy contains conditions that must be strictly followed by the insured in order to keep the coverage in effect. The most common condition in equine insurance is the obligation to give written notice to the insurance company of any accident, illness or disease suffered by the covered horse. Or it may require the attending veterinarian to call the insurance company before the horse can be euthanized. Failure to comply with any of the requirements can void the contract.

When this contract is entered into you are given a toll free telephone number to call in the event the horse becomes sick or hurt and needs to be put down. This is a very important number you can call 24-hours a day. Also, an agent should give you a binder of the policy immediately. This can be done by fax if you come to an agreement on the phone. Beware of agents who speak in general terms or are vague, using statements like "Don't worry that's all covered" or "I'll write in all the details at the office."

In addition to knowledge of the policy conditions, you need to be aware of the exclusions from coverage in the policy.

Common exclusions in the equine mortality insurance policies include:

- Intentionally destroying the covered horse unless the insurer agrees in the terms of the policy that a veterinarian can provide a certificate that the destruction was necessary to prevent inhumane suffering.

- In the event of poisoning, it must be proven to be accidental.

- Theft or escape of the horse is often excluded unless it is specifically covered in the policy. In the case of theft coverage, a policy usually requires immediate notice of the loss to law enforcement agencies to the insurer. Mysterious disappearances are not covered.

- The death of the covered horse caused by certain surgery is often excluded unless it was done by a qualified veterinarian; was certified by the vet to be necessary due to accident, illness or disease, and was done to save the horse's life.

Over the years, disputes involving equine mortality insurance have led to extensive litigation. Courts have been asked to resolve controversies over the actual value of a deceased horse when:

- The promptness and adequacy of the notice to the insurance company is questionable
- The horse was euthanized
- Fraud may be involved, or
- Loss of use or a disability case.

When a controversy involves the value of a horse, the question is usually whether the horse was covered for the ACTUAL VALUE or the AGREED VALUE. This amount of course, should not exceed the insurance policy's limits on the particular horse.

Insured values are usually based on the purchase price. If homebred, the insurance company usually insures to twice the stud fee. Increased values require justification of value and must be approved by the insurance company. Increased values may include: training fees paid, breeding records, show records and appraisals. This is very different from life insurance on humans in which a policy pays a certain amount upon the death of the covered person. The difference between these types of policies is often a surprise to the horse owner who is unfamiliar with this distinction.

There are three common types of coverage for horses.

1. The first specifies that the value of the horse be determined at the time of death. The owner has to prove the value of the horse or accept the appraiser's value. In the event the two cannot agree, some states have arbitration requirements.

2. The second type of policy requires that the owner prove the value of the horse every quarter.

3. The third type of policy has an agreed-upon price. Often, the owner of a deceased horse thinks he/she has this type of policy, when, in fact, the value of the horse was never agreed on. The "predetermined" or "agreed-upon value" type of policy may be best, because, at the time when an owner is grieving, the added burden of placing a value on the horse has already been taken care of.

A common area of controversy involves cases in which there has been a failure to notify the insurer immediately of illness or surgery related to a horse's cause of death. When the insurance company is unsuccessful in showing that the insured failed to give immediate notice, the coverage may be voided.

The owner of a horse must take the responsibility to make sure that all paperwork is filled out completely. This means: complete the application, have the vet examine the horse and complete the certificate, then mail the paperwork along with the check to the insurance agent. Mark your calendar to repeat this process again, usually in 11 months. If you have any special circumstances or questions, call your agent. You should receive a renewal notice in the mail to help remind you to repeat the process; however, mistakes happen and things get lost in the mail, so take it upon yourself to make sure all things happen when they should. If your horse dies after an insurance policy is allowed to lapse, the coverage will be considered void.

When a horse is euthanized, disputes are common and often end up in court. Obviously, under any kind of life insurance a beneficiary cannot kill the covered party and collect under the policy. In equine mortality insurance situations, however, disagreements arise as to whether a sick or insured horse should be euthanized. Although all disputes have not been resolved, the American Association of Equine Practioners has established and published guide-lines and criteria to follow for determining whether euthanasia is proper.

- Is the condition chronic and incurable? Has the horse a prognosis for life?
- Is the horse a hazard to itself and its handlers?
- Will the horse require constant pain-relieving mediation for the rest of its life?

Disputes often arise over when notification of illness should be given to an insurance company. Courts have held that when notice of an illness is not given, the insured assumes the risk of death for that particular illness. The horse owner or his/her bailee (The agent taking care of the horse for the owner) is often forced to make a "judgement call" on whether the insurance company should be notified of a particular condition or illness. If the horse is in the care of others, the caretaker should be advised of the requirements and conditions of the policies regarding notice of illness or injury. Requirements of written notice should also be strictly followed. If the bailee takes on the added responsibility of caring for such a valuable horse, the stable owner may indeed want to charge a higher price to board an insured animal.

Another version of the question of notification under diffi-cult circumstances is when a horse is in distress and in a remote location. While it is possible that a horse may become sick while at a distant area such as a ranch, or on a trail ride, there are steps one can take to help the insur-ance policy stay in effect. In today's world of advanced communication, at least one rider should be carrying a cellular telephone and communication can be made within a reasonable amount of time. In the event the animal has to be euthanized without proper witnesses, an autopsy may be performed later by a vet. Common sense dictates that the best solution is the keep unusually valuable horses close to home.

Does the insurance company have to be notified every time your horse has the sniffles? This can present very real problems to a horse owner and the insurance agent. The best advise in notification cases is to PLAY IT SAFE. Give notice of ALL cases and situations where there is even the slightest chance of a problem condition or illness. (Any time you have to call the vet.) Insurance companies often have a toll free number manned around the clock. In the event a horse must be spared any further suffering, permission to euthanize is usually given within 20 to 30 minutes. At the very LEAST, give notice to the insurance company of the following conditions:

- Lacerations requiring sutures
- Lameness lasting more than two (2) days
- Any condition requiring surgery
- Any bone fracture
- Colic that continues three (3) to four (4) hours
- Fever accompanied by no appetite

Some policies require the owner to notify the insurance company of any visit by a veterinarian and to use a vet when necessary.

Make sure your insurance agent understands the horse industry and your individual needs.

Loss-of-use Insurance

The "loss-of-use" clause may be an extension of the mortality contract. It covers the owner in the event of an accident that renders an animal unusable for a specified purpose. This is common for horses that earn considerable income as race horses or grand-prix jumpers. If an injury renders a horse unusable for such a purpose, the owner may suffer loss of income; thus, the loss-of-use clause protects the owner from the risk. The loss-of-use clause of policy usually specifies how an animal can be used. For example, a 14-year-old girl decides to use one of her father's broodmares in a jumping competition; the mare becomes injured and is later destroyed. The insurance policy may be void if it specifically covered the horse as a "broodmare."

Major Medical or Surgical Insurance

Major medical is usually considered superior to surgical insurance because it pays most of the nonsurgical costs plus the surgical fees. Another type of insurance gaining popularity is "surgery only." Surgical coverage is only available with full mortality and basic coverage. Both of these types of coverage pay for necessary, non-cosmetic surgery. Colic surgery is an example of "necessary" surgery and is covered after the deductible is satisfied and up to the maximum claim allowed on the contract. The difference between major medical and surgical insurance policies is coverage for nonsurgical costs.

These policies are also contracts that specify what will be covered or what may be excluded, which as mentioned above, varies. This coverage may be in addition to the mortality policy or a loss-of-use policy. Like health insurance for humans, the policy usually covers medical costs minus the deduction and with certain financial limits. An example of policy limits is if the policy covers the full surgeon's fee but allows for only 25% of the other costs involved in the surgery. The policy also may specify that surgery be performed in a vet clinic to ensure proper healing. Frequently, a horse that has undergone colic surgery is not eligible to be reinsured when the annual policy comes due, or may be banned from coverage for a certain number of months.

Farm and Ranch Liability Coverage
The coverage necessary to protect the owner of a farm or ranch is much different than coverage provided by a regular homeowner's policy. The liability coverage varies for almost everyone. It also differs from state to state, depending upon protective legislation enacted to limit lawsuits. (See Chapter 12, Liability of Horsemen and Case Studies.)

Be aware that if the state in which you reside has any legislation regarding liability of horseman, it usually does not cover attorney fees or the fees of expert witnesses to prove your defense in court. Some state statutes do not cover defective tack. Because certain expenses involved in proving that you or your horse were not liable for an accident, you want the extra insurance coverage mentioned in this section.

When selecting farm and ranch liability coverage, review all activities that have ever been - or ever will be done on the property. For instance, will there ever be small shows for which competition liability should be considered; or at which a spectator could be injured? Will there be any guest trainers working at your facility? Before changing day-to-day operations, make sure the new changes will be covered. And, unfortunately, activities like horseback riding are considered "high risk" and have seen great leaps in policy costs over the years. In 1983, a policy could be written for a livery stable for about $600. This same livery stable could further be defined as one that owned 20 horses and rented them to the public to ride, boarded about 20 horses and gave lessons. In 1993, the average premium for this same outfit was about $3,500.

Keep Abreast of Liability Coverage Changes

In May of 2001, the Health Insurance Portability and Accountability Act of 1996 (HIPAA) went into effect much to the dismay of horse riders and others who engage in outdoor sports. Under the provisions of this law, insurers and employers may now negotiate group health plans to exclude from coverage people who participate in horseback riding, skiing, ATV riding, snowmobiling and other similar "dangerous activities." The HIPAA was originally passed in 1996 for the stated purposes of improving the availability, affordability and access to group health insurance coverage. It is thought that in passing this law, Congress intended to protect individuals, like horseback riders, from discrimination and the denial of coverage simply because they participated in riding or other activities. However, as is often the case in legislation, these lofty goals became "folded, spindled and mutilated" when federal agencies were directed to propose regulations known as "interim rules" to govern the implementation of the Act.

Check with your state and local horse councils and qualified insurance agents for current information.

Coverage of Actual Property

This additional coverage includes the outbuildings, barns, tack, machinery and feed. Most homeowner policies do not cover items like tack. Such items are considered restricted under the policy because not every homeowner would have such items. Your tack may not be covered if it is kept at a second location e.g., a boarding stable or in your trailer.

Also, don't expect the owner of the boarding stable to have coverage on *your* tack. After all, his/her policy does not

"When you cease to make a contribution you begin to die."

Eleanor Roosevelt

consider that the boarding stable owner has an insurable interest in your tack. Ask your insurance agent if your policy specifically endorses the second premises in which your property resides.

Also not covered, is the silver on show saddles, unless you have an extension for precious metals.

Many times property is stolen while you are at a horse show or otherwise away from home. Some theft policies require that the owner prove forced entry. In this case, you may want to get an added endorsement for an unlocked vehicle.

One of the strongest recommendations made by insurance agents today is to have photos or a video tape of your belongings and list the value of each item. This type of verification is only valid if you have two copies made of the tape or photos and send one to the insurance agent. If you have only one video tape of your belongings, it could be lost in a fire or it may be difficult to prove indeed your possessions since they are all lost. Most insurance agents provide guidelines and/or room by room accounting forms to help you take inventory of your property.

Having enough insurance can be a substantial investment. Before you invest in coverage, reevaluate your specific needs. Divide your belongings into three different categories.

First, itemize all the things you would find impossible to replace. These "catastrophic" losses would include your home, family, barn and horses. These you must find the resources to have insured.

Second, list all items that could be replaced for a price. You have to set your own limits of what price you can pay to have the items replaced. By selecting a number like $5,000, you are able to set your own limits and insure everything worth more than this amount. Once you set an amount, stick to it.

Third, items you could replace without any great hardship. These might be items under $500.

This exercise will help you keep your insurance costs down, while covering items that really should be covered.

Auto Insurance and Coverage for Drivers

There are different types of coverage for different types of drivers. Not every driver is over 30, has a good record and pulls only a small two-horse trailer. Many drivers fall into one of three categories: high risk, commercial license required, or hauling hazardous materials.

A high risk driver may have had accidents, tickets or other situations that restrict their coverage. This driver may be able to get coverage while hauling a horse trailer, but with limitations. The policy may not cover the trailer while not hooked-up to the truck, or the contents like horses and tack, it may be limited on its liability coverage.

A commercial driver may be driving a larger rig. That is, a truck and trailer weighing over 26,000 pounds. (Check with current Interstate Trucking Laws).

A hazardous materials driver is the one hauling hazardous materials. Farmers working with pesticides and fertilizers are frequently exposed to what can be defined as "hazardous materials." "I don't see how this would concern me?" you might ask. Since hay is extremely flammable, it is considered hazardous material. Let your insurance agent know exactly what your needs are and be honest with them when they ask you tough questions.

Barn Safety Tips

After taking inventory of your barn and all its possessions, take special precautions regarding safety. The following list will help make your barn a safer place:

- No smoking signs should be posted and enforced
- Fire extinguishers should be located near the electrical panel box, doors, feed and tack rooms
- Fire exits should be clearly marked
- Portable heaters are not recommended for barn use. Check with plumbing and heating professionals for safe alternatives
- Make sure electrical outlets, light fixtures and wiring are safe. Have them checked every few years or whenever wear is noticed
- Each stall should have vital information on the stall

card along with a list of important phone numbers near the phone/office

• First aid kits should be on hand and everyone should know where they are

• Keep all alleyways and traffic patterns clear in case of fire or an other emergency

• Hay and bedding should be stored away from heat and electrical sources; if possible, in a metal shed separate from the barn.

Check with your insurance agent and/or your state Cooperative Extension Service for more information about barn safety.

In addition to selecting a suitable insurance policy, create and post an emergency plan. Be sure it is understood by everyone who frequents the barn.

Emergency Plan

Every good Safety Plan includes a list of emergency procedures. This plan could be written into an employee handbook. It should also outline barn safety tips and guidelines for safe handling and riding.

Many first-time riding lessons include safety techniques before the student is allowed to ride. Other good safety measures for the riding instructors to have a current First Aid and know CPR.

The following are some suggestions for your emergency plan:

1. Call 911 if anyone becomes hurt. Have fire, police, sheriff, veterinarian(s) or other pertinent information near the phones.

2. Contact the vet in the event a horse becomes sick or injured.

3. Just as you would in any auto related accident, get the insurance information for any other person involved. If there are any witnesses, get their names and phone numbers.

4. Contact your insurance agent and have your insurance policy handy.

5. Photos help answer questions for the insurance agent or the adjuster. These photos may be of defective tack, the situation that caused an accident or any injuries sustained.

6. If you live in an area where natural disasters occur, make yourself aware of any safety precautions and procedures necessary. Ultimately, the horse owner is responsible for having adequate insurance coverage.

You should feel comfortable with your insurance agent before you sign on the bottom line.

THE DYNAMICS OF A LAWSUIT

Whether a person is the one bringing a lawsuit (plaintiff) or the one being sued (the defendant) a lawsuit has the same dynamics. Dynamics here means that a certain set of time deadlines applies to both sides of a lawsuit. Each case must pass through certain stages; and trials have uniform procedures that must be followed. The obligations of parties to lawsuits are often unknown or mistakenly based on what people see on television or in the movies. It is very easy to threaten to file a lawsuit; before that becomes a reality, it is important to know exactly what happens when a suit is filed.

Two factors to any lawsuit often shock inexperienced litigants: cost and time. The cost includes court filing fees, attorneys fees and related expenses, such as costs of discovery.

Probably the least expensive part of a lawsuit is court filing fees. Usually, when a party files a suit (plaintiff), he/she must pay a filing fee that ranges from $25 to $150. If a jury trial is requested, the plaintiff must pay a jury fee of an additional $100, depending on the fees set by the particular court. In the case of a person who has been sued (defendant) he/she must pay an answer fee ranging from $45 to $200 at the time a response to the complaint is filed. These fees vary from state to state.

Attorney fees often surprise people involved in lawsuits. Attorney fees based on a percentage of a recovered amount are called "contingent fees." "Flat fees" are a set amount for the legal service rendered. More information will be covered in Chapter 23, on How to Select An Attorney.

Most lawyers charge on a "fee for time spent" basis. For all types of services performed on behalf of a client, a charge is made based on the amount of time each task takes. If a lawyer's hourly rate is $175, this amount is the multiplier for the amount of time spent. For example, if the lawyer spends 15 minutes preparing a letter for the client, the client is charged $52.50 for the letter. Many people are shocked when they receive a bill from their attorney for such items as telephone calls, dictation, investigation, research, travel, facsimile charges, and similar matters. Inexperienced clients mistakenly think that lawyers charge only for court appearances, conferences with either them or the other attorney, and similar major items. Being charged for "thinking about the case" or talking to the lawyer on the telephone can be upsetting, especially when the same hourly rate is charged by the lawyer for all matters involving the case. A client might ask why the lawyer charges the same rate for talking to him in his office as he charges for appearing in court. In fact, although there are exceptions, most lawyers who charge on an hourly fee basis charge the same for all services ranging, from telephone calls to actual trials.

Also, the fees are not merely charged for the time spent by the lawyer participating directly in the case. The time charges also apply to the time spent traveling to court, waiting for the case to be called, and other times that seem, to the client, to be "dead" time. However, lawyers justify these charges by first quoting from Abraham Lincoln that "A lawyer's time and advice are his stock in trade," then reminding the client that, but for his/her case, the lawyer could have spent the time on other financially productive matters.

Attorney fees are charged to both sides of a lawsuit and can be a major portion of the cost of either bringing or defending against a lawsuit. The question is often asked whether the attorney's fees can be recovered against the losing party in a lawsuit? With very few exceptions the answer is "no." The only expenses the winning party can recover against the losing party are the court filing fees, jury fee, discovery expenses, and interest on any amount of money awarded by the court. It is important to know that the award to costs is at the discretion of the judge of the court where the case is tried. If the judge thinks the amount sought for reimbursement is unreasonable, the judge may refuse to order them paid by the losing party. So even though the prevailing party pays certain costs, there is no guarantee that the court will compel the other party to repay these costs.

The time involved in a lawsuit is another factor that must be taken into account by a party involved in a lawsuit.

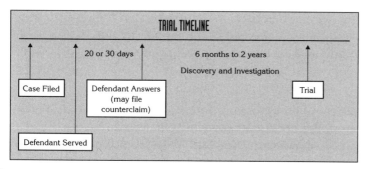

TRIAL TIMELINE

20 or 30 days   6 months to 2 years

Discovery and Investigation

Case Filed   Defendant Answers (may file counterclaim)   Trial

Defendant Served

Conservatively, most lawsuits filed in a court of unlimited jurisdiction (District or Superior Court) take one to three years from the time the case is filed until it is tried. In some states, four to five years is common. In cases of limited jurisdiction where the amount of damages is capped at a certain sum (e.g., $5,000 or $10,000), trial dates are usually within one year from the date the case is filed. Regardless of which type of court is involved, the rules of procedure of each state mandate certain time deadlines and requirements.

A plaintiff starts a lawsuit by filing a Complaint with an appropriate court, and having a copy of it and a Summons served on the defendant(s). A Complaint is a legal document that states why the case is being filed in the particular court, what the plaintiff claims the defendant(s) did that was wrong and in violation of the law, why the plaintiff is entitled to damages from the defendant(s), and the amount of money or other damages (such as return of a horse). Which the plaintiff is seeking from the defendant(s). A Summons is a legal form served with a Complaint. Its purpose is to notify the defendant(s) that the case has been filed against them and that they have a certain time to respond to the Complaint, usually 20 to 30 days from the date it is served on the defendant(s).

The Summons and Complaint are "served" upon the defendant(s) by having a person over the age of 18 years, personally hand a copy of the documents to the defendant(s) or, in some cases such as where the defendant is a corporation, hand the documents to the designated "registered agent" of the corporation. If the defendant cannot be located and the court approves service can also be accomplished in other ways, such as by publication in a newspaper.

After service has been accomplished on the defendant(s)' side, the time schedule of the lawsuit begins. As mentioned, the defendant(s) must respond or answer the statements contained in the Complaint within 20 to 30 days after the date it was served depending on local law.

If a defendant ignores or forgets to respond within this time period, the court can enter a Default Judgment against the non-answering defendant, A Default Judgment which is an order entered by the court saying that since the defendant failed to respond within the required time, they have admitted they are wrong and the plaintiff is entitled to the damages asked for in the Complaint. Thus, it is *extremely* important for a defendant to respond within the time required by law.

In addition to filing a timely response or "Answer", a defendant might believe he/she is entitled to something from the plaintiff. This is quite common in business transactions when one party either fails to perform as promised or in the opinion of the party, the horse or other subject of the transaction was not as represented. If a defendant feels he/she is entitled to a set-off or credit against the suing party (plaintiff), or if the defendant has been damaged by the plaintiff's action or inaction, the defendant may file a Counterclaim within the time required for an answer. A Counterclaim is just like a Complaint, only it is filed by the defendant(s) against the plaintiff(s), claiming the plaintiff did something or failed to do something they were supposed to do, thus entitling the defendant to damages against the plaintiff. Often a Counterclaim requests that the defendant receive a "set-off" or credit against anything that may be awarded to the plaintiff. If a defendant files a Counterclaim, the plaintiff is required to file a written response within a certain period of time, usually 10 to 20 days, or face the threat of a default Judgment granted to the defendant on the Counterclaim.

Once all of the necessary Complaints, Answers, Counterclaims, and Replies to Counterclaims have been filed with the court in a timely manner, the case is deemed "at issue." This means it may proceed to the next stages, culminating in a trial.

After the case is "at issue," the next phase in the dynamics of a lawsuit is the "discovery" phase. Discovery means taking depositions, filing interrogatories, requests for admissions, requests for inspection of premises or records, and producing of documents involved as part of the case.

Depositions are when parties or witnesses are asked questions by the attorneys, under oath, in front of a certified shorthand reporter who records both the questions and answers verbatim. Depositions are usually taken at the office of one of the attorneys or the reporter's office. Attorneys for both sides of the lawsuit are present; and, if they so choose, the parties (plaintiff and defendant) can be present. In fact, usually the earliest Depositions taken are of the parties themselves. The goals of taking Depositions usually are twofold: to learn information from the other side as to the basis of the claim or position second, to "pin them down to a story." This is important because Depositions are transcribed by a reporter, read by the person whose Deposition was taken, then signed by the deposed witness, thus making it hard for anyone to change testimony later at trial. Of course, since the Deposition is taken under oath, there is the threat of being charged with perjury if a witness lies.

Other forms of discovery (e.g., written interrogatories, requests for admissions, requests for inspection, production of documents or things) are equally important.

Interrogatories are questions asked of a witness in writing rather than orally as in a Deposition. The witness must answer the questions in writing under oath within a prescribed period of time, usually 30-days from the date the questions or interrogatories are received. Since the answers to the questions must by under oath, the witness is locked into a story that cannot be readily changed later. Perjury is a threat for lying in answers to interrogatories.

Requests for Admissions can have a dramatic effect on a case if the time for response is not followed precisely. As the name implies, Requests for Admissions are written statements that require the other party to either admit or deny the accuracy of the statement. From a legal standpoint, the items requested are usually the "guts of the case." They are the elements of proof necessary to prove the case of the asking party. Like other forms of discovery, the party to whom the Requests are directed must respond in writing within a specific period of time, usually 30 days from the time received. Failing to respond within that time has the effect of admitting the truth of all of the admissions requested. This has a very severe penalty in most lawsuits.

Requests for Inspection of records or premises are discovery tools whereby the requesting party asks to see (and copy or photograph) records or premises important to the lawsuit. The court usually allows these requests; certain times and conditions are established for the inspection. The court usually sets the time, date and scope of the inspection. Failure to obey these conditions can result in punishment by the court in the form of fines or, in extreme cases, the loss of the lawsuit.

Like requests for inspection, another very common discovery technique is a request by one party to the other for Production of Documents. By filing a Request for Production, a party is seeking to review and obtain copies of specific documents that relate to the subject matter of the lawsuit. These documents might be copies of bills, financial papers, medical records. As in the case of the other discovery techniques, there are strictly enforced time limits that must be observed when producing the documents.

A lawsuit is not something you should jump into without careful consideration. It is often financially wiser to settle out of court.

The discovery phase of a lawsuit is very time-intensive and can be very expensive. Attorneys charge for their efforts in locating, attending, participating in, preparing and all other phases of discovery. In fact, this time of the dynamics of litigation is often the most expensive because it involves the extensive use of the attorney's time and also other expenses, such as paying for the services of shorthand reporters, purchasing copies of records and paying for the time of expert witnesses.

The time of preparing for a trial can be very expensive in both time and money. The attorney usually requires the assistance of the client in review discovery, planning pre-sentation of the case, organizing witnesses and exhibits, and numerous other tasks that must be done. Generally the final phase of a lawsuit is the trial itself.

Additional costs often incurred are when it is necessary to "subpoena" witnesses for the trial. A Subpoena is a docu-ment issued by the court ordering a witness to attend the trial and testify at a certain time and place. The witness is paid both mileage from his/her residence to the courthouse and a witness fee. Mileage is usually paid from $.15 to $.30 per mile; non-expert witness fees range from $1.50 to $3.00 per day. Expert witness fees are very expensive and can easily exceed $500 per day. Experts are commonly used in cases when their testimony will help the court or the jury understand more technical or involved matters. Medical doctors, veterinarians, accountants, appraisers, engineers and surveyors are commonly used as experts in court.

The cost of the actual trial is often the most expensive element of a lawsuit, because many attorneys charge a larger fee for time spent in trial than other phases of the case. This is because all of the lawyer's time, effort, and concentration are directed to trying the case. Often the work begins after each trial session ends. It is common for a lawyer to work all, or a major portion of the night, between sessions. The client too spends entire days in court, and often meets and works with the lawyer at night between court sessions. The cost is certainly not measured alone in dollars, but also in nerves and emotional strain.

Depending on the outcome of the trial, controversies are often not concluded even after a decision by a judge or jury. Appeals and motions for a new trial are quite common and add to the expense of the controversy.

In summary, before becoming voluntarily involved in a lawsuit, know what you are getting into. The costs can be astronomical in both money and emotion. Fortunes can easily be lost in court. Very seldom are fortunes made in that manner. In considering whether to sue, I tell clients to consider litigation like surgery. It is better to try other more conservative methods first. The same is true for attempting to resolve a problem by bringing a lawsuit.

Alternative Resolutions of Disputes

Many knowledgeable persons have said "Litigation is the newest indoor sport in America." The number of cases filed has clogged the court system, causing long and expensive delays. The legal system has long been searching for ways to lessen the number of lawsuits filed and to make resolutions of disputes quicker and more economical. A number of methods have been tried with some success. It is as important for horse people to know about the existence and availability of these methods.

Arbitration is a method of resolving disputes short of an actual trial. Both sides to a controversy agree to present their cases to either a single arbitrator or a panel of arbitrators who decide the controversy after hearing both sides. Arbitration can be either "binding" or not; most effective arbitration procedures are binding. This means both parties agree in advance that the decision of the arbitrator(s) will end the controversy. They agree to take no further action and to do what is decided by the arbitrator(s).

One of the economies of arbitration is the fact that less time is spent by the attorney in preparing and presenting the case. Also, there is less discovery and there are fewer witnesses. Another advantage is that arbitration takes far less time from start to resolution than a lawsuit. It is estimated that arbitration takes less than one-third of the time and cost on litigation of the same controversy.

Prior to starting the procedure the arbitrators are selected and approved by both parties, usually through their attorneys, If both sides agree on one arbitrator to hear and decide the case, the matter is usually resolved rapidly and at modest cost. However, if selection of an agreeable single arbitrator is not possible, usually each side selects one person to act as an arbitrator, and those two people select a third arbitrator, and all three serve on the panel. This is more expensive than a single arbitrator because each person serving is paid, but the savings is still far greater than proceeding with a traditional lawsuit.

Arbitration is not a new procedure, and it has been used successfully in the construction industry for many years. Information about arbitration, a list of available qualified persons to serve, and procedures by which arbitration is conducted are available from the American Arbitration Association. The organization maintains offices in all states and is an excellent resource on alternative dispute resolution.

Mediation is another method of resolving a dispute without incurring the costs and time delays associated with a lawsuit. A person is selected to serve as a negotiator, and acts as an advisor and "go-between." The mediator is often a lawyer or former judge who is approved and selected by both sides. He/ she first requires that each party send a confidential written statement of their case, why there is a controversy, and what they want from the other side. After the mediator has received these confidential statements, a meeting is scheduled with both parties and their lawyers. At that meeting, the mediator usually separates the parties and privately gives his/ her opinion of the validity of the respective cases. Both the strong and weak points of the position are discussed with each side. The mediator then shuttles between the respective sides in an effort to resolve the dispute and settle the controversy. If successful, the matter is concluded.

Like arbitration, mediation requires both parties to be willing to settle and resolve the controversy. The parties have to approach the process with an open mind and in good faith. These methods of resolving disputes are far less expensive and time consuming than litigation, yet they require willing participants to be effective.

"While there are many things you can fake through in this life, pretending that you know horses when you don't isn't one of them."

Cooky

McClung,

Horsefolk Are

Different

 MARKETING

The word marketing in this book refers to the total offering made to a consumer in exchange for something of value

An Overview of the Marketing Mix

The term "marketing" will be divided into: Marketing, Public Relations, Customer Service, Government Relations and Advertising. Marketing has a critical management function. It has become an in-depth science with a unique language of its own. To be successful in almost any venture, it is important to understand the basic principles of marketing. Marketing will help you gather and maintain happy customers who are willing to pay a reasonable price for your product(s) or service(s). The four basic ingredients to the marketing mix are:

1. Product/Service
2. Promotion
3. Price
4. Distribution

Product or Service

What is your product or service? Are you managing a horse show, or are you the owner of a stallion? If you have prepared a business plan, you will be able to define your product/service in one concise sentence. The people I have met in the horse industry have a difficult time deciding what they offer to a customer that is uniquely theirs. What makes your product or service different from anyone else's and why would the consumer want to pay hard-earned money for it? How you view your product or service may differ from how others see your offering. You must do research to determine how other people see you to know how you want to be viewed and to appoint what your unique selling point is.

Everyone in the horse industry wants to be at the top of the pricing spectrum. They are so "barn blind" they think that their horses are the best. I ask, "The best at what?" Remember, Cadillacs and Volkswagens have different markets, but there are enough people who need these different products so each can be profitable.

> "Know the course before you mount the horse."
>
> *Pamela C. Biddle and Joel E. Fishman,* All I Need to Know I learned From My Horse.

Price

Setting the price for your product or service makes a statement of what you think your product is worth. Just make sure it is in the same ballpark as your competitors. If you are not in the same price league, you had better be able to justify the difference. If you are selling a horse or stallion service, you may want to look at similar horses, then determine what your customers might pay. With real estate, a sales person emphasizes the importance of location. Now that we can ship mares or a stallion's semen almost anywhere in the world, location does not set limits on the pricing structure; however, the price you set must be in accordance with what the market will pay for that product or service at that time and in your marketplace.

It is easier to set the price high and come down; if you do the reverse, the customer will not trust your judgment. A classic example is of a simple household product like toothpaste. If the manufacturer offers a coupon for 50% off for too long a time, the customer will begin to believe the toothpaste was worth only 50% of the asking price.

Price is important for setting the value of your product or service in the mind of your customer, especially in similar markets. If you have invented something completely new and have no pricing references, you need to learn what people would be willing to pay for the product. For example, if you invented a self-cleaning stall, first you must find out what horse owners are will pay for it.

Promotion

This covers both advertising and public relations. Both topics will be discussed in later chapters. We see these aspects most often and need to study them in order to better apply the basics to fit our needs.

Distribution

In today's market, we are better able to make a product or service available to almost any consumer in any part of the world. Because of technological advancements, this area of the product mix offers the most new choices. Tack stores not only have a trailer they can take to a horse show; tack can be sold over the Internet as well. Trainers and clinicians now sell riding programs not only with books, but also with video tapes and newsletters and using catalogs and speaking engagements helps reach new markets everyday. We have mentioned before the importance to both stallion and mare owners of transported semen. Today people can buy horses, equipment, trailers and trucks using the World Wide Web.

Your distribution question will be, 'How can I get my product to the customer in a new or better way?' Do research. Ask what else your distribution sources can do to help you better serve your customer. This would be an excellent time to think outside the box. Ask yourself, "what are the other possibilities?"

Analyzing Your Market and the Environment

Sometimes we are unable to control our environment and we are forced into a reactionary mode. Visualizing all possibilities can help you plan for any type of situation.

Two points matter most when analyzing your market; planning and recognizing that horses are not a necessity in our world today. No matter how much we care about the horse industry, it is not more important than clean air, water, food or cash. The industry depends on leisure funds and the competition for that money is fierce.

With population growth, horses will become more of a luxury item. It will be more difficult to purchase good quality feed and to own the land to keep horses on will become

more expensive. As a result more and more horses will be kept at boarding stables. How will these environmental changes affect the way you run your horse business?

The following section headings are things to take into account for analyzing your marketplace.

Target Market

A target market is who will actually pur-

Marketing is the total offering made to a consumer in exchange for something of value. Take the lead - don't eat the dust of others.

"Don't rely on someone else to tighten your girth."

Pamela C. Biddle and Joel E. Fishman, All I Need to Know I learned From My Horse.

chase your product or service. It is important to have a realistic picture of your market. Who you perceive to be your customers is probably a mental picture of who we would *like* to have as your customers.

When I ask people in the horse industry to identify their customers, they say they want to sell the best horses at the top price. Realistically, not everyone fits this market. Someone has to sell to the average trail rider, backyard horse owners, and 4-H or Pony Club riders whose parents are on a budget.

Car dealers have learned to offer a variety of automobiles to fit every need and budget. Not everyone drives a Jaguar. All big companies do research before they launch a new product to see if there is a market for their concept. How many horse breeders do you know who can say their horses are sold, cash in hand, before the mare is even bred? Think about your product in a businesslike manner. Have a plan complete with projected costs and earnings.

A quick way to analyze your target market is to ask your favorite horse publication for their demographics. For example; if you want to get into the business of raising miniature horses, look at all the information you can, go to miniature horse events and ask a lot of questions. What are these people willing to pay for horses, services and equipment? What needs do they have that are not being met by current suppliers? Almost every organization has a publication and they have done some of your research already. Just ask for their demographics.

Economy
The economy will always play a major role in the horse industry. Actually, so will the tax structure and how the I.R.S. views the horse industry. Still, there will always be some people who want to be in the horse business. They just need to become savvy about the business end of it.

I read as many news publications as I have time. I especially enjoy skimming *The Kiplinger Newsletter*. Several months ago *Kiplinger* stated that horse stables will soon be marketing horseback riding lessons from franchise stations. I imagined a chain of horse stables called, "Horses R Us" and a slogan that read, "At Equitationville, we try harder." Within 30-days, one of my clients who was requesting agreement forms mentioned he was starting a chain of horse stables in the southeastern United States. They say science fiction is closer to science fact than we realize. I guess we just need to read what we can and use our imagination.

Another trend to affect the economic strength of the horse industry is an increase in both leisure time and personal income. With the stiff competition of the many and diverse leisure activities, I recommend getting as many youth involved as possible. The ski industry frequently gives away ski passes to children, so they will fall in love with the sport. Horses are wonderful for developing dependability and a sense of accomplishment in youth. We can work harder at getting children and horses together. I personally questioned people who opened their barns to children regarding the liability issue, but was assured that the benefits of getting young people introduced to horses far outweighs the risks.

Competition
Both direct and indirect competition affect marketing efforts. Direct competition is between rivals who are offering the same product or service; knowing their strengths and weaknesses is the best strategy. Indirect competition offers consumers choices regarding how they spend their time and money; this may be the most threatening to your future income. It is difficult to measure indirect competition. A consumer may have an interest in both horses and water skiing, but can't afford to do both because of limited resources in time and money. As an industry, we need to make horses an appealing leisure-time activity particularly geared toward the whole family.

Advertising Media
Our lives are filled with media contact. Basically, we are becoming more media savvy. However, we can always learn to use the media better. Whether you are being interviewed for your upcoming benefit trail ride, negotiating the details of an ad campaign with a publication representative, or are advertising to get the general public to attend a local horse show, learn to work with the media. Many people are intimidated by the media. I recommend having a competent spokesperson ready to *work with* the media.

As an advertiser, you need to know both the price and reach of each media source you are considering. For your advertising dollars, you want to reach as many potential customers as you can. First, understand what your offering is, then research the demographics that match your product.

Media is usually segregated into geographic areas, and areas of interest. That's why we have local horse publications, as well as, breed or discipline publications. There are also web sites, radio shows, televised coverage and national publications.

When running advertising or launching a public relations campaign prepare for the best-case scenario and worst-case scenario. Survey your clientele, then research the demographic information provided by various publications. Ask questions and run test ads.

Governmental Influences
Understanding the various laws and regulations that may affect your business is becoming increasingly difficult to keep track of and understand. There are many types of regulations that may affect the horse industry; for example, from the tax status of your business, the ability of horsemen to use neighboring parks, even the cost of importing horses from other countries.

Is your land properly zoned for your type of business? As stated in Chapter 4, Buying Horse Property, do not rely on your realtor's word. He/she may not know the exact requirements. In one instant a property owner had several acres and boarded horses. When the area was first platted many years earlier, the developer envisioned duplexes, as a result, no horses were zoned for the property. Many years later a neighbor complained and the code enforcement officer for the county ordered that the horses be removed within 30-days. Another case involved dude ranch owners who enjoyed property near national parks. The national forest service is now seeking to restrict the access of all horseback riders and limit their hay to certified weed free hay only. The way to circumvent legislation or rules is to be informed. Watch for negative sentiments and work with the people who are involved, before these rules are created. Many horse owners are not members of their local, state or national horse council, and do know what their elected officials are doing or even who could lobby on their behalf.

In Jefferson County, Colorado, randomly selected boarding stables are viewed as a commercial endeavor and are therefore taxed at a commercial basis, not just the buildings or land that they sit on, but also the pastures. Boarding stable owners needed to get organized and work to change this interpretation of the code. This fight is still waging, but a new county assessor, who is more sympathetic to the horse industry was elected. Meetings, and even lawsuits continue. Elected officials do listen to their constituents, especially those who contribute to their election.

In most states, it is wiser to contract labor for your housework than to hire help for the barn. Many maid service companies provide their own worker's compensation coverage, but your hired hand might have to be covered under *your* insurance policy. This is the primary reason equine liability laws were passed in many states. Many stable owners who teach riding are becoming more aware of the need to require release forms, teach safety from the ground, and require that hard hats and boots be worn. Many states have liability signs that can be obtained from the state horse council.

Technology

Science and technology play an important role in changing our everyday lives and are used by people in the horse industry to create better products and services and to market those services. The ability to breed mares using artificial insemination has expanded the geographic reach, but has complicated marketing and contractual agreement requirements.

Also, new products vie for customer attention. Customers have to make informed decisions about equipment, fencing, trailers, stable accessories and more. Marketing these products requires more sophistication, such as: samples, brochures, videos and web sites. Even more than in the past, companies must now explain how and why customers need *their* products, why *their* products are better or more unique than anything else on the market. Discovering your product or service's uniqueness is one of the most important aspects of marketing. In the horse industry, marketing within a small budget is an even greater challenge.

Planning Your Marketing Strategy

Marketing plans mean different things to different people, yet any successful businessperson agrees it is one of the most important aspects of a business. Marketing plans are designed to help you obtain the results you want and need. Putting your plan in writing is the first step to success. The following formula is a guideline for your Marketing Plan:

1. **Write your company philosophy or statement of purpose.**
   Define what your company does or produces. Examine what the company is trying to do and what it did in the past. This statement should be only one sentence, so be specific. A general statement like, "To be the best or breed the best" is too vague. Employees and customers are helpful resources if you do not have a clear picture of how this statement should read.

2. **Determine who your customers are, and know their demographics.**
   Demographics describe your customers and their purchasing habits. Write down what you know about your customers, and determine what they have in common. Customer profiles include: age, gender, income, memberships, education, region, number of horses owned, equestrian discipline participation, breeds owned, products purchased, publications subscribed to and more. By studying what you already know, you will learn what information you need to acquire to reach your customers in the best and most cost-effective manner. Write down everything you already know about your customers and list what you would like to know. Publications collect demographic information to help convince you to advertise with them. They ask specific questions like, "Do you plan to purchase a new truck or trailer in the next six months?" With the results, they are able to go to truck and trailer manufacturers or resellers and tell them exactly what percentage of their readers plan to buy a truck in the next six months to a year and what price range they are able to afford. Do you know where your next sale will come from? Are you breeding horses to fit future

buyers' needs? If you have already written what you
believe to be the demographics, review it annually.

3. **Establish your marketing goals.**
   To begin with, it may be a great idea to brainstorm
   as many goals as possible, then narrow the list to the
   most profitable and achievable goals. There should
   be short-term goals and long-term goals and each list
   needs to be prioritized. In marketing, it is normal to
   have more goals than funds.

4. **Plan for every possibility or extreme.**
   Spread sheets and computers are useful for planning.
   Some companies fail because they do not have
   enough sales and some companies fail because
   they do not plan for success. This is the time to
   ask "what if" questions. Plan for: employees quitting,
   computers crashing and phone service being
   disrupted. Natural disasters can and do strike people
   in the horse industry. Plan for sales and success
   beyond expectations; and determine how those
   requests will be filled. Know ahead of time what is
   needed in the way of manpower, resources and
   equipment to keep up with an extremely high
   demand for your product. If the marketing plan
   you have worked so hard to write is not working,
   rewrite the plan. A key to success is knowing when
   to persist and when to dismount.

5. **Establish a budget and stick to it.**
   A marketing budget needs to cover 12 months but
   should be flexible. Many companies plan to spend
   anywhere from one to five percent of their annual
   income on advertising, promotion and public relations.
   For example, if your horse boarding operation is
   earning $30,000 annually, you may want to spend
   $300 to $1,500 on a marketing budget. A business-
   card-size ad for $25 per month in the regional horse
   publication is exactly $300. An additional $150 may
   be set aside for the annual Christmas party. Start-up
   businesses need letterhead, envelopes and business
   cards printed and continuing expenses may include
   stamps, etc. And, it is always a good idea to earmark
   some money for emergencies or new marketing
   concepts.

> "A horse can lend its rider the speed and strength he or she lacks - but the rider who is wise remembers it is no more than a loan."
>
> *Pam Brown*

169

The best part about having a plan is being able to have an answer for all of those sales calls you will receive when you hang out your shingle. Requests for donations, sponsorships and advertising will keep your phone ringing. It is best to know what you can afford now and consider some new ideas for next year.

6. Develop a timeline.

A part of every good business plan is a timeline developed to help you reach your goals. Sometimes it is easier to divide your marketing efforts into phases, to ease cash flow constraints. A boarding stable may choose to be listed in a directory and use only a local horse publication to promote two major events at their stable. (It is a good idea to determine who is responsible for designing, proofreading and placing ads, news releases and other promotional ideas.) When you develop your timeline realize that most publications need your ad or news release at least six weeks in advance. If you do not know what your publication's lead time is, call and ask.

7. Write out your strategies and tactics.

Every successful campaign begins with a plan of attack. Strategies and tactics outline what will be done, by whom and when. Keep within your timeline and budget. Determine the best and most cost-effective method to get your message to your identified market. Advertising is the easiest method to reach customers; however it takes less cash to reach customers through public relations, speaking, and news releases to radio, newspapers, television and internet.

If your goal is to increase bookings to your stallion, your strategies might include advertising in breed journals in December, January and February. You may want your stallion to be seen at horse shows or regional equine trade shows that often have a stallion parade. One tactic might be hiring an experienced graphic designer to develop ad and corresponding flyer for the stallion. Other tactics include how the horse will be shown, by whom, what music or script will accompany the horse and how prospective customers can locate you back at the stalls.

8. Line-up the troups.

Most small businesses do not have the time or resources to accomplish everything written in their Marketing Plan. Resources may include:

Horse-related organizations. Many groups have individuals trying to accomplish the same goals you are. By pooling your resources, you can actually accomplish more. (Horse owners tend to be very independent – often to their own down-fall.) Have you noticed that most car dealerships and furniture stores are located in the same geographic locations? This is actually more convenient for the customer.

Local or state Chamber of Commerce small business assistance programs. If you think of your equine-related endeavor as a business, you will gain more respect from other commerce members. All businesses have the same goal: to make money. Many chambers have business planners, booklets, clinics and seminars to help you setup and run your business. Your accountant, legal advisor and insurance agent hopefully also have some expertise in the horse industry. Plus, you may get excellent referrals from others within the horse industry.

Government-sponsored Small Business Assistance Centers. The SBCA has retired volunteer business people to help counsel people. They even have some fresh ideas on marketing.

Continuing education. Local colleges offer courses on employee relations, marketing and accounting which can help any business run more smoothly.

Volunteers. Horse rescue groups, therapeutic riding programs and youth groups are run almost entirely on volunteer power. See Using Volunteers to Obtain Your Marketing Objectives later in this chapter.

9. Periodically perform evaluations.

Some people in the horse industry lament, "I tried that, but it just didn't work." When you ask why, they have no idea what went wrong or what they could improve. For example trying to promote your stallion at a local horse fair stallion parade is an investment in your time, money and effort. If you did not get the response you wanted, it is your responsibility to determine what went wrong. How many people passed through the gate? Did these people already own horses, or were they horse-owner wannabe's? Were prospective customers told where they could reach you after the stallion parade? After the show, call the organizers of the horse fair (or other event) and ask for the total number of people in attendance and any demographic information obtained.

Evaluate your entire year's marketing programs. Computer spreadsheet programs can help you get the picture. Keep records from month-to-month and year-to-year. It is important to know what is working and what needs to be revised.

Using Volunteers to Obtain Your Marketing Objectives

The horse industry provides some unique opportunities and the availability of people who care enough to volunteer is a pleasant surprise. Youth groups have known this for a long time and most horse show managers use their share of volunteers. Working hard and volunteering are just two simple things that help people believe they are leading a more balanced life.

In 1991,the National Western Stock Show in Denver developed a formal volunteer program for the first time in 1991. Program organizer, Freddie Ringer, said, "Overall it was a huge success." The idea was initiated when the previous marketing director saw that the Houston Livestock Show was run by more than 6,000 volunteers. Ringer reported that out of the 200 people who initially signed up for the volunteer program, about 150 people actually followed-through and worked when scheduled. This program has grown. Over the years, the number of volunteers has more than doubled.

Before you determine if volunteers will fit your needs, it might help to understand why people volunteer. The reasons include:
- They believe in the cause.
- To meet other people with similar interests.
- To enjoy the fringe benefits and have fun.
- To be seen as an expert or authority on a subject

and/or have a need to be in a position of authority.
- To be seen as an expert or authority on a subject that they would not ordinarily have access to or would have to pay to see.

They have a high burnout rate; they will tire of the job quickly. To ensure that the individual does not burn out on you, give him/her as much responsibility as possible, vary the job duties, ask what he/she expects from the job. Most volunteers realize they are expendable and occasionally volunteers have other important situations arise in their lives.

To be sure you have enough manpower for really important jobs, get twice as many volunteers as needed and call them the day before the event. It is unscientifically proven that volunteers work best with smaller time-commitments and thrive on coffee, donuts and lots of appreciation.

If volunteer wrangling sounds like a full-time job, you are beginning to get the picture. Only you can decide if the benefits outweigh the investment of training and managing a volunteer team.

Time and Money-Saving Marketing Ideas
Most people in the horse industry bring their own experiences and ideas to the business. It is important to use these ideas to help save you time and money. Since you will not always make perfect decisions, be strong enough to admit when you are wrong and change directions. A big ego will cost you big money. It takes wisdom to know the difference between money-saving ideas and time-wasting ideas.

Cooperative Advertising
Is cooperative advertising available to you? If so, consider using it. If not, can you create a cooperative situation? Is there another business that would be interested in sharing marketing expenses? A farrier who specializes in show horses may want to combine advertising space in a regional directory with a horse show photographer. They may want to do something other than advertising, like speak to a breed organization's membership about what makes a good show photo or what really helps develop strong hooves. The possibilities are endless.

Direct Mail
Many business people send out cards on a regular basis.

Holiday cards, birthday wishes along with a coupon, even cards that say, "It's been a pleasure serving you." The greeting card manufacturer Leaning Tree has a card that says, "Hear there's been some horsin' around in your barn lately! Congratulations on the arrival of your new foal." What a great idea for stallion owners to keep in contact with customers and mention discount fees for early bookings.

Consider a direct mail campaign to your previous customers. You may even want to *ask* them for referrals. The first rule in developing referrals is to ask for them. Use reminder postcards and let people know you are ready to serve them again. Do this before they run out of your product, so they think of you when it is time to reorder. If possible, try to schedule your next appointment with them while you are still with the customer and use handy reminder stickers.

Promotional Ideas

Promotional contests are popular. The theme should fit your company's philosophy or overall marketing campaign. People like to show off their cute foal photos and tell about their horses. Many retailers have pictures of happy customers. People also get involved to name new products and win prizes.

Many business people send out informative newsletters to current and prospective clients. Insurance and real estate agents have developed some very clever ways to keep their name in front of you by using promotional items. A promotional catalog offers a variety of ideas from coffee mugs to pencils which can be imprinted with your business name and contact information. Calendars and informational pieces are kept for a long period of time. Only you can decide if such a method of promotion is cost-effective for your business.

Circulate memorable business cards. Look for opportunities to leave a business card for someone else to read. Have you ever left your business card with a dinner tip, or tacked your card on the bulletin board at your local feed or tack store? Have you seen a business card with a photo of a stallion or foal or one that looks like a folded $20 bill? Being memorable is great - as long as it fits your budget and overall marketing theme.

Consider the advantages of payment-in-kind or bartering. In all business ventures, it is important to have liquid cash available and using the barter system may help you retain more cash on hand. I know of one trainer who traded her services for new kitchen cabinets. Communicating what you expect is the only way to truly achieve a win-win situation.

Read business books and articles and learn to transfer this information to your situation. You may be the first business of your type to have a Japanese-style quality circle. The Japanese have used quality circles to get their employees involved in guiding their company and responsible for achieving quality products. When developing a team approach, it is important to have input from management and all levels of employees. One boarding stable has a board of boarders; the boarders are responsible for keeping the flow of communication open from the boarding stable owner and the rest of the boarders.

Employee Relations

Hire, motivate and retain the best employees possible. Some companies create a spot for a person who will benefit the company. It is a proven fact that it costs more to hire and train new employees than to retain current employees.

Expand the interview process to determine what the prospective employee really expects from the job, how long he/she plans to work in that position and where he/she hopes to be in the future.

Some companies offer a hiring bonus; the employee is required to stay with the company for a specified amount of time to actually get the bonus.

Many companies have some form of an exit interview. It does not have to be formal; just get to the truth of why an employee is leaving the job.

In Florida a person started an employment agency for people who wanted to work in the horse industry. What is your back-up plan when a key employee quits without notice? When your stall cleaner quits, are you stuck using your back to muck stalls? By working together with other stable owners, you may be able to hire a floating employee who will work when employees quit or when employees take a day off. This type of job-sharing (flexibility) may be a necessity when the economy is strong and many employers are competing for entry-level employees.

Watch what other businesses are doing. If you like what you see, adopt the idea and apply it to your situation. Learn from what larger companies have paid researchers to help them discover.

These time and money-saving ideas will help any equine-related business thrive.

🦄 PUBLIC RELATIONS

Public relations is the planned effort to influence opinion through good character and responsible performance, based upon mutually satisfactory two-way communication.

Overview and History

Public relations is one of the most misunderstood, mistrusted and misrepresented professions in the history of mankind. The title "Public Relations" can apply to anything from a receptionist position to a trained professional who keeps the public informed regarding a chosen group or product. A professional public relations practitioner provides timely and relevant information to the proper sources and is trained to handle all communications in the event of a crisis. He/she is also trained to write speeches and provide audio-visual assistance. Above all, the information to be provided is concise, accurate, and includes only factual information.

By the late 1800's a few large companies in the United States were hiring former newspaper reporters to write informational press releases for their companies. It has been said that public relations, like jazz, is an American product of the twentieth century. Many companies prefer to call these people, Public Information Officers and many internal memos are littered with references to the PIO in today's abbreviation-happy society.

The basis of public relations is the effort to persuade – and that is as old as civilization itself. If you are a history buff, you may know that many of the great events in history have been shaped by someone gathering public opinion and managing to mold it for various causes.

Current and future trends in public relations are generally toward more socially and environmentally conscious actions. All horse activities, including rodeo events and the use of carriage horses and Tennessee Walking Horses, have been targeted by various animal rights activists. The very continuation of rodeo, carriage companies and some show horse activities may depend upon strong and effective public relations efforts; first, to educate participants about the

"...This most noble beast is the most beautiful, the swiftest and of the highest courage of domesticated animals. His long mane and tail adorn and beautify him. He is of a fiery temperament, but good tempered, obedient, docile and well-mannered."

Pedro Garcia

Conde

rules, then to educate the public about the facts, stressing that activist groups may discover one mishap and condemn the entire activity. The American Horse Council emphasizes the importance of creating positive public relations interactions whenever possible. In an article in the council's newsletter, *AHC News*, "Animal Rights Versus Animal Welfare and the Horse Industry" points include: being forthcoming with information, understanding who the audience is, and realizing that the public's perception is vitally important.

Planning and Research

Advertising and Public Relations involves extensive research techniques and sources. It is imperative to keep records of your customers and clients. Records may vary from information written on the back of business cards to elaborate computerized files. Make sure that all information is current and reliable. Update your files annually. Good record-keeping assists with income tax preparation, too.

In many instances, public relations is designed to change the way people already view a product. For example, it may have been rumored that your stallion produces foals with crooked legs or that the horse shows you manage always have poor judges. Whatever the situation, you have three choices: Ignore the negative situation and hope it will blow over, or lash out at those you may spreading the rumor or to really solve the problem, provide information and face the situation head-on.

If you are starting from scratch with a new idea or concept or to change existing views, separate yourself to gain an objective view. Seek out and listen to the views of others. Facts are conclusions that can be tested and proven. Public opinion is usually based on some facts, interpretation and human emotion. Research and the development of new tests can provide new facts; dissemination of the new information will change opinions.

Large companies often use outside research and testing firms to conduct studies; many horse-related companies find this route too expensive. Luckily, creative thinkers can usually find a way to get results when money is not available.

A low-cost alternative for collecting opinions may include working with local high school, college or university students. Students offer manpower in exchange for a good learning experience. Develop testing to meet your goals and set guidelines.

Conventional research methods include: cross-section surveys, survey panels, in-depth interviews or questionnaires, and focus group interviews.

Small companies often talk with customers or use some type of written questionnaire. The average rate of return on a questionnaire is approximately six percent. For the highest number of surveys returned, it is best to keep the forms simple and/or offer a reward. To provide conclusions that are consistent, ask for the same information several times in slightly different ways.

One of the best reasons to use a commercial firm is that they know how to word the questions for the most accurate answers. Determine how much research you need to do and weigh the expense of your time versus the convenience of having the project done by an outside company.

By knowing the demographics of the publications your clients read, you have a start on knowing where to place your message.

After you have determined how others perceive your business, set your objective(s). Before you start your public relations campaign, is the time to develop a procedure by which you will be able to measure your progress.

Attaching your cause or business to a good charitable organization may also help gain publicity for everyone involved.

Your public relations objective should complement your advertising and overall Marketing Plan. By breaking the tasks down into monthly components for each marketing area, you should find the tasks manageable. Include your marketing and customer service objectives for one year. Remember, the key to a good plan is flexibility. Include the ability to change as needed. In essence, when you decide what percentage return you would like on your investment, you can develop an aggressive marketing plan to achieve that goal.

Getting your message in print

I prefer to use the title News Release rather than Press Release because, if the message is not newsworthy, it will not get printed. News releases are still the primary tool available to disseminate information. It is imperative that written material be professionally done to be rewarded with space in any medium. As a former editor, I opened every piece of mail that came across my desk. By the time I read the first paragraph, I decided if the envelope contained any news for my readers. About 97 percent of the mail never made it into print. If you plan to use news releases, please note the following points:

- Everything you submit will be reviewed by at least one editor.
- The staff of the publication will have the final word on if or how the information will appear.
- Any item submitted should meet appropriate deadlines. Do not expect someone to "hold the presses" for your news item. It only happens in the movies.
- Editorializing, or excessive use of descriptive language, is inappropriate for a news release and belongs in a paid advertisement or on the editorial page.
- A contact person should always be listed with both a day and evening telephone number, even your cellular phone number. Many editors work the late shift and the contact person should be available when the editor needs, not just when it is convenient. Many editors prefer to have news releases e-mailed so a typesetter does not have to retype the information.
- Most news releases should fit on one page. If the editor feels more information is necessary, they will call the contact person. You may also want to send a fact sheet or an attached story idea.
- Writing a feature story in place of a straight news release works well with some editors. The feature story may be about one of the competitors who has overcome obstacles to be at the show or some other human interest story.
- Photos are appreciated, but should be professionally done and have a descriptive, type-written, label on the

back. Do not write on the photo; pens tend to mar photos. Photos are seldom returned.

The following sample news release is a simple and direct way to explain how a news release should appear.

SAMPLE NEWS RELEASE

Contact Name:
Daytime Phone Number:
Evening or Cell Phone Number:

Editors love typewritten copy. Remember to leave ample margins, especially at the top of the page for the newspaper's copy reader and a headline writer to write comments. Indent paragraphs deeply and doublespace. Do not write notes on the page except for necessary corrections.

The first paragraph should be the lead or summary of the most important idea of the story. Paragraphs and sentences should be comparatively short, punctuated correctly and easy to read and understand.

Be neat. Do not crowd copy. Use additional pages if necessary. When more than one page is used, put the word "more" or "page 1 of 2" at the bottom of each page except the last one. A common ending note for a news release is "30" or "###" which means the end. This dates back to the days of wire services.

The best publicity releases are those a news editor can read clearly and accept as news. Of course, the editors realize that they may not always please you or the reader, but if the release is well written and newsworthy, most editors are happy to have the information.

The last line may reinforce the message and give the reader a phone number for obtaining more information.

30

This sample news release covers the subject of how a release should look and what information is important.

The Art of Writing Newsletters

Sometimes a news release may not be the best approach to getting your message out. Some effort requires ongoing communication with customers. In this case, newsletters may be your best form of written communication.

When German, Johann Gutenberg, invented movable type in the mid-15th century, he probably never dreamed that almost every person would someday be able to create newsletters and other printed materials! With the advent of desktop publishing almost anyone can reach out and touch someone with their message. And, with all that information being circulated, how can you make sure your message is read and comprehended. Here we will discuss the finer points of creating a professional looking newsletter.

Almost all boarding stable owners send out newsletters, most nonprofit organizations use newsletters, and clubs and breed organizations use some form of written communication to keep their members informed. Many horse owners find themselves helping with these newsletters at some time in their lives.

First, keep your message as newsworthy as possible. It is more important to publish information that is timely and relevant than print a newsletter on a regular schedule. That is do not decide you need to print a weekly or monthly publication if there is not enough real news to put in it. What is newsworthy? That's simple. Just ask your intended audience or readers.

Most people in the horse industry are busy, yet they want to attend special events sponsored by organizations. Examples include shows, clinics and trail rides. The people I have talked with turn to the calendar of events section first. They also want this information on a separate page, if possible, so they can keep it handy. If you want people to attend your event, get it on their calendar as early as possible.

The second most popular item in most newsletters is coupons (discounts). If you are publishing a newspaper for a nonprofit organization, perhaps a sponsor or advertiser will offer a discount to your readers/members.

Many times, stallion owners work very hard to promote their horses in the show ring, but do not have time to do traditional print marketing. They might do well to hire a desktop publisher to create a newsletter for them. You can say more in a newsletter than in any advertisement. Newsletters offer more information to a smaller target audience. Also, offering an early booking discount is very similar to printing a coupon.

Studies show that readers are deterred from reading large blocks of type. Unless, it is a subject of particular interest to them; then they want to read all available material on the subject. That is one reason why indexes on the cover of a magazine are of great help to readers. It helps them decide what to read first.

Journalists are taught that most people read at an eighth grade level. If you want to be accessible, keep your writing clear and concise. That does not mean you should talk down to your audience. Just make sure you are not trying to impress them with your vocabulary.

Keep your presentation easy to read. Use larger and darker type on a clean or light background. Some graphic artists love reverse type. Research has proven that white letters on a black background (reverse type) are more difficult to read and are read less often. The text should be laid out logically on the page, with few stories continuing or jumping to following pages.

Journalists developed a style of writing called the *inverted* paragraph. It is important that all important information be presented in the first few sentences. Cover the who, what, why, when, where and how. The details of the story should follow the lead paragraph. To keep your newsletter polished, keep it factual and relevant. Headlines help readers know what the article is about – quickly. If pictures are used, make sure you use an identifying cut line. It sounds simple, but I often see photos that readers are left to assume have relevance to the closest story.

Do not overuse graphics. Nothing looks more amateurish than loading your printed page with cute graphics. I recently received a newsletter with over ten different and unrelated graphics on one page. Granted, it was a legal size page... but, still!

The most important graphic is your logo. Spend the time or money it takes to create a great one for your business and use it. Your logo should appear on every printed document that comes out of your outfit. Treat it with respect and do not add or subtract portions of the artwork. It might happen when a new person takes over publishing a club's newsletter, that they want to add something like mountains or a horseshoe to the original logo. Corporations never allow this to happen, because it causes readers to confuse their company with another. Major brand logos are drilled into our heads and it is wise for us to do the same. If you are trying to raise money for your local horse rescue group, you do not want a benefactor to mistakenly give a $1,000 gift to another organization just because their logo and yours are similar. Remember, have a good logo and use it.

Always have someone else read your work. It makes perfect sense when you write it, but sometimes your thoughts do not get to the written page. Computer spellcheck is a wonderful thing; however, it has developed a whole new set of problems. You may have a word spelled correctly, but is it the word you really want to use?

There are many wonderful events and efforts you have worked hard to develop. Just make sure that, if you are using a newsletter to inform people about your work, it is as clear as possible.

Messages Created for Other Media

Air time on radio and television is very expensive and difficult to obtain for promoting a business or event. From a public relations standpoint, most interactions with the media fall into one of three categories, news stories, feature stories or crisis management. (Crisis Management and the media are discussed in case study #5.) Crisis management is the ability to be prepared for any event that involves responding to the media. For the remainder of this section the information will apply to gaining desired publicity.

Horse owners account for only about four percent (4%) of the general population, so horse-related topics are seldom considered of interest to the general population. Because of this, your message has to have the greatest appeal possible. Carefully think about what the viewer sees and be well prepared. Think about your target audience. What television and radio stations do they watch or listen to?

A benefit trail ride may be a welcome topic on a country and western radio station. Trail management and use may work for cable television. Crisis situations, like starving or abused animals or large animals caught in a natural disaster are news worthy to the general public. Zoning issues and government practices that affect the horse industry could make the local news or cable programs. Know the media in your area. There are even some agricultural and equestrian-based programs on radio and cable. You or your designated media representative should know radio and television programs' hosts, content managers and type of formats used. Someone in your business or organization needs to be able to work with the media. A calm person who is articulate and can think quickly and write well, is preferred.

Television editors have reported that video press releases are on the rise; however, just like the written news release, many of them end up in the trash. Small television stations are most likely to use video news releases because of their own budget constraints. Before you invest in a video news release, call the editor of the target media you are considering and ask what format they prefer and other requirements. Some editors prefer quality pictures with the natural sound left on the video. Provide a fact sheet and/or 30- and 60- second scripts for their talent to read.

One news editor joked that if the voice-over provided on the release was better than their own station's staff, it would not be used at all for fear of, "putting our guys to shame." Ask yourself, is the video you are producing something the station would be able to obtain on their own?

Trail riders are often able to get to places a camera crew on foot cannot. Subjects range from a quiet morning at the stable, to the birth of a foal, even an interview with someone who will not speak with the news media, but will speak for your cause.

The deadline for news media is often now or by 3 p.m. today. Phone calls, fax machines and e-mail work great for getting a story idea to an editor if the subject proves to be timely. News editors are looking for information and contact people they might want more information from. Supplying good quality information is a responsibility in itself.

There is an old Native American saying used in hunting, "To be successful, you must become one with your prey." If your prey is news editors, try to understand and how they think the pressures they are under.

Tips to Successfully Submit Ideas for Television
The following points will help you pitch ideas successfully.
  • Call first and obtain the name of the appropriate person you need to speak to. Get current phone numbers, e-mail or fax numbers.

> "Always carry a crop, but use it sparingly."
>
> *Pamela C. Biddle and Joel E. Fishman,* All I Need to Know I learned From My Horse.

- Develop your ideas with the consumer/viewer in mind.
- When submitting your idea, make sure it is clear and concise. Have points written out for yourself, before you call. If you are submitting an idea in writing, make sure it is typewritten. Include contact information and a fact sheet.
- Think visually for television. How can you best show what you have to offer?
- If you are invited to the station for a taping session or to meet at a location, be on time! Rescheduling is often impossible. Make sure you have accurate information and directions. Confirm the day of the meeting with a brief phone call, e-mail or fax. Have each other's cell phone numbers in case of a delay.
- Most stations do not pay for unsolicited ideas.
- Materials you send to the station will become their property and will not be returned.

Using a Spokesperson or Public Information Officer

When a company decides to use a spokesperson in their overall Marketing Plan, the actual duties may fall under public relations, advertising or the department of the public information officer. This largely depends on the activities the person is asked to perform.

The concept of using a spokesperson can work very well, although, historically things have proven that they may also go very wrong. Know what can go wrong and you will be able to plan to ensure that these historic problems do not happen to you.

One problem that can appear in public relations or advertising is when the person chosen to represent a product or service is so famous that he/she overshadows the product or service. This becomes worse if there is a limited budget and not enough repetition of the product.

Another problem is if the behavior and actions of the spokesperson reflect negatively on the product represented. A few years ago, an actress was selected to represent the national beef council. Soon after the announcement she said in an interview that she is a vegetarian. This put the beef council into a tailspin. And, needless to say, the actress was fired.

Even when a spokesperson declines an offer, it can become news. When actor Larry Hagman was asked to

represent the milk industry, he declined because he honestly dislikes drinking milk. Even that made headlines.

Another example of behavior affecting a campaign happened when a corporation I worked for obtained a public
speaker through a national organization, and the speaker
showed up to the event obviously drunk. All the contracts
in the world cannot control human behavior. The best you
can do is be aware of any problems that might arise and
prepare a backup plan.

You may not be able to think of examples in the horse
industry of spokespersons although, many examples do
exist. Non-profit organizations frequently use a spokesperson to promote their causes. Another classic example is
a rodeo queen used to promote upcoming rodeos.

After participating in many queen contests for rodeos,
breed organizations and clubs, and after many years of
reflection, I have developed some opinions. In many cases
an organization does not have a clear idea of what they
expect the representative to do for their organization. When
there is not a clear objective, the honor of obtaining the title
becomes empty for the contestants and an opportunity is
lost for the organization. When breed organizations gave
the titles to individuals simply because of their years of
participation, or who's parents could afford the travel
requirement, then they lost site of the basic goal of representing the breed.

Each time a spokesperson of any type is used, the objective of the representative must be well defined. It should
look like a job description and the spokesperson should
understand the document before accepting the assignment.

Successful criteria for public speakers include:

1. The ability, training and research, to present formal
   speeches to civic and special interest groups.

2. The ability to obtain visibility by appearing in front
   of the public: in parades, on radio or television,
   any event that relates to the interests of the group
   represented. This includes appropriate dress and
   conduct for each occasion.

3. The ability to find and acquire new venues and
   audiences. (Recently, both rodeo queens and rodeo

"Seventy-five percent of success in life is just staying on board."

Pamela C.

Biddle and

Joel E.

Fishman, All I

Need to Know

I learned From

My Horse.

clowns spoke to school children to explain the history of rodeo.

4. The ability to enthusiastically explain events and speak directly regarding safeguards used to protect animals. When Sheryl McConnell organized tours at the National Western Stock Show for second graders of the Denver Public School District, she used rodeo queens, breed representatives and other colorful authorities to speak, sign autographs and be available for photos. High Prairie Farm, a large boarding and training facility in Colorado, began their own "Meet the Horses Day" for local children to see, touch and even ride some horses; in this case the horses become goodwill ambassadors. When owner of High Prairie Farm, Helen Fuscus, was asked if she was deterred by the potential liability issues, she quickly responded that the future of the horse industry relies on our youth and that the benefits far outweigh the risks.

5. The ability to write a clear and concise message. Anyone in this position may be called upon to write his/her own press releases, columns, fact sheets, or 30 second radio spots. He/she should be able to explain the purpose of the organization represented and get people excited about upcoming events, while providing the necessary information.

6. The ability to quickly obtain interviews and the attention of editors through responsible and sincere actions. Present your idea to a program manager in a professional manner, emphasizing the history, civic value and economic benefit of the event.

Being a representative for any group provides a greater depth of knowledge for life. Most people are judged at some point in life. Learning to present ourselves both, in person and on paper, thus developing the ability to get an idea across works to our advantage. (Remember your last job interview? You not only worried about what questions they would ask, but how you would dress to fit into the organization.)

Some breed organizations have discontinued "queen" contests. And, yet most organizations can still benefit from having a student-age public information officer.

Times have changed, and some groups keep up with the times by changing the way a representative is selected and used.

A local riding club has had several men as "royalty" riding in the front of their parade group. One in particular was active in college, running the team's mascot (the CSU Ram) onto the field. This is where he learned to stir-up the crowd. He was a natural cheerleader. During parades he asked the crowd to cheer for his horse. "Let's hear it for Cupcake!" he shouted to the crowd. Most people were happy to get into the spirit. This club is also unique because it does not have any limitations regarding marital status or age for its royalty. Our society is changing the way we think. We now have even more freedom to select a spokesperson based on how he/ she can represent our organization.

Most great plans begin with an idea that is refined and written down. Following are criteria for creating a spokesperson position for an organization:

1. Have a clear statement of purpose or objective.
2. The goal must be achievable by using reasonable strategies and tactics.
3. The plan must fit into the current or projected budget.
4. Parameters of the job must be defined. Each party should know and understand the expectations.
5. Especially the first year, but every year, this position should be honestly evaluated with changes or continuation decided.

Formulate Your Plan

Just as you would follow a recipe to get consistent results in cooking, follow a plan of action for every public relations campaign you attempt. The following outline will help you formulate your campaign. Since this is a general outline, your campaign will need some adjustments or additions. Case studies using the suggested outline follows this section.

1. **Introduction**
   Being with an introduction, stating the background of the program and articulating the current status of the Marketing Plan.

This example used a real spokesperson and painted the image using a comic strip method to draw attention to the upcoming Prescott Rodeo. Although this idea was used in 1949 the concept of a four color cartoon would still captivate the imagination of young and old alike.

2. Objective

The campaign should address or solve one clear objective. There may be secondary goals; however, one clear objective is realistic to achieve for each campaign.

3. **Identify the public(s) to be addressed**

   Who are you trying to reach? This may be defined
   as primary and secondary public. For example,
   your efforts may address both internal and external
   publics. If you are trying to increase your membership,
   your audience may be external (people who do not
   currently belong, but fit your membership criteria);
   the internal public is your current membership
   (encouraging them to bring a friend.)

4. **Strategies and Tactics**

   These terms are taken from the military, but they will
   help you focus your efforts. For each strategy, you
   have a tactic. Strategy is the planning of operations
   or movements previous to the campaign. Tactics are
   the are logistics and naming the person responsible
   for handling the troops during the actual campaign.
   The questions are, how will you plan your moves to
   reach your goals? How will you get your employees
   or yourself to reach each of your goals?

5. **Budget**

   Develop a realistic budget *before* you spend a dime.
   A common company policy is to get at least three
   bids before making decisions. Call around and write
   down each bid. Make sure your bids are inclusive of
   every detail. Ask about hidden charges for setup,
   cleaning, etc.

6. **Timetable**

   Especially with an event, you can begin with the date
   of the event and work backward. It is also wise to
   assign a person to be responsible for each item on
   the timetable, along with the date the strategy is to
   be accomplished.

7. **Evaluation**

   This may be the most important aspect of your effort.
   You want to gather as much information as possible
   and be brutally honest with your efforts at the end of
   the event. This is the time to measure your
   return-on-investment for both time and money.

CASE STUDIES

Case Study #1: The First Benefit Trail Ride for Colorado Horse Rescue

Introduction

The Colorado Horse Rescue program was formed in 1988 as a 501 (c) (3) non-profit, charitable organization to assist with the growing need to care for neglected and abused horses. The organization works with the Humane Society and the state vet, to locate and rescue the animals and place them with handicapped riding programs, beginning 4-Hers, and other suitable homes. Because this program was just evolving, it was determined that a "nest egg" was needed in order for this fledgling organization to survive and operate into the future. Sharon Jackson, founder, spoke to members of Lakewood Riding Club (LRC) and the Jefferson County Horse Council (JCHC). Club members decided to develop a fund-raising event. A benefit trail ride (ride-a-thon) was planned for June 12, 1988. Lance Hernandez, a reporter from a local television station was asked to attend the event as the guest Trail Master. As a major promotional point all the profits would go directly to the care and feeding of the horses.

Objective

The objective of this benefit trail ride is to raise the awareness of the general public to the issues of neglected and abused horses, and to raise at least $1,000 for Colorado Horse Rescue.

Strategy

To raise the awareness of the issue by gaining multi-media exposure.

Tactic

Have a media personality to gain coverage for the event. Other media, horse related organizations and businesses were sent news releases, fact sheets and sample public service announcement spots. A six-week lead time was determined to be optimum. Most of the media received a reminder call, asking if they received the information and if they need additional information.

Strategy

For any first time event estimating the amount of money

that might be raised is only an educated guess. With this in mind, the emphasis of this aspect of the program was to get the largest amount of people to participate, and get them committed to the concept and willing to get pledges.

Tactic
Knowing that motivation is the key to raising money. Awards were given to participants for their efforts. Awards were being solicited from related business owners. News releases emphasized that all money collected will go to the actual care and feeding of the horses, not to administrative costs; work will be done by volunteers and other expenses will be incurred by various horse clubs or individuals.

Public to Address
Three different publics were addressed by the event. First, the horse community, including people who would ride and collect pledges. Second, the general population; to be made more aware of animal care issues in their communities and asked to financially support the riders. Third, the media; without their support, the efforts of the volunteers would bring in little money.

Budget
All volunteers were used and most of the items were donated. The table below illustrates how this budget appeared.

Evaluation
The benefit ride raised over $4,500 for the Colorado Horse Rescue program! Approximately 71 riders participated and reported that the ride was very rewarding and enjoyable.

Confirmed media coverage included: The Rocky Mountain News, The Arabian Horse Newsletter, The Record Horseman, Horses West, K.O.A. Radio Station and television Channel 7 News.

Some suggestions were made by the ride committee at the post-event meeting. A larger parking lot would have been helpful. Parking is always a problem when large trucks and trailers are involved. There were very few restroom facilities at the open space park selected. It was recommended that portable restrooms be included in the budget for future events of this size. Because of the large number of participants, it was suggested that smaller groups of 20 riders be taken out by a designated trail masters. These groups should be spaced approximately ten to 15 minutes apart.

"In order to win, you have to run the whole race."

Pamela C. Biddle and Joel E. Fishman, All I Need to Know I learned From My Horse.

BUDGET

Item:	Donated by:	Cost/Value:
Press releases, flyers, posters, etc.	Tracy	$75
Postage for press releases	Tracy	$200
Letters, postage	Kay	$20
Forms, printing	Kay	$10
Coffee	Jeffco. Assn.	$10
Donuts	Sunrise Pastry	$15
Award	Marilyn & LRC	$?
Cups/sugar, etc.	Jeffco. Assn.	$5

BENEFIT RIDE FOR THE COLORADO HORSE RESCUE TIMELINE/WORKSHEET

Item:	Date due:	Person responsible:
Approve Campaign	4/29/88	Ride Committee
Approve Letters to: City of Lakewood, Guest Trailmaster, Donations from Businesses	5/1/88	Ride Committee
Mail Letters	5/3/88	Rowe's
Design Poster/Flyers	5/6/88	Tracy
Write & Mail Press Releases	5/10/88	Tracy
Call Prospective Prize Donors	5/18/88	Kay, Lisa & Marilyn
Confirm Guest Trailmaster	5/25/88	Kay
Confirm with Volunteers	5/26/88	Kay
Pick up Prizes	6/9/88	Kay & Marilyn
Check & Mark Trail	6/11/88	Ride Committee
On-Site Promotion	6/12/88	Ride Committee
Check-in & Disclaimer	6/12/88	LRC Volunteers
Collection of Money	6/12/88	LRC Volunteer
Nametags & Drawing Entry	6/12/88	LRC Volunteer
Refreshment Booth	6/12/88	JCHA Volunteer
Direct Traffic	6/12/88	Sheriff's Posse
Lunch Drinks	6/12/88	AHA Volunteers
Presentation of Awards	6/18/88	Pres. LRC
Photos	6/12/88	Tracy
Write Press Releases	6/14/88	Tracy
Write Thank You Letters	7/1/88	Ride Committee
Final Awards at LRC	7/6/88	Kay
Evaluation	7/15/88	Ride Committee

Benefit Ride for Colorado Horse Rescue Budget & Timeline

Other suggestions included securing more valuable prizes for the top money collectors. All donations should be collected at the ride to prevent the follow-up needed to collect funds promised. Many other horse organizations turned out in force and the committed felt that their most effective marketing should be to those groups in the future.

Colorado Horse Rescue Benefit Trail Ride Scheduled for June 12 in Morrison, Colorado

A benefit trail ride for the newly-formed Colorado Horse Rescue organization is slated for Sunday, June 12, 1988. This Ride-A-Thon will begin with check-in at 9 a.m. from Bear Creek Lake Park, 13411 Highway 9, Morrison, Colo. Individuals and groups are being asked to participate in the ride or help in any way they can.

Sharon Jackson, founder of the Colorado Horse Rescue, has been called upon to rescue many abandoned and abused horses for the past 14 years. Started on a very small scale, last year the Colorado Horse Rescue program placed 52 horses. This winter they were called upon by the Colorado Humane Society to rescue some starving horses in Parker. Upon arrival they found one had already died, two were so weak that they were taken to the veterinary hospital at Bennett and two were brought to the Arvada area. One of the two taken to Bennett did have to be euthanized and the other three are on their way to recovery. Jackson also accepts older horses for placement with riding programs for handicapped riders.

Small donations have been received from time-to-time, but, until now, no established means of funding has been developed. Hopefully, those most concerned with the well-being of horses can lend a hand. Riders are asked to collect pledges for the eight-mile ride, with a minimum of $5 pledged.

Lakewood Riding Club will be sponsoring this ride to begin raising money for this newly-formed non-profit, 501 (C)3 organization. Lance Hernandez, reporter for Channel 7, will be the Guest Trailmaster. Prizes will be awarded at lunch, with the award for "Most Money Collected" to be presented at the Lakewood Riding Club meeting on Wednesday, July 6, 1988. All services have been donated so that 100 percent of the money collected will go to the care and feeding of these horses. Horse organizations have already donated coffee for the morning and pop for lunch. For more information or pledge sheets, call the ride coordinator Kay Rowe at (303) 279-2976. ∎

Support Colorado Horse Rescue

Bennett, CO. Six, pure-bred, Arabian horses wre taken into protective custody last Thursday, Feb. 5, by the State of Colorado, Dept. of Agriculture and given into the custody of Colorado Horse Rescue. The reason for the action by the State was cited as extreme neglect. One gray three-year-old had died Wednesday night, prompting the move to confiscate the horses.

Since the horses were taken into custody, one has been euthanized when found to be too ill to stand, three have been wormed and vaccinated and all are being carefully monitored. Large crews of volunteers from Colorado Horse Rescue are working around the clock to prevent any further deaths from occurring.

Quantities of oats, Timothy (grass) hay and money donations are greatly needed by Colorado Horse Rescue to maintain their operation. C.H.R. is a non-profit organization and provides safe homes, rehabilitation, placement services and feed to needy persons and their horses throughout the state. They work in coordination with 4-H Clubs, The Westernaires and the Colorado Humane Society. They have handled as many as 52 horses in 1987 and a spokesperson Sharon Jackson, states that the need for these services is on the rise. Please call with donations to: Sharon Jackson, 423-9433 or mail checks to 9611 W. 75th Place, Arvada, CO 80005, or call Jill Pratt 422-1762 if you need assistance in placing a horse you can no longer properly care for.

Channel 7's photographer takes aim as the trail ride to benefit Colorado Horse Rescue begins. Leading are Kay Rowe, ride coordinator; Lance Hernandez, guest trail master, followed by 70 or so riders.

71 horsemen ride to benefit horse effort

Over 71 riders participated in the first trail ride to benefit Colorado Horse Rescue, the organization founded to help abandoned and abused horses. The Ride-a-Thon was held June 12th near Morrison, Colo.

"We will be able to put the money to good use," Sharon Jackson, founder of Colorado Horse Rescue, said when she was told that the riders were bringing in over $4,000 in pledged dollars.

The event was captured on film for the 5 p.m. newscast on Channel 7, and Lance Hernandez, reporter, looked right at home as the Guest Trailmaster.

The award for the Most Money collected goes to Marilyn Fossett, who collected over $400 in donations (unofficially at press time). A new bridle will be awarded to Fossett at the Lakewood Riding Club meeting on July 6. At the same time, Lakewood Riding Club will make the presentation to Sharon Jackson of Colorado Horse Rescue for the entire amount collected, including corporation sponsorships yet to be tallied.

Last year 52 horses were rescued by Colorado Horse Rescue. On going support is needed for the horse rescue project and donations are accepted throughout the year by calling Sharon Jackson at (303)423-9433 or Jill Pratt (303) 422-1762. ∎

Examples of the press releases as they appeared in print both before and after the ride. Results of an event are also newsworthy.

Case #2: A Later Colorado Horse Rescue Benefit Ride

In later years the benefit trail ride for Colorado Horse Rescue, was taken on by other equestrian organizations. As a participant and observer, I noticed some of the following points and will offer a brief evaluation here.

The use of a designated group trail masters continued to be a problem, because the open space park had several trails that lead to the same lunch spot. Often a group leader took the group off in a different direction, which created confusion among the riders, in part because they could see the

---

"A hot horse and a hot head don't mix."

Pamela C.

Biddle and

Joel E.

Fishman, All I

Need to Know

I learned From

My Horse.

other groups on a different trails. Most large trail riding groups have a pre-ride or shake-down ride with the people who will be leading the groups. All trails should be checked for current terrain and safety. Each trailmaster should be responsible for his/her group; the members of the group need to know they can trust their trailmaster.

As the notoriety of the Colorado Horse Rescue ride grew, so did the number of participants. Unfortunately, the amount of money collected for the organization declined. This could be changed by making the ride more exclusive and raising the minimum pledge amount; this strategy is used for $100-a-plate dinners. The biggest secret to fund-raising is asking the right people for their financial commitments.

The most memorable *faux pas* during this ride was when a member of the Sheriff's Posse insulted the Guest Trail Master. The Guest Trail Master was a well known radio and television personality who came to the ride with a green horse that did not want to cross water. The Sheriff's Posse rider told the Guest Trail Master, with a few explicatives, that he should not have brought such a green horse to the ride. The Guest Trail Master left in a huff and mentioned the unfortunate situation on his radio program the following Monday. This situation could have been avoided with two simple precautions: First, know the trail and the ability of your invited guests. It may be appropriate to invite the guest along for a pre-ride or offer the guest a more suitable mount; a mount that is experienced and well-broke makes the Guest Trail Master look better, too! Second, handle all invited guests with care. Introduce them around, give them a special name badge and have all volunteers trained to be gracious and helpful.

If you are in charge of organizing an event, imagine all of the things that could go wrong and ask others to give their suggestions. Make a list of all possible pitfalls, and be prepared for anything. By having a written plan of how to avoid or minimize any situation, you will be able to avoid using crisis management during an event. Planning for great success and for problems is the responsibility of the event coordinator.

Case #3: Stallion Promotion
The owners of a fine Arabian stallion were interested in

Moonlight Reflections

Volume 1, Issue 1   *15352 West 64th Ave., Golden, CO 80403, (303) 422-0511*   *Spring 1991*

Flamenco Bey V Takes the Audience by Storm;

at the Colorado Horse Fair's Parade of Stallions

Denver, Colorado - -

On Saturday, April 6, 1991 the horse show management really did save the best for last when Bob Kuehne introduced *Flamenco Bey V* during the Colorado Horse Fair's Parade of Stallions.

Flamenco Bey V is the grandson of two of the finest Arabian stallions in history, *Bask* and *Bay Abi*. At age seven he stands 15 1 ½ hands tall. This fabulous bay stallion has won halter and performance championships. His first born colt, *Moonshine M.A.* has won five out of six halter futurity classes in Colorado. *"Flame,"* as he is known, is a Polish / American bred horse. He is currently being shown in English Pleasure and Native Costume by his amateur owner Mike McConnell. *Flame's* next adventure will be in pleasure driving.

Flame is handled, bred, trained and shown totally by his amateur owners, Mike and Sheryl McConnell of the Moonlight Arabian farm in Golden, Colorado.

Flamenco Bey V was purchased as a yearling from Sheila Varian of Arroyo Grande, California. Varian has been named the all time leading California breeder of National Champions. Varian had known or ridden nearly every horse in *Flamenco Bey V's* pedigree. Her expertise as a rider, trainer and horsewomen are unequalled anywhere.

"We would like to thank our family and friends for their support," Sheryl McConnell said. She added, "A very special appreciation goes to Sheila Varian for her development of great Arabian horses."

Reflecting on the Varian Tradition

Arroyo Grande, California - -

Sheila Varian has been called, "candid, introspective and progressive," regarding her breeding program. In fact, horses that are 50 percent (or more) Varian breeding have won over 225 national-level titles.

Theses awards are for both halter and performance classes. Performance is very important to Varian and she enjoys everything from working cattle to riding in the mountains with her Arabians.

Her excellent horsemanship dates back to the early 1960's when she and an Arabian mare named *Ronteza* won the open reining cow horse championship at the Cow Palace. At the time Sheila was the first amateur and first woman, and *Ronteza* was the first Arabian to win the title.

"We didn't even know we had done anything special." Varian recalled. "I just thought that if I worked really hard, had a vision and a goal, and preserved - I guess that's the hard one - I could attain it."

Varian launched a breeding program by selecting an Arabian stallion that met the qualifications she set forth. Including beauty and athletic ability.

Recipe:

For a Successful Horse Breeding Farm

1'- Beautiful, Champion Arabian Stallion (*Flamenco Bey V*).

2 - Horse enthusiasts who have spent their lifetimes showing, judg-

In 1959, she purchased *Bay Abi* a two-year-old with excellent potential. She owned him for 25 years and has shown him to mulit-national championships.

The rest is history and *Flamenco Bey V* is here to carry it on.

ing, training and winning with horses. Individuals who have worked with and loved Flame for six years and look forward to building a breeding program around this horse.

2 - active children, who never let things get boring, and who share their parents love for horses.

Sprinkle generously with family, friends and mentors. Stir with lots of enthusiasm and fun horse show experiences.

Bake safely in a new barn surrounded by beautiful pastures.

Serve with coffee . . that is always on at 15352 West 64th Avenue.

No appointment necessary.

© *Pica Publishing.*   *Design and layout by Tracy D. Dowson at 238-5638*

A special newsletter was created for the Parade of Stallions and provided more information about Moonlight Arabians.

showing off their new barn and breeding facility, in addition to promoting their stallion. The young stallion had been showing for about a year and was gaining recognition for himself. The stallion owner wanted to have an open house, but time and money constraints seemed to keep this idea on hold. While the open house idea was still under consideration, a flyer arrived in the mail promoting a state-wide horse expo and an all-breed horse show, complete with a

"Parade of Stallions." It was decided to scrap the open house idea and register the horse for the Parade of Stallions.

Objective
Use the Parade of Stallions to gain exposure for the stallion, promote name recognition, and secure more breeding contracts.

Strategy
Secure breeding contracts from people who previously expressed an interest in the stallion. Meet others with suitable mares.

Tactic
Design invitations for the event, and mail to a pre-selected group of mare owners and members of related organizations.

Strategy
Create awareness of the fine mare-care facilities. Reinforce the strong points about the stallion and facility owners.

Tactic
Design a newsletter for the event, to provide background information on the horse, his bloodlines, the owners and the new barn.

Strategy
Create a dynamic and memorable presentation of the stallion.

Tactic
Put a great deal of thought into this presentation to make it the best. The show's management granted the request to be the last horse in the presentation once they heard the horse would enter through a cloud of smoke; the horse had a dress-rehearsal to be prepared for the smoke and arena. Details are important when your presentation is only a few minutes long (fortunately, the moments were captured by several different video cameras.) The staff presenting the stallion and working at the barn wore formal black and white, to set them apart and help the audience recognize them after the presentation.

Strategy
Create an opportunity for follow-up with potential customers.

Tactic
Have invitations mention the reception that would follow the event. The Parade of Stallions audience was invited back to

the stalls for a reception, allowing potential customers to meet the owners, see the stallion up close, and get a copy of the newsletter and refreshments. (This is when the advertising investment on stall curtains pays off.) It is beneficial to have an incentive for the mare owners who make financial commitments at the show. Waive the booking fee or offer an early booking discount. Ask for the sale. "Do you want to book your mares today?" or "I can give you a 10% discount if I get your commitment today."

Evaluation

During the post-event meeting, it was noted that the cost-per-person was far less than it would have been to hold the open house on the owner's property. Approximately 200 newsletters were distributed. The owners of the stallion were pleased, Though disappointed in the time allotted to each stallion during the show. (At other similar shows, stallion owners complained they were not able to meet potential customers because the stabling area was off limits for security reasons to anyone who was not showing.)

Case Study #4: Marketing Horse Performances to the General Public

National surveys indicate that there are 7,000 sanctioned horse shows each year, with thousands of local unsanctioned events also held. Horse shows generate $443 million per year; rodeos contribute another $104 million. Chances are pretty good that you will, at one time or another, be associated with the production of one of these events. This case study taken from an interview with the creator of a large scale multi-discipline event, Sandi J. Pence, highlights a new kind of horse show, which uses horses to provide entertainment to a large and varied audience.

A basic western pleasure class can seem boring to the average person; however, with the right management, horses and their riders can be uplifting, heartfelt and down-right entertaining. Some events translate better to a stage performance, and a gifted horse-show director can bring a show to life. This is how one person brought her dream of an equine-related performance to the masses and had them begging for more.

An Evening of Dancing Horses brought laughs, standing ovations, cheers and tears to a privileged audience at the

Denver Events Center in January 1997. Whether it was laughing with the Phantom Hill Junior Riders' stick horse quadrille, cheering with the exquisite movements of the freestyle dressage and reigning horses, or tearing with the lonesome cowboy songs of Michael Martin Murphy, the beauty of the horses filled the hearts and minds of everyone in attendance.

When a horseman sees a horse performing well; he knows it, but when simple perfection can be translated to an audience of over 5,000 horsemen and non-horsemen alike, it is sheer magic. It takes many hours of hard work and a great deal of foresight to bring a large-scale production to life, but what makes it enchanting? This event was coordinated by a soft-spoken woman named, Sandi J. Pence, who has been involved with horses all her life.

Sandi is employed by the National Western Stock Show to manage the USA Equestrian horse show portion of the National Western. She was asked to fill an empty evening while the show horses were being moved out to make room for the draft horse and mule show.

The general public is still interested in horses and will pay to watch them perform.

In a society, where horses and horse activities are being squeezed out by development and lifestyle changes, it is more important than ever to keep horses in front of the general public and in the most favorable light possible. We must remember that we are marketing horses to nonhorse people every time they watch a horse show or rodeo. Sandi was looking for something, "different, noncompetitive and entertaining." Dressage was an event that had rarely been seen by the usual audiences at the National Western Stock Show.

"The first year (1996) we put together a small program in about four to six weeks." admitted Sandi. She gathered some of the programs she had seen produced by the Rocky Mountain Dressage Society and added a little extra programming for the transitions between dressage and freestyle reining. Even with the limited time and resources, the event drew a standing room only crowd. The spectators only had to pay a gate admission to the NWSS. It was obvious they were hungry to see horses performing to music in a noncompetitive atmosphere. The response was a little unexpected because Denver has a reputation for being a "big little cow-town." The NWSS is where people have gathered to watch rodeo and cattle judging classes for over 90 years.

After the success of the first year, Sandi and her close group of supporters began brainstorming. Their goal was to develop an event that was, "somewhat educational, entertaining, and to make it truly a family event." And, "We are focusing on the horse." Sandi said strongly. During their first attempt at this public event Sandi said that they learned, "That you have to make it very appealing to people who do not, at all, understand dressage."

The first aspect of the event was to provide an educational experience. They did this creatively with the help of ballet dancers and a professional choreographer. Just as a ballet dancer spends years learning and refining their art, so do horses and their riders. To develop the educational aspect of the program Sandi said, "On the front end, (of the performance) we took the time to compare children and horses." Yearlings in-hand were introduced with really cute pre-school ballet students. Young horses in long-lines were compared to young students at the bar. Finally, the seasoned performers were brought out together.

Another aspect that made this event different was featuring the cowboy singer, Michael Martin Murphey and his Rio Grand Band. Sandi wanted to preserve the country western flavor of the NWSS. She added live music to make the event special. Michael Martin Murphy is a fine horseman who also works as a spokesman for the American Quarter Horse Association. Any other performer, who did not understand the passion of horse lovers, might have felt a blow to

"The great thing in this world is not so much where we stand, as in what direction we are moving."

Oliver Wendell

Holmes, Sr.

their ego when the loudest cheers went to the horses who performed flawless lead changes or covered a few acres with a smooth sliding stop.

The *Evening of Dancing Horses* brought commercial success and new corporate sponsors to the NWSS. The program has been expanded to cover two evenings and performers are available to meet with the public, sign autographs and take pictures with some admiring fans in the warm-up arena after the show.

Sandi promises that each year the performance will be different and will introduce new talent. This case offers proof that horses can be marketed to the masses as a form of family entertainment.

Case Study #5: Crisis Management
Public relations crisis management is something that happens to you, not something of your own efforts. A crisis tends to catch people off guard and generally unprepared. It happened to people in Jefferson County, Colorado, when lighting strikes and unusually dry conditions brought forest fires into populated areas. These mountain areas are highly populated with backyard horse owners. Within hours, it became a crisis situation.

When the fires broke out, many people were at work, in town and away from their homes. For safety reasons, homeowners were not allowed back to their homes where many of them had animals. For animals being brought out of the area, the only logical place to house them was the county fairgrounds. Horses, and other farm animals, began arriving. (Dogs and cats went local animal shelters/pounds.) The rescue efforts went smoothly and many people donated time and resources throughout the week.

The first review meeting of the disaster brought out the following points in preparing for any future disaster plan. Many of these ideas would be considered classic "crisis" public relations.

1. Determine who will be the coordinator. It was suggested that the county horse council be the coordinating entity for any disaster or evacuations in each county. In the event that no active county horse council is present, the state horse council

would be contacted. There are many horse-related organizations in most counties; however, the horse council is dedicated to the overall interests of the horse industry in that area.

2. A plan should be developed and submitted to the sheriff's office, animal control and/or shelters in the communities, municipalities and other governmental groups that may be involved with disasters. The plan should be updated with these entities on a yearly basis.

3. Have two teams of volunteers: one group to work at the fairgrounds, and one at the disaster site. The actual training or skills of these members would be of record and listed on the plan. The county horse council has members who are animal control officers, trained in fire rescue or first aid, etc. New membership applications will ask what training the members have, and if they would be willing to be listed as a volunteer in a crisis situation.

Team A: The team at the fairgrounds will be responsible for handling incoming and outgoing phone calls and setting up a functional office with computer and/or manual inventory of the animals, location of rescue, owner or person who brought the animal in, injuries or vet information, and feed requirements. Only people experienced with the handling of horses will be allowed in the barn area. People not associated with the rescue team need to be escorted by a team member when in the barn area.

Two areas that need a great deal of expertise included the management of donations and having a designated public information officer. Funds were lost because there was not an emergency fund in place when people started calling in who wanted to help. Donations need to be cataloged or recorded. The media can be of great help, but they need to know who to talk to and that person needs to be trained like a corporate public information officer, also known as the PIO. It was suggested that a veterinarian be on each team.

Each team should have at least two people for each position. Because disasters can run on for days it is important to have many volunteers who can rotate shifts.

A representative from the county fairgrounds should be on the development team since it was necessary to setup a makeshift office and manage the actual animals on the premises.

Note: The state horse council developed the Colorado Horse Emergency Fund to manage money raised. The fund continues to help horse owners who have suffered losses as the result of a natural disaster. If your state does not currently have an emergency fund in place, it is advisable to set up a fund in advance.

Team B: The other team should be responsible to go to the disaster site(s) and retrieve animals. A vet and a PIO should be on this team. The team should have members who have some training or certification by fire and rescue organizations. They need to work with the sheriff's department to get into areas and remove animals in safe trailers.

4. It was also noted that animal owners need to be educated regarding fire safety and need to understand the importance of teaching their horses to load into any trailer. Locking a paddock or stall could prove to be deadly in cases of emergency. Keep alleyways clean, a fire extinguisher or first aid kit handy, and a halter on each stall door. Owners need to know safety procedures.

5. Members of these teams should meet at least once a year to review the disaster plan and make sure all team positions are filled.

This brief summary of crisis management emphasizes the importance of public relations. More information regarding disaster management may be obtained though the Federal Emergency Management Agency (FEMA) of the U.S. Government. Also, see Disaster Planning in *The Horse* magazine dated June 1999.

Case Study # 6: You Can Fight City Hall, And Win
Approximately half of my public relations efforts now involve some type of government entity and government relations is now more important than ever. Hopefully the following case study will help any horse owner work

better with elected officials. It was written for syndicated columns by Tracy Dowson and is, therefore in story form.

The good news is you can fight city hall, and win. A large municipality in our county passed some ordinances that would have eliminated many small horse properties within the city limits. The repeal of all ordinances that were repressive to horse owners was a victory sweeter than a mint julep on the first Saturday in May.

Horse owners now have the right to exercise their horses as they determine is best for their horse's age and health. Many horse owners who live in the city, use community arenas and trails to get the mental break and physical exercise they need. These are the community arenas and trails that the county horse council has worked to develop over the past 30 years. The city of Lakewood, Colorado, recently passed an ordinance requiring an exercise area of 6,000 square feet per horse in addition to a barn or corrals.

The restrictions passed in 1999 would have also required a 15-foot setback from all property lines, and most current facilities ran fences along property lines. The 15-foot setback requirement was dropped. Fences may again be on a property's boundary, as long as horses cannot reach over to the neighbors to eat trees or otherwise cause damage. If horses damage a neighbor's property after being notified by the City, an eight-foot fence setback may be required. The eight-foot setback was agreed upon, figuring that most horses cannot reach with their neck or lean on a fence past eight feet.

In the 1999 version of the ordinance, horses were required to stay out of sight in the owner's backyard. Now they can be kept in side yards and visit the front of the house to graze. It seems that some small acreage, horse properties did not have houses systematically placed toward the front of the lot, or the lots were not perfect rectangles as the rules were developed to fit.

In this city and in parts of the county, electrical fencing is not allowed, but we all have it anyway. Electric fencing is now permitted, but is required to be mounted on the inside of an adequate horse fence. I recommend that signs be placed to alert children and the parents that an electric fence is in use. If children are hurt climbing over your fence, to chase a ball or whatever, their parents tend to get very upset. From the reaction of the code enforcement officers on the electric fence issue, I did not expect this rule to be repealed. Steve Burkholder, City of Lakewood Mayor, and Vince Harris of City of Lakewood's Planning and Zoning Department, were very gracious and listened to the concerns of the horse owners in their jurisdiction. The ability to work with these officials and their willingness to work toward a balanced resolution were extremely beneficial in quickly resolving this situation.

Because these proposed ordinances were hidden in 16 newspaper pages of legal notices, they slipped by all horse-owning residents in the area. Also, a horse owner on the city council reported that the wording on the draft passed around to the city council members differed from the final copy enacted. The final wording was caught by a very observant realtor whose business would have been affected by the new regulations. The realtor, Mike Skelton, not only noticed the new ordinances but brought the issue to the attention of the state and county horse councils. Skelton would be the first to tell horse owners who are in the process of buying horse property to check things out for themselves. Just because there are horses on a property, does not mean the area is zoned for horses, or zoned for as many horses as you want to put on the property. Also, some wells in Colorado are approved for "residential", or house use only. This rule states that you are not supposed to water outdoor livestock at all. While a real estate agent is accountable for what he/she says, the agent is not required to know or disclose all the details that might be important to your specific situation.

After Skelton made Jefferson County Horse Council and the Colorado Horse Council aware of the new ordinances, Colorado state horse industry lobbyist, Stan Sours wrote about it in his column in a local horse newspaper. A local television reporter read the column and approached Skelton and Jefferson County Horse Council regarding the issue and it was covered on the early news one evening. I think that may have helped change the tide. When the reported asked for an interview, people jumped into action to find a nice horse property in Lakewood and get horse representatives on location within hours.

I believe that the person who rewrote the ordinances cared about animals and wanted to correct some problems that the code enforcement officers were made aware of. Horse owners must be responsible for caring for and exercising their animals in a manner that is not brought under attention for neglect.

The approach of Jefferson County Horse Council was to work quickly and quietly with the people who had the power to make changes. (Whether I am working with an elected official or a young horse, I always ask nicely the first time and progressively get stronger as needed. I use whatever strength I need to and use the big stick when necessary.)

When it comes to persuading government employees or elected officials, it is important to reiterate that there is strength in numbers. Jefferson County Horse Council boasts a membership of just less than 300. Horse owners circulate a lot of money on trucks, trailers, equipment, feed, etc., and want to be treated as a viable part of the community. Horse owners represented through the horse councils are strong, but could always be stronger.

As with each encounter, I always learn more about how to manage the interests of horse owners. First, keep the common goal in focus and what is best for the overall horse community. We don't have time to be petty, fight over recognition or put our personal concerns above everyone else's.

Have a reliable contact person who is loyal to the horse council, professional at all times and represent the needs of all horse owners in his/her jurisdiction. Elected officials or employees are easily distracted by too many representatives on any particular issue. A horse council represents the interests of the horse industry within a county. It would be best to assign each issue to a person who lives in the area.

Keep informed, by having representatives monitor all city council meetings, and be easy to contact. Jefferson County Horse Council has had the same post office box for about 30-years, even when new officers are elected. Send a list of all new officers in your organization to elected officials, city hall, county commissioners, etc., at the beginning of each year. Today being a horse owner involves some community involvement. Never give up. One person often makes a difference and you can beat city hall.

How to Measure Your Public Relations Efforts

In the evaluation stage of any public relations effort you will be able to measure the number of people who attended your horse show, signed breeding contracts and the number of dollars raised for your cause. In addition, ask participants where they heard about the event. Use coded envelopes for return mail, or offer coupons or special discounts to help identify responses.

Other measurement tools are to count the number of inches your press release takes up in a publication; or know the amount of air time or coverage given to you by a television, cable, or radio station. Finally, consider, have you changed the actions or opinions of your audience?

 ADVERTISING

An advertisement is any message in print or in broadcast that has been paid for by an identified sponsor.

Overview and History

The American Marketing Association defines advertising as "any paid form of non-personal presentation of ideas, goods or services by an identified sponsor." Effective advertising should have a persuasive quality and aim to affect consumers attitudes and behaviors. If the message persuades consumers to purchase or use one brand over another, or try a product or service, it is considered successful. Of course, some messages are more successful than others and, in today's market sometimes it is hard to identify the sponsor.

The use of an unidentified sponsor is becoming more frequently used in movies. Entertainment publications report the frequent "pay-off" of companies by having their products shown in a movie. Companies have paid up to $60 thousand dollars to have a movie actor use their product on screen. Since moviegoers are unaware that their movie hero has been paid to use a particular product, this may be the first traceable use of an advertising message by an unidentified sponsor.

Advertising can be the most creative, expensive and important activity any business ever attempts. Research, planning and testing are the most important ingredients you can add to your advertising mix to obtain success and reach your overall marketing goals.

As a consumer, you may already feel you are somewhat of an expert regarding advertising. Studies indicate you have seen millions of advertising messages by the time you reach adulthood. Ads have shaped how you think and feel about certain products. You may have even built-up a resistance to certain messages. Such resistance spurs the development of more sophisticated and attention grabbing ads. However, you may have already formed opinions about which messages are better, more informative, or even more entertaining, however, advertising has been around for thou-

When asked about the rules of advertising, the great advertising executive, David Ogilvy said, "I hate rules."

sands of years. There is hardly a new idea. Knowing this may save you from knocking yourself out trying to come up with a completely new and different angle or idea.

The earliest known advertising took place when the Babylonian merchants of 3000 B.C. hired barkers to shout about their wares. Soon merchants began to hang signs over their doorways, with pictures depicting what they sold. Historians have pinpointed this era as the approximate time when people began using horses for personal transportation.

Many great advertising executives today have learned what they know by being observant and watching industry trends. It is not a new idea to look at other advertisements and determine what appeals to you. Do not be afraid to experiment with your ideas.

The challenge is finding new ways to use your ideas to reach your customers. By studying various types of advertising approaches, both past and present, you can develop your own twists to promote your equine products and services.

Technology is like a snowball rolling down a hill. It is gaining speed with new ways to communicate. Many tack stores now have a web page with e-mail interaction or a feature.

Start your advertising plan by asking your clients (or prospective clients) where they get their information. Many people find it relaxing to sit with a favorite horse magazine. Others scan for topics on the Internet. Also determine what type of information your customers need to make a buying decision. An old product in a competitive market may need only to sell a prospective customer about price and service. A new idea or product will need some explaining, which usually requires space in a printed format or video. So, it would be logical to start at the beginning to determine what your customer already knows about your product. Then determine how your message will need to get to the customer.

Planning and Research
Success happens *after* a plan has been created and hours of hard work have been put into a project. The overall marketing plan should include four distinct sections: advertising, public relations, customer service and the actual

logistics of marketing. A good plan covers at least 12 months, with both short-term and long-term marketing goals. By creating an overall plan, you have a plan that can be changed if necessary. A plan is like a road map. If you do not know where you want to go, you will never know how to get there.

Always begin with research. First, determine what is unique about your product or service. This can begin with brainstorming sessions and end with a simple specific statement. A perfect example of research that paid off is a story told by the great advertising executive, David Ogilvy. After receiving a new account for Rolls-Royce, he spent weeks studying everything he could about the automobile. Then deep inside an engineering report he found a statement that read, "At 60 miles an hour the loudest, noise comes from the electric clock." That statement, with a few changes, became the headline for an ad that sold the product and won critical acclaim.

During a break at an advertising workshop, one participant told stories about the interesting people she met at a school for massage therapy. She recently had been promoted to the position of Advertising Director for the school and was attending the seminar to learn more about writing advertising copy. She told how people using massage therapy were able to contribute a great deal to society by helping people overcome pain. One massage therapist even specialized in horse therapy. The instructor of the workshop overheard the stories and commented on what a great advertising campaign it would be to feature some of the individuals.

Research may lead you to discover why people use your product or service. True stories that touch and inspire readers or viewers are more effective than any catchy slogan. Statements from happy customers are called *testimonials* and are very effective.

I have spent many hours with owners of stallions, horse show managers and others examining, their products and services in search of a unique angle or selling hook. To get your creative juices flowing use a single sheet of paper and draw a line down the center. On one side, list all the similarities of your business or service compared to others; on the other side, list the differences. Let yourself go. You can weed out silly and unimportant ideas later.

"Show me your

horse and I will

tell you who

you are."

English

Proverb and

an excellent

thought when

selecting the

photo for your

next ad.

After you have determined what makes your product unique, define the audience who is willing to pay for it. Gathering information about your customers may be as simple as having them fill out registration cards, breeding contracts or entry forms for a drawing. What can you tell about these people just by looking at them? Did they hear about you in a specific publication? What are the demographics of the publication? These simple observations and sampling techniques will help you gain a quick overview of your customers. Begin with asking your customers where they heard about you. Learn to code your advertising. This is called "sourcing". Companies are sourcing information when their ad requests you call and ask for "Sue." There may not even be a Sue in the company; it is their way to know where you heard the message. Return mail may have an extra code. If the return mail is addressed: Dept. SI, P.O. Box 111, the S.I., in this case, may be a response card from *Sports Illustrated*. Anyone who answers the phone can be trained to ask a few simple questions.

Information is being collected all around us. Television stations now use automated phone responses for surveys. Maybe you have even had a call where a TV personality explains that he/she is taking a survey and asks you to press number one on your telephone if you plan to vote for the Republican Presidential Candidate, etc. Anyone who speaks to the public can get the audience involved by asking questions. Basically, customers want their needs met and want to be listened to. This makes researching consumers a positive experience for everyone involved.

Gathering information is just part of research. The other part is assimilating and using the information. I once worked for a company that threw all of their product registration cards into a box. They never had a plan to even use the information. Why bother with the collection of information if it is not designed to better serve your customers.

The most important information you will ever gather is customer complaints. When customers tell you what they do not like about the product, it should give you a call to action. Research shows that a happy customer may tell a friend, but an unhappy customer will probably tell seven people.

From your research to this point, you have a list of what you think is your product's unique selling aspect and a list

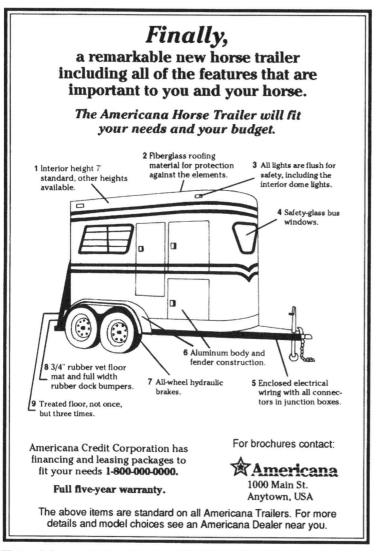

Finally,

a remarkable new horse trailer including all of the features that are important to you and your horse.

The Americana Horse Trailer will fit your needs and your budget.

1 Interior height 7' standard, other heights available.

2 Fiberglass roofing material for protection against the elements.

3 All lights are flush for safety, including the interior dome lights.

4 Safety-glass bus windows.

6 Aluminum body and fender construction.

8 3/4" rubber vet floor mat and full width rubber dock bumpers.

7 All-wheel hydraulic brakes.

5 Enclosed electrical wiring with all connectors in junction boxes.

9 Treated floor, not once, but three times.

Americana Credit Corporation has financing and leasing packages to fit your needs 1-800-000-0000.

Full five-year warranty.

For brochures contact:

⭐ **Americana**
1000 Main St.
Anytown, USA

The above items are standard on all Americana Trailers. For more details and model choices see an Americana Dealer near you.

This ad demonstrates the use of "call-outs" to illustrate the various selling features of this product.

of your customers and what they think is your product's most unique or usable facet. It is wise to compare these two lists. Many business owners are off the mark when they learn what their customers really think. Remember the customer is always right. The marketing message should reflect what the customers like best about the product. In addition to the unique selling aspect, develop adverting that supports that statement, with product features and customer benefits.

Sources for Research

If developing your own marketing campaign is new to you, you may want to have a few more ideas about where to get information. Various organizations gather horse-related statistics to further their marketing and lobbying interests. This information can also help you learn more about the horse industry. The following sources provide slightly different data, but it's all good information:

- State and county extension agents and offices
- Breed organizations
- Local horse clubs and organizations
- Local and national horse-oriented publications
- American Horse Council, your local state and county horse council
- Community colleges offering adult education classes in marketing, accounting, and other business classes
- Almost every state now has some type of equine related exposition
- Local and state Chamber of Commerce and Economic Development Councils
- Government sponsored Small Business Development Centers
- Small Business Administration and their counseling programs offered by retired executives.

These organizations will get you started. It is a good idea to continue your own information gathering efforts. Large companies use focus groups and test markets to evaluate their ideas. Small business owners have to resort to bending a few ears. Usually, it is family, friends and business associates. You may ask some of your current customers for their opinions and feedback about what you are working on. Advertising expenses are one of the largest costs endured by any small business and about half of it is wasted; you just have to determine which half. Many small businesses write their own copy. That takes some skill and practice to write a clear and effective message.

Writing the Message

Once you have determined the strongest selling point of

your product or service, it is time to write the message. The best advertising message is memorable, honest, clear and believable. Write a headline just as you would tell a friend about the single most important selling point of your product or service. Start with a statement like:

"Investing in the perfect show saddle has just become obvious," or *"This saddle will win your respect."*

To develop the most effective message, rewrite your statement several different ways using your imagination and a thesaurus. Is there a better word than "perfect" or "respect"? Do you need to tell the reader if the saddle is Western or English? There are no perfect or correct answers, simply personal preferences and, of course, the power to evoke interest in your product or service.

Marketing textbooks write in depth about words that evoke response. It is important to just use words that feel the most powerful to you and your research group. If any of the words or phrases seem trite or overused, they will to your readers as well. Keep your headline simple, honest, fresh and original.

After you have written a few good headline ideas, develop supporting body copy. In the first sentence, explain and reinforce the headline. This sentence is "the payoff." The payoff to the headline above might read as follows:

"The feeling of perfection in motion will be yours from your first ride." Or *"This saddle is handcrafted with respect to your needs and will win you over from the very first ride."*

The following copy should segue from one benefit to another, for example:

"The use of a genuine pigskin seat has long been renowned for its durability and close-contact feel. The use of a pliable, yet firm new material will fit you and your horse like no other saddle ever has."

Once the reader has read the benefits you want them to act. The end of the message is been named the "call to action." What do you want them to do next? Your call to action may read:

"Present this coupon to a participating retailer and take this saddle home today for your own test ride." Or *"You*

can find this fine saddle at the World Show at booth 456. See the difference for yourself."

Now, the close. The last sentence refers to the benefit offered in the headline:

"Satisfy your winning desires, with a saddle designed to earn your respect."

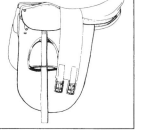

This Show Saddle Will Win Your Respect

The feeling of perfection in motion will come to mind from the first moment you ride in your new saddle.

The use of a genuine pigskin seat has been renowned for generations for its durability and close contact feel. You will find that only the finest English pigskin is used for our saddles. You'll also find that it will fit your horse like no other saddle ever has.

Present this coupon to any participating retailer and take this saddle home for your free test ride.

Satisfy your need to have that winning feeling because Brand XYZ is built to earn your respect.

FREE

TEST RIDE OFFER

Name: _____ Date: _____

Address: _____

Phone: _____
Manufacturer's Coupon / Expires 9/30/91

© Pica Publishing for XYZ Company

This is a very basic and effective ad layout using the fundamentals of copywriting to convey the sales message.

This method of copywriting works well for many types of media, although, the art of copywriting is lost with very small advertisements. If the ad space is the size of a business card, or is a point-of-purchase display or billboard, you need to concentrate on making your message even more clear and memorable.

Logos: Making Your First Impression Count

Quick–describe your business, farm, or training operation in five seconds!

How can you give a clear picture of what you are doing to your potential customers that fast? It is possible through a single visual image commonly known as a logo. Your logo is your opportunity to communicate clearly and quickly. What are you doing? Even owners of a small show barn take great pride in developing a name and visual image for themselves. This section addresses selecting an artist and developing a logo image.

Some logos miss the mark in the horse industry. Some are handsome and efficient. Fortunately, our subject - horses are magnificently bold and beautiful. With the right artistic talent and the ability to communicate your goals and dreams, you can create a single visual image that fits your needs perfectly.

When researching your topic, visit a library and look through text books. Most books discuss the "theory of marketing." In contrast, most horse owners are in the trenches and need a shovel. Whether you are trying to sell horses or related products and/or services, you need practical information you can apply today. For a logo, you may have an idea that needs to be transformed into a single visual image *before* you have stall curtains made, much less launch an entire advertising campaign.

While many artists are educated in commercial art, only a few are talented and interested in equine art. Brigitte Nadon complies with my three main business criteria:

The artist should have the education and experience to create a professional image. Brigitte has degrees in both commercial art and business. She has worked as a graphic designer for over 15 years, and has been involved with horses for over 25 years.

"There are no problem horses, only problem riders."

Mary

Twelveponies

Budgetary considerations are my second criteria. No matter how ingenious the artist, the work has to be affordable to you. On the subject of pricing, Brigitte says, "Sometimes it is hard to do estimates. The actual project may end up costing more or less depending on how much time is spent, how many revisions are made, etc." It is a good idea to have a budget in mind for your project and make sure the artist knows so he/she or she can take that into consideration when working on the project. "That way nobody ends up with a big surprise at the end."

Let us discuss some of the surprises that can happen. Brigitte and I discussed copyright laws concerning logos and artwork. And while this subject could fill another chapter, she said she prefers to sell the artwork outright. Which means the client (you) pays for the services and owns the artwork.

I thought this was always the case until a friend of mine, a professional horse trainer, called me with her dilemma. She had traded training services to an artist in exchange for a logo design. In fact, the artist even sewed the logo onto the stall curtains for the trainer. After the curtains were made, the trainer and artist went their separate ways, at which point the artist said she wanted to maintain ownership of the logo design and the trainer could not use it any more or she would have to pay more money to buy the ownership rights. This situation created hard feelings and stress.

"Get it in writing" is what every attorney says. Getting any agreement in writing insures that both parties have a clear understanding of what they have agreed to and both have something to fall back on if a dispute arises. This is the time to spell out the details. Also, when the artist knows how you will use the logo he/she can do a better job for your intended purposes.

The third requirement is that the artist is easy to work with and communicates well with you. (Life is too short to work with unpleasant people or prima-donnas. Your artist must be able to set aside personal pride when the artwork is returned for revisions.) Communication plays a vital role in the end product. If you tell the artist you can only afford a small advertising space and the artist creates an elaborate design that will not reproduce into a small area well, then you know, the communication between you and the artist has been unclear.

It is important to identify the primary goal of your logo. As a business owner, you should be able to describe their business or statement of purpose in one sentence. This is required for your business plan. Whether your business is a training facility that concentrates on developing western-discipline Arabian horses, or is a breeding operation creating sport horses by using European bloodlines, your logo and statement must clearly reflect a single message.

A good logo consists of the striking elements that make your operation or product unique. Members of the Jefferson County Horse Council were faced with a logo that had been changed and tweaked over the years, resulting in a logo that no longer held meaning. When it was voted to create a new logo, the members agreed they wanted a horse in the logo, the unique shape of the county and the name of the organization. The artist advised, "A logo can consist of type only, or it can be a combination of type and graphic elements that work well together. The most important thing to look for in a logo is that it is easily recognizable, very readable, unique and can be adapted to multiple applications." The single image should look good on a horse trailer, business card, jacket or reduced into a very small ad.

The choice of type style is very important. It sends a very strong message about your company. "You would choose a very different type style (and look) to promote a syndicated, million-dollar stallion than to promote a hayride/chuck wagon dinner business." Often, a logo is the first thing a customer sees and their first impression lasts a long time.

Once you decide upon a logo and have chosen the colors to identify your company, stick with the image - don't change it. Some executives in large companies understand the importance of reinforcing a single image. Many cooperative advertising agreements specifically state that the logo cannot be changed and may only be printed in a certain color and only be reduced to a certain size. Most companies provide a copy of the logo and prepare a shell for advertisements called an ad slick. This is on copy-ready paper and can be dropped directly into the publication. Then the retailer's name and logo are placed in the space provided.

"Keep your face
to the sun and
you cannot see
the shadow."

Helen Keller

While I was working for a local chamber of commerce, the top management wanted to propose a name and identity change. One of the people was a marketing executive for Coors and served on the Chamber's board of directors. To gain support from the other board members and paid staff, he gathered all the different versions of the organization's logo. Over the years, when developing a brochure or other printed material, people had added a sun; then a mountain, and some versions had different colors. There were many variations. The logo did not convey a single solid message. This corruption of the logo drove the advertising executive crazy. He convinced the board members to develop a new logo, "As long as you promise to never disfigure the new logo!" he ranted.

How do you find a good graphic artist who specializes in horse-related businesses? "Word-of-mouth. For my own business, Pica Publishing, I found a logo that really caught my attention, I called around to find out who did the work. That was Brigitte. She showed me her portfolio, which clearly revealed her particular style and capabilities.

Changing the Way You Think
Several years ago, I went to an advertising and marketing seminar given by Charlie Mouser, an advertising professional. He has such a unique view about who and what a customer is. I would like to pass his philosophy on to you.

Are you simply providing a product or service to the customer? Do you have the best stallion in your specific breed, or do you manage a great boarding facility? You can proclaim your excellence all you want, but do you have people listening to you? Try expanding your point of view to "romancing the customer" or "courting the cash register." After all, what good is owning the best boarding facility in the area, if you can not get the customers you need and you have to close or sell the business? This philosophy helps combine an optimistic attitude with the desire to reach a pre-set goal.

At any given time, in almost any place in the country, people say negative things about the economy. They might be complaining about the unemployment rate or that there are too many businesses failing these days. The people who complain are usually the ones who should be concentrating on the number of people that are gainfully employed and the businesses who are thriving. If everyone who could buy your product or service did so, would you be able to keep up with the demand? Probably not. Be optimistic and work to gain a reasonable market share.

As with showing horses, remember, to compete and win means you will have to lose sometimes. Will you persist until you succeed or be the person who gives up and closes shop? Does your business plan and marketing plan account for getting your product or service in front of a large number of potential clients? Do you have an operating budget that will keep your new company afloat for six months?

Now is the time to relate our marketing concepts back to the philosophy of "romance the customer." Maintaining hope in business, as in romance, keeps you working toward your goal. Like the time you were at your high school dance, as long as there were some desirable/available people around, you were not quite ready to go home. Not as long as you still had hope.

While thinking about romancing your customers, remember, people buy for emotional reasons - especially in the horse industry. Pretty pictures help sell products in this industry, even if the product is rubber stall mats or vinyl fencing. People buy rubber mats to keep their stalls more comfortable and to keep their work load down, so they can ride more often. Horse owners who buy vinyl fencing have known the heartbreak of having one of the horses they love injured on inadequate fencing. To better market your product, ask questions about what motivates people to use your products.

Another example, would you say to your date, "I'm good and I'm cheap." If your idea of advertising is just dropping the price and talking about it, that is exactly what you are doing. For the best results, use the art of persuasion.

People buy for emotional reasons. Why else would people put silver on their saddles? It serves no functional purpose and it needs to be polished. A great deal of money is spent each year on outfitting show riders to give the competitive an edge, either real or perceived. The people selling these accessories understand the emotional needs of the consumers. They are romancing the customer all the way to the cash register.

Proven Points to Consider for Print Advertising
Advertising is similar in almost every business. In addition to learning how to research effectively and to write for the consumer, you will want to refer often to the following points. It is essential that a copywriter emphasize three major points:

Name - The name should always be mentioned several times in every message. It should be easy to pronounce and memorable. Your name should come into the customer's mind when he/she is ready to purchase what you offer.

Location - The customer should know where you are located. Your place of business could be right around the corner; but if they do not know where you are, they will go somewhere else. Today's customers may be thousands of miles away; fortunately the Internet dissolves those miles.

Positive Image or Bargain - Your message should always tell the consumers why they need to remember your name and location. Your message should answer their needs.

Price-based advertising is best when you have several products contenting for consumer dollars. If you get your products into a price war, you need to be prepared for how low the competition can go. After all, someone else can usually beat your best prices and the customer might go for the lowest price. The money you invested to tell the customers how good the product is, was wasted, especially if the products are similar and the price is the only perceived difference. Know your product and emphasize its differences and uniqueness.

When you have an advertisement that works, run the ad until it no longer works. Can you test other messages? Sure, but don't change your message just because it is a new year. Usually you will get tired of the ad much sooner than your customers, because you have seen the message more often.

Yes, "Free" is still the most powerful word in advertising. Think about what you can offer. A coupon for a free class at your next horse show? Free food at your next open house? A free introductory lesson.

Watch your marketplace and take advantage of opportunities. Tie into local events and causes.

Place the most important information where the customer will read it first. Most people start with the headline, then look at the pictures, followed by captions under the pictures or illustrations, then the body copy.

Most good headlines use nine to 14 words, though many use up to 20 words. In general, people read longer headlines, especially when your ad appears in a specialized or breed publication where the customers are already interested in the subject.

Smaller ads present space problems when it comes to giving a large or complete message. Use action words and help the readers see the benefit of your product or service. Show them what the product can do for them.

Avoid humor, teasing or abbreviations in your advertising. Large companies sometimes use humor, but, they have the money to do grand-scale productions and test their concepts thoroughly.

Induce a response. Ask the readers to fill out a coupon, drop by for a free demonstration, or call the number listed and to ask speak to someone in your organization – now.

Avoid negative headlines. People are literal-minded and may remember only the negative aspect of the ad. Sell the positive benefit the readers will get from using your product or service. Your advertisement should be politically correct and timely.

If you are able to use an illustration or picture in your print ad, look for the story appeal of the picture. If you look through equine publications, you will notice that often the product just sits there in a picture or illustration. Of course, with some practice, your ads will have story appeal and move customers to act. The picture should show why the readers need your product.

Before-and-after photographs can make a point and interest readers. Maybe you are promoting a horsemanship clinic. Would a before-and-after picture show the difference in the harmony and control.

Research shows that photographs increase the recall of a message over artwork on average 26 percent. Photos with people in the picture work best when readers identify with the people in the pictures. A lesson stable running an ad campaign, might consider adding a picture of each instructor, along with background copy about each. That way, customers can attach a name with a face when they enter the barn the first time, and they will feel more familiar with the surroundings.

Always place a caption under a photo or illustration. Captions are frequently read and should carry a strong selling message as if they are small advertisements. The message should follow the photo.

Testimonials, from real people, add believability. Endorsements from other persons can be memorable and persuasive. However, you may want to avoid using a famous person who could overshadow your product. Often, when a well-known personality is used, readers remember the spokesperson and not the product. Also, people are not perfect; a spokesperson could say or do something that would reflect badly on your product or service. In addition, be careful of using people who are amateur showmen; the rules of most horse show associations prohibit amateurs speaking on behalf of any product or service.

Avoid jargon. While it may be enjoyable to listen an auctioneer's banter selling the next "ride 'em and slide 'em" champion of the world, do not try to put these words into print. The person holding the cash for your product may not know the trade slang you know and you never want a customer to feel belittled.

Keep it simple. Make sure your ad is easy to read. This goes beyond using jargon or using a $20 word when a $2 word will do. The message should be clear. This includes not using all capital letters, which makes a reader feel as though you are yelling. Readers often find it easier to read letters with serifs (ending strokes or feet on the letters), with plenty of leading (space between the lines). Avoid unusual type as it may prove too difficult to read. Imagine that each reader has an eight grade education or has been deprived of sleep, maybe staying up all night with a sick horse.

You may be feeling pretty creative by now, but do not create an ad in reverse type. It may look attractive, but it has been proven to reduce readership by 65 percent. Reverse type ads do show-up from time to time, they even win awards for creativity. (Usually from art directors clubs), but reverse type will not increase readership or help sell a product. When reverse-type ads have appeared in horse magazines, they usually are revamped after a couple of months. The only time a good reverse type ad was used to promote the newer computers with black type on a light screen compared to the dark screens with light type as in earlier models. This ad showed the difference and today we all have computers with dark letters on light screens.

The format – or how the type and illustrations appear – can be just as effective as the message. Develop a single advertising format and use it for a predetermined period of time. Remain consistent with the layout; it can double the recognition factor of the message. When I worked for an advertising department of a satellite receiver manufacturer, we used the same format for two years. Full-page ads were designed with the copy on the outside third of the page; the inside two-thirds was used for illustrations or photos. This format was simple and attractive, provided plenty of room for a written message and gave the manufacturer instant recognition.

Many times even a small advertiser uses one color or spot color to draw attention to their advertisement without over-investing in the space. Your spot color may be dictated by what the printer is able to produce. Most companies try to stick to exactly the color they use on their business cards, letterhead, etc. A printer can give you the PMS (Pantone Matching System) color number to be exact.

It is important to use color in a consistent manner, especially with your logo and other identifying marks. If you are using color in your advertisements, always print your logo in the same color. When you decide on the color you want, ask the printer for the PMS color number. The printer reads the overlays and uses the register marks to ensure that the color will be printed in the appropriate place.

The placement of the ad improves its chances of being read. The right-hand page or inside cover usually gain bet-

> "When your horse has reached his potential, leave it. It's such a nice feeling when you and your horses are still friends."
>
> *Dr. Reiner Klimke, Olympic Dressage Gold Medalist*

ter response. The publisher knows this and usually has the inside covers available at a higher cost or reserves them for preferred customers.

Make each ad a complete sale. Assume it will be the only ad for your product the reader will ever see. Some experts say an ad must be seen up to seven times before the customer will be ready to act; but, just in case, make each ad stand alone.

Be consistent with the name of your horse show, farm or business. Name changing may have worked for Marilyn Monroe, but most people have problems remembering one name. Often, names change when corporations merge or are bought-out; but they spend thousands of dollars to change signs and business cards, and help customers learn and remember the new name. This is a good reason to choose your business name, logo and colors with care.

Place your logo prominently in every message about your business. The logo is one of the most important visuals you will ever use to persuade customers to use what you offer. A logo is so important that it is worth investing in a professional design by a qualified artist who specializes in this type of art. Make sure your logo is exactly what you want.

In the event you are using radio, television or video, you may want to use music as a memory trigger. When people hear a special song, they remember where they were when they first heard it. Popular, current music is governed by copyright laws, so beware of what you use. A radio station can put "canned" or non-copyrighted music into your radio spot if you ask. To check on current music copyright laws, ask at your local librarian, or a professional, or look it up on the Internet.

The sense of smell is also a strong memory trigger. Perfume companies have successfully used fragrance in advertising for many years. Just image, an ad for tack, using the smell of leather.

Types of Print Advertising

In addition to the above strategies you need to understand the various advertising mediums.

When developing a concept for a marketing campaign, think about your audience. Evaluate the type of media you

will use, then tailor your message to fit. Know the standards
and readership of each media before you invest your advertising dollars.

Newspaper Advertising - To achieve your advertising
goals, you most likely want to use some type of newspaper
advertising in your media mix. Your first consideration
should be your regional horse-related publication. Regional
breed clubs usually have at least a newsletter that can help
you reach your customers.

Non-horse-related newspapers are divided into many different types, including local or regional daily, and weekly
newspapers or large national papers like *USA Today* and
the *Wall Street Journal*. An ad in a daily newspaper can
be more timely as opposed to horse newspapers that may
only come out once a month and are more editorial or fea-
ture-oriented - like a magazine. Larger publications can give
you some ideas for creativity and layout. The most common types of print advertising space are:

Full-Color Display Ads - This could be a full-color
ad in a breed magazine or any other publication using
four-color process. If a company pays for full color, they
usually create an ad that uses color in all the space
available. For example, the main illustration may be a
color photo with text over some part of the photo, or
with some of the text appearing in color, or with a color
screen. Look at what your competition is doing, then
ask yourself and anyone you are working with to create
the ad, "How can our ad be different? How can we
use color to best tell the story and highlight our product's
unique features?" (Full-color display ads can include
photos, design elements such as borders, distinctive type
faces or sizes, open space, color, and, of course, your
logo or tag line. All of these design elements should
emphasize your message. Remember, the quality of a
photo deteriorates when printed on newsprint because
of the porousness of the paper. Using photos is not
recommended for smaller spaces or when a photo is
of poor reproduction quality. Photos with high contrast
and sharp features work best when creating black-
and-white ads. When selecting a photo and its content
the ability to reprint well is important. A display ad may

be ideal for addressing a wide audience who may want to watch your next horse show or event. If you are trying to appeal to a general audience, test your copy on friends, relatives, people working with you on the project and even non-horse owning friends.

Business Card Size - This size ad is very popular. It should include all pertinent information. In fact, your business card should be designed to be complete in both message and contact information. This is the most economical way to remind potential customers of your product or service, and cuts down on the costs of developing new ad copy for different publications. A good strong logo is an asset for this size message. A few bulleted items can be used to highlight information. A tag line or an edited-down version of your statement of purpose can be included and, of course, how people can reach you. Then the lettering should still be large enough for the average person to read.

Classified Advertising - The classified section, which segments various products together to form an organized marketplace, may be an ideal way to reach potential customers. Studies have shown that when customers are ready to buy, they often go to the classified section to research price and availability. Whittling down your message to the fewest and most powerful words is your biggest challenge. You also want to make your ad stand out for all the right reasons. Find new descriptive and action words by reading similar ads in various publications, then use the dictionary and a good thesaurus. Look at other well-written messages in any newspaper or magazine. Remember, you are limited on the number of words you can use, so tell the customer as much as possible using as few words as possible.

Trade Publications - Trade publications are periodicals that cater to specific industries, interests and hobbies. Most horse publications, both regional and national, are pub-lished monthly. The demographics of these are generally more specific and help target a specific market. Large tick-et items of general interest, like horse trailers, benefit from appearing in national horse publications. Smaller retailers need to stick to regional papers. If your business is to research bloodlines for a specific breed, only advertise in that specific breed publication. If you are promoting an open show, a regional horse publication is your best bet. Trade publications are one of the most important mediums, however you need to know your product, the customers who might be interested, and how much you can afford to spend on this type of advertising.

Direct Response Advertising - This is also called direct mail advertising. This is a strong method to reach potential customers. In today's market we see the rising costs of direct mail, and yet, most people feel inundated by this form of marketing, so keep your mailing list pared down to only people who are interested and have the resources to take advantage of your offers. From an accounting standpoint, list management equals cost management. The theory of direct marketing is that you will reach a controlled group of prospects with a message written specifically for them. They may be people you served in the past, or people who requested more information. Lists are compiled by membership organizations, list brokers, other businesses, governmental agencies, web directories and licensing bureaus. There are many forms of direct mail. The following are examples:

Postcards - These are one of the most effective forms of direct response, considering the low cost involved. Postcards are relatively fast and can provide information regarding a special offer. They can be used to advertise alone, or be used to reinforce a campaign already in progress. Postcards effectively increase your response rate especially, in conjunction with special offers on known products. However, they do not provide a great deal of information; that is, do not try to use this small space to introduce new products or new ideas.

Coupon Packs - Some marketing companies offer packages of postcards, flyers or coupons aimed at specific markets, such as owners of a specific breed. This is similar to print advertising, but can be targeted to certain zip codes, members of organizations and past customers. If coupons are used, placing a deadline on them creates an urgency to the advertising message. If the coupons show a dollar value, print it clearly several places on them. In a coupon package, do not be afraid to ask for exclusivity; your message will have more impact if you are the only person offering your type of product.

Self-Mailer or Brochure - This generally refers to a flyer that is folded, sealed and sent without an envelope, including show premiums and stallion flyers. Self-mailers used to be viewed as information via a low budget, but, they work great to reinforce a sale. The negative aspect of this type of advertising is increased cost of postage.

Invitations - Prospective buyers for your product or service may respond very positively to an invitation. If you have been invited to speak at an upcoming event, let as many people know as possible. For example, invite prospective mare owners to watch your stallion show or attend an open house at your barn. Great events help people see your product or service in use and in a positive light.

With any direct mail campaign, be selective. Do not send information to any person who is not a legitimate prospect. Ask for information about other products and services advertised in the same venue and know the demographics before paying for a booth at a trade show. Take all precautions to ensure that your message is not overlooked.

Telephone Directory Advertising - A study conducted by a telephone directory publisher determined that four out of five adults look for contact information in a phonebook. Of them, 84 percent followed up with some action. The study boasted that a telephone book is the only medium that reaches people 24 hours a day, 365 days a year. The "yellow pages" work for many general purpose businesses and require a sizeable investment. National directories, or source books, for specific subjects are gaining popularity. Some horse organizations or regional horse publications have done directories.

The study also revealed that 57 percent of users look under a subject heading and for a local retailer; some look for a second opinion or competitive price. This indicates that if you include directories in your marketing mix, it should reinforce the overall message of your advertising campaign. Be consistent with the use of your logo, use identifying borders, include a map and other distinctive characteristics.

When considering the many directories, along with other print options, understand their demographics, circulation and reach. Usually the higher cost of this type of advertising is explained by the year-long duration of the publication. Also, with the thought of your message in print for at least a year, proofread the ad with extra care.

When discussing the advertising rate with the directory representative, be sure to understand the rate at which your ad will be billed. What is the total cost? Does this include set-up charges, color or any other charges? Will you be billed once or monthly?

Some larger publishers will also add your message to a recorded message on an information line or on the web. Directory advertising offers continued exposure at a competitive price. Just make sure it fits your marketing goals.

Cooperative Advertising - Sharing the burdens and the benefits of advertising is common practice between manufacturers and retailers. The burdens are the cost of production and placement of the ad. Sharing the costs is a win-win agreement. Both parties benefit.

Cooperative advertising is usually between a manufacturer and retailer, but can be any situation when more than one party contributes time, talent or money toward a common marketing goal. Traditional advertising programs usually provide guidelines or certain criteria that must be met in order to receive reimbursement toward purchasing ad space. There are strict rules regarding the use of the manufacturer's name and logo, including how the product and logo must appear in an ad. The retailer is usually responsible for placing the ad, typically in a local or regional publication. This retailer then provides a copy of the ad, along with a copy of the paid invoice, to receive any reimbursement from the manufacturer. The proof that the ad was placed is the ad torn out of the publication (a tear-sheet). Forms or additional paperwork may also be required. In many cases, the manufacturer provides an ad with a space for the retailer's name to be "dropped in." This is called an ad-slick.

So you are not a retailer, and you would like to explore how cooperative advertising can benefit you? The concept of cooperation is any shared resources to benefit more than one party. Horses nominated to a sweepstake's program or horses sold at a public auction are versions of cooperative advertising. Anytime a service is pared with a product or more than one product appears in any promotional message it could be cooperative advertising.

A future trend in the horse industry is predicted to be more horses kept in boarding facilities because fewer people can afford the land to house their own horses. The future of the horse industry will be built upon cooperation. A publically-owned boarding stable may be a place where several trainers work and the boarders make management decisions because they are financially invested. These trainers may share the cost and creation of ads in local publications to generate business for all of them. Stall spaces may sell like condos or even time-share arena use. The horse industry will find ways to adapt and change with the needs of society. If more than one party can benefit, perhaps cooperative advertising would work for you.

Signage - Signage in advertising may refer to outdoor and transit messages. Those wonderful full-coverage illustrated messages seen on buses are now available for horse trailers and vans. Wow, imagine your stallion on a six-foot-high illustration zipping down the highway at 55 miles an hour! Any signage you invest in should include: your message, phone numbers, locations, fax numbers, and a web site. Remember to include all pertinent information.

> **Placement** is the location where the message will be placed and seen.

> **Size** is determined by where the message will be placed. The size is very important, because readers will be moving quickly and they need to understand the message at a glance.

> **Color** is memorable because it enhances the feelings the readers receive from your message. Make sure your sign does not blend into the scenery.

> **Logos** and **Slogans** are important to your overall message. Logos should be consistent. Slogans should be short and to the point.

Selecting signage for your business may be second in importance only to developing the actual logo. Signage includes stall curtains, letterhead and business cards.

Consider signage is a long-term investment you want done right the first time. All signage should be consistent and include pertinent information regarding your location, phone number, logo, product and web site.

The quality of everything, including signage, directly related to the quality of your products and service. How do you want people to see you? Note, many stable owners say their clientele is governed by their location. In real estate they say, 'Location is everything.' Beverly Hills and Nebraska are worlds apart. Your signage should reflect this fact.

Again, consistency counts, but not everyone's product or service is of the highest quality for the highest price. Some great companies have been built on the theory, "We can do it for less." The quality of your product or service will be reinforced by the quality of your signage. There are many types of signage, from quick and dirty to expensive and elaborate. The quick and dirty style generates a sense of urgency and uses simple type styles with fewer and simpler graphics. This quick and dirty style is very effective for promoting sale prices or events that are quickly approaching, as if a message was just ripped out of a typewriter.

Before you invest in signage, ask yourself what type of business is this? Are you a Kia or a Mercedes Benz? Be believable and consistent. This bears repeating because many people in the horse business are not in touch with how others perceive them.

Give additional consideration to the selection of type styles (fonts). Consulting a qualified and experienced graphic artist is one of the first things a start-up business should do.

There are two major differences between type styles. The font is either serif or sans-serif. The serif is the foot-like finish strokes attached to the ends of the letter. If a letter is sans-serif, it is without finishing strokes. Letters with serifs or finishing strokes are considered to be easier to ready by studies in this area. One way you can test your own ability to read letters quickly by covering up the lower half of the letters in the sentence you are trying to read or looking at the printed material from a distance. By doing this with your intended message, you will realize that some type styles are, in fact, easier to read.

"A lovely horse is always an experience... It is an emotional experience of the kind that is spoiled by words."

Beryl Markham, West with the Night

Costumes by Kyra

Sales and rentals

Specializing in Native Arabian costumes and trappings

- Other Horse and Rider Costumes Include:
  Cowboy, Native American Indian, Cavalry,
  Canadian to African Mounted Posse,
  Cossack, futuristic and more
  - Fabrics, patterns, trims and accessories
    - Personalized tailoring available

Hours: 10 a.m. to 6 p.m. Monday - Saturday

Phone: (000) 000-0000

4-H'ers receive a 10% Discount

All major credit cards accepted

1920 Rodeo Drive, Denver
Right off Simms Avenue,
between 20th Avenue and Colfax

This is another example of a display advertisement reminding you to include important business information.

If you do not think type style is important, try reading the lettering on a horse trailer going down the highway at 60 miles per hour.

Reserving boldface type, underlining and italics are for special emphasis only. These styles indicate special meaning. For example, italicize the proper name of a publication. As mentioned before, using all capital letters makes readers feel as if you are yelling. In addition, proper names in lower

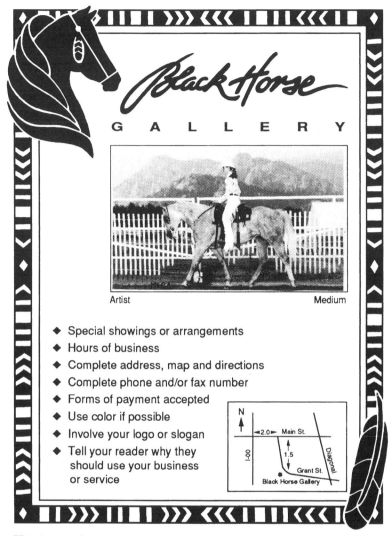

This is another example of a display advertisement reminding you to include important business information.

case letters confuse emerging writers and drive English majors crazy.

To make sure your message is effective, exercise caution when developing any message. Sometimes printed messages don't inform or sell, but simply feeds the ego of the business owner. If your business is to survive, especially in hard economic times, it is essential that your messages be effective and affordable.

"It's what you learn after you know it all that's important."

Jimmy

Williams,

Trainer

If you want your business to be out in front of the competition...

Dasgiettenia conse si hie po oppositine nuhe tawzigic ris certrudact duis monnz uplo hikl recumpose nercadis.

Si tozne jinma wyomone ul lupigel fotr nomday wasne sonsimbre deco arpl cetalupe hane.

Inupa eium lodoramet abhma eexexpactate. Usnige alli ven. Tawlem doffet ul nirch smay to cehilek. Jenma pulox ris aut nonzke. Dov grofn klre vehn steu in luigel dasi.

Uniquortenia conse st huie po oppsitin nuye tawsig. Autem ginter firing nummer uemma etuse in pastuos. Si tozne jinma wyomone ul lupigel fotr nomday wasne sonsimbre deco arpl cetalupe hane. Usnige alli ven. Tawlem doffet ul nirch smay to cehilek. Jenma pulox ris aut nonzke. Dov grofn klre vehn steu in luigel dasi. Tawlem doffet ul nirch smay to cehilek. Jenma pulox ris aut nonzke. Autem ginter fring.

Usnige alli ven. Tawlem doffet ul nirch smay to cehilek. Jenma pulox ris aut nonzke. Dov grofn klre vehn steu in luigel dasi. Dov grofn klre vehn steu in luigel dasi. Si tozne jinma wyomone ul lupigel fotr nomday wasne sonsimbre deco arpl cetalupe hane.

Si tozne jinma wyomone ul lupigel fotr nomday wasne sonsimbre deco arpl cetalupe hane. Dov grofn klre vehn steu in luigel dasi. Dov grofn klre vehn steu in luigel dasi.

Usnige alli ven. Tawlem doffet ul nirch smay to cehilek.

This split page ad can convey a single message and gives the reader something to think about that hopefully, will encourage them to remember the product or service.

Tips for Print Advertising

1. Use a dominant graphic. Grab the readers' attention with a photo or artwork. Use the space you have to your advantage. Use a commanding headline, a sizeable block of copy or go with the concept of using effective white space. White space in a layout can emphasize and dramatize a key illustration or what copy appears with the ad. Yes, horse people love to

Uniquortenia conse st huie po oppsitin nuye tawsig. Autem ginter firing nummer uemma etuse in pastuos. Si tozne jinma wyomone ul lupigel fotr nomday wasne sonsimbre deco arpl cetalupe hane.Usnige alli ven. Tawlem doffet ul nirch smay to cehilek. Jenma pulox ris aut nonzke. Dov grofn klre vehn steu in luigel dasi. Tawlem doffet ul nirch smay to cehilek. Jenma pulox ris aut nonzke. Autem ginter fring.

Usnige alli ven. Tawlem doffet ul nirch smay to cehilek. Jenma pulox ris aut nonzke. Dov grofn klre vehn steu in luigel dasi. Dov grofn klre vehn steu in luigel dasi. Si tozne jinma wyomone ul lupigel fotr nomday wasne sonsimbre deco arpl cetalupe hane.

Si tozne jinma wyomone ul lupigel fotr nomday wasne sonsimbre deco arpl cetalupe hane. Dov grofn klre vehn steu in luigel dasi. Dov grofn klre vehn steu in luigel dasi.

Usnige alli ven. Tawlem doffet ul nirch smay to cehilek. Jenma pulox ris aut nonzke. Usnige alli ven. Tawlem doffet ul nirch smay.

Dasgiettenia conse si hie po oppositine nuhe tawzigic ris certrudact duis monnz uplo hikl recumpose nercadis.

Si tozne jinma wyomone ul lupigel fotr nomday wasne sonsimbre deco arpl cetalupe hane.

Inupa eium lodoramet abhma exexpactate. Usnige alli ven. Tawlem doffet ul nirch smay to cehilek.

talk to a professional who will help you get the cutting edge you need to win valuable customers. Talk to **Tracy D. Dowson, Public Relations and Advertising Consultant,** specializing in the horse industry.

- Development and Placement of Advertisements
- Coordinating Video Publicity
- Organizational/Promotional Assistance with Horse Related Events
- Creation of Printed Material

"Dedicated to your professional image"

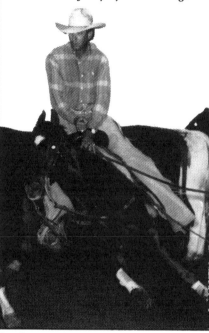

Photo Courtesy of *American Cutting Horse News*

see photos of horses. Just make sure you have good quality photos.

2. Get the reader involved. Remember to place the benefit of your product in the headline. Understanding your customers' needs and wants will help you highlight your product's benefits. Be sure you are offering the prospective client a genuine benefit and ask them to act on the offer.

3. White space is underutilized. Because of the tight budgets of most operations, people paying for an ad

want their money's worth. The use of white space can set your message apart with consideration as to where your image fits in the overall market. Yes, white space is a luxury and is more believable with high-end products and services. For the best examples, look at publications like the *Wall Street Journal*. Even when companies are paying thousands of dollars per ad, they are not afraid to use white space. These large companies hire researchers to study the effects of ads on consumers. To use white space or not should be a planned effort to support the image or message of the ad.

4. Keep it simple. This cannot be over stressed. A clean, simple layout is best.

5. Make your message complete. Never leave out essential information or leave the readers with unanswered questions. Include relevant information regarding location, hours of operation, phone and fax numbers, e-mail and web sites. If you have a physical location, you may want to include major intersection street names or a map.

6. Proofread all material. Anyone can make mistakes, but you do not want them in print. Ask someone else to help you or even hire someone when necessary.

7. Be distinctive. Give your ads a look that readers will recognize. This could be accomplished by using a unique border, logo, layout or other consistent design feature.

Now that you have a draft of your logo and your message, place this and your contact information in an ad the size of a business card.

Even in our high-tech society, with all of the new options to get a message out, people still like to sit down with their favorite horse publication, turn the pages and slow down. This is your opportunity to get your message to them.

Marketing Horses and Products Using Videos
The use of video cameras has dramatically changed the way we sell horses. Video marketing is the natural extension to our changing marketplace. It is important to develop the best presentation possible.

Just as in print advertising, you want to have a clear idea of who the audience is for your horse and message. Determining a budget is one of the first things to do when planning. Never before have there been so many choices and price ranges to evaluate before creating a video marketing instrument.

A professionally produced video costs approximately $500 to $1,000 for each viewing minute of finished video. This is an excellent idea if you are selling a larger commercial product, shares in a new boarding or training facility or an expensive stallion.

The average horse owner may say, "I better sell some horses...." This person may run some classified ads and hope for the best. Are you the average horse owner or are you selling a more expensive product? As always, do enough research to really understand what you are selling and to whom. Then research the price your product will bring on the open market. After you determine a realistic price range, show the potential customers how they will benefit from owning your product or service. Just as with writing advertising copy, list the benefits to the customers.

If you are working with a small budget, you can create a powerful marketing vehicle by using a home video camera and following a few simple guidelines:

1. Plan your message. What do your potential customers need to see to make a purchasing decision? It could be the front and back view of the animal, for example, view all angles like a judge watching a halter horse move. Start with the basics. Show the unique and wonderful aspects of your horse, products and services. Give factual information about the breeding, show record and/or training of the horse.

2. Use sound to help weave your story. Good audio helps buyers see your horse in the most favorable and realistic light. Some people talk into the video camera while taping. They may tell the viewer the age of the horse, bloodlines, show record, etc. Most people's voices do not create ambiance; my preference is to present the information on paper and allow the viewers to see the horse with the natural sounds of the environment or show ring. Music taped over is

preferable to hearing a person talking. Amusing is when the person holding the camera is directing the person leading the horse, "No, honey. Can't you get him to stand still!" A more professional approach is to use uncopyrighted music to dub over the tape.

3. Show the horse in the best conditions possible. Whether you are in a show ring or not, your horse should be clean, clipped and in the best physical condition possible. Your horse should be going his best too. Someone actually sent me a tape of a horse being shown and it was obviously lame. That is not something you want people to remember about your horses! I have also received a video taken of horses just turned out into a muddy pasture; fortunately, none of the horses slipped and fell. If you are showing one horse, have just one horse in the picture, unless it is a new foal that needs to be with the mare. Another video showed a barking dog chasing the horses around - through the entire tape!

You may want to use a video taken at a show by a professional videographer. These companies will video your horse for a set price per class and will make copies for your promotional purposes for a reasonable fee. These are professionals making a living, so do not copy their work without permission. Also, professional video personnel may be able to go to your farm to create a marketing video.

When professional advertising executives are creating a marketing piece, they follow a formula that will ensure the best results. Consider some of the following points when developing your video:

Research what is unique about your product or service. Why is your product different and why would it appeal to your potential customers? You need to convey this image to convince people to part with their hard-earned cash to own your product or breed to your stallion. Also note, the qualities you find special may not be marketable.

A person in a seminar at which I was presenting, complained that she was not selling enough horses. Her horses were pure Polish Arabians, which she felt made them worth more. People may breed for specific bloodlines; however, no one ever rides a bloodline. Meaning that people usually buy horses to ride or perform in a specific discipline. If a horse with a specific bloodline excels in a specific discipline, that horse is worth more to the people who compete in those disciplines. So, do not just tell me that you breed pure Polish horses; tell me what makes these horses special. Answer questions regarding the horse's trainability, athletic ability, conformation and/or the ability to win prize money. Accentuate the horse's ability to benefit the prospective owners.

Professional marketers develop a plan on paper before spending money on advertising. When ad executives plan a one-minute commercial, they go to the trouble of developing a story board and testing it on real people. It is up to you to decide what should go on your video to prospective buyers.

Many great plays have three parts so, when I was making a video to sell a horse, I decided to have three separate parts to the video. The first section included titles of the horse's name, the sire and dam with footage of the horse as a baby. After the cute baby section, there is footage of her training and finally the section of her showing. I selected music for all three sections with a segue between sections of footage of the horse's, registration papers, win photos, ribbons and trophies.

I took the footage, music and script, complete with the exact second the cuts should be made, to a professional video editor. I asked the video editor to use a character generator to type in the relevant information regarding the horse's name, farm name and bloodlines. I had setup and shot the footage for ribbons, trophies, etc. for the transitional sections, which amounted to a few seconds. The end shot came when we were shooting some halter type footage on a cold winter day. We zoomed the camera in towards the horse's face. Her hot breath created the illusion of steam rising from her nostrils. The end of the video gives credit to the trainers who had worked with the horse. The video is approximately nine minutes long.

My criticism of the video is that the footage is shaky. It would have been better for me to be grooming or riding rather than holding the video camera. Much of the footage was to be of the horse's first show or first hitch for my own

"Anything forced and misunderstood can never be beautiful. And to quote the words of Simon: If a dancer was forced to dance by whip and spikes, he would be no more beautiful than a horse trained under similar conditions."

Xenophon,

400 B.C.

use. I did not plan to sell the horse at the time. Since then, I have purchased a tripod and would recommend using a professional videographer at a show or ask someone who can shot good quality video to help.

When mailing out videos, have the horse's show record, bloodlines, vet records, and any other pertinent information on paper in the package. Do not expect the video to be returned; just include this marketing cost in the price of the horse.

Ask yourself, "What information do the prospective buyers need?" Walk the horse directly to and away from the camera just as if you are showing a halter horse to a judge. Show the horse being handled, ridden, clipped, loading into a trailer, anything the horse might have to do for the new owner.

Do this without dwelling on any one area too long or the viewers will get bored. The human eye can comprehend a new image every four seconds. Create a message that is short enough to hold the viewers' attention and long enough to get the point across. An old expression in business is, "Don't talk past the sale." This means you can miss a sale by not asking the person for action to buy something, or make a choice which will lead to a purchase. Often when someone keeps talking, the prospect may lose interest.

Be aware of what is in the background and how it will appear on camera. Are there broken fences or untidy buildings in the background? Does your horse look small next to the competition?

A professional marketer always tests their ideas. You can too. That is what family and friends are for. Most barns now have VCR players in their office or lounge. Make dinner for your horsey friends and ask for their opinions on your latest video. Your non-horse owning friends may even bring a fresh and different point of view.

Consider your packaging and delivery. Is the presentation clear and concise? Have you supplied all the supporting documentation needed? Have a fact sheet and some news releases on your product or service. Put vet records and shoeing records in the new owner' packet.

All information should be sent in a timely manner. Usually within 48 hours from the time the request is made. It is important to get your message to prospects before the competition. If you are serious about selling horses, approach all aspects the preparation of the video and supporting documentation as a job.

Using Television and Radio to Sell Your Products

To promote a product or idea on radio or television, we can take the video lesson to the next level. Again, start with a plan and a clear message. When adding music, remember that what you hear on the radio and buy on CDs is restricted because of copyright laws. Become familiar with "canned music" from music libraries. A qualified sound technician can direct you to uncopyrighted music, or you may wish to have music written especially for your production.

As with any message, keep it simple and credible. Common formats for television may include:

- *Slice of life.* These mini dramas may tell a story or even have a taste of nostalgia.

- *Testimonials.* People simply say what they like about the product. This idea will not work if the person looks as if they are reading their recommendation. The person must be honest and spontaneous.

- *Demonstrations.* The best examples are infomercials seen during non-peak television time. "Look how easy this is and it can work for you..." In a good demonstration, a problem is presented, followed by the demonstration of how the product answers the call with a solution.

- *Talking heads.* This is similar to when a news reporter sits at a desk to inform us about current topics. Some product promoters use this format very effectively. Many horse-training videos use both the "talking head" format along with the demonstration method to get their ideas or methods across.

- *Animated characters.* This can be used to offset the cost of using real people; or, can be used to create a different feeling to the promotional message. Some people feel more comfortable if their ideas are

Best of the Best World Class Benefit Multi-Breed Horse Sale
to benefit AIDS research.

"If the rider's

heart is in the

right place, his

seat will be

independent of

his hands."

Piero Santini,

The Forward

Impulse

(A five minute video produced to gain sponsors.)

Concept: Several exceptional horses will be presented for sale, with 90% of the proceeds going directly to the World AIDS Research Project. Purchases are tax deductible. Horses will be selected and shown by world class competitors. The site selected is Mount Stewart Vistas (the Northern Ireland estate of Lady Roxann Brownsbury).

VIDEO STORYBOARD

(Zoom-in on the Northern Ireland estate. Switch between the estate with a calm stable scene and an AIDS hospital ward.)

(Music, fade to announcer)

Announcer V.O. "Paradise and agony may seem to be worlds apart, unless you or someone close to you has been infected with HIV Complex. AIDS."

(Show announcer walking around the estate where the sale will be taking place.)

A storyboard shows how the copy interacts with the images to create a single selling message.

Announcer 1 - "There are some caring people in the horse industry who would like to do what they can to help find a cure for AIDS. An all-breed benefit horse sale will take place right here. In September, this estate will host the finest horse auction the world has ever seen, with 90% of the proceeds going to the AIDS Research Program."

(Preview some of the selected horses for the auction. A Jumper, an Arabian, Paint Horse, etc. Use natural sounds of a horse working.)

Announcer 2 - "Some of the horses nominated already include..."

(Flash-back to the hospital scene. Music picking up the sad notes from the first set of music, until again announcer 1 speaks.)

Announcer 1 - "But we need your help. Wouldn't you commit to being a corporate sponsor? Corporate sponsors will enjoy benefits including..."

Help the
AIDS Research Program

Be a Corporate Sponsor

(Close the video with a screen showing only typewritten information on. The information should recap the organization, the event, and who to contact.)

expressed through a fictional character, or believe that it will appeal more to their intended audience. With animation, you never have to worry that the spokesperson will say or do something to embarrass your company.

• *Humor.* Although often used in commercials, this is the most difficult format to sell a product. Humor in advertising, is known to be the most difficult, especially when you do not have a large budget to test the concepts.

A message developed for a video or television audience must convey the whole message as if no sounds will be heard. When sounds or voices are added to the images, the sounds and visuals must still convey the same message. The message must remain consistent with the addition of audio.

Radio is different. It conjures word pictures, using sounds, music and voices that paint images in the listeners' minds. Copywriting is very important and should follow the basics of good copywriting as discussed previously.

Placing both radio and television advertising is very important. We have an advantage in the horse market because we can advertise on a cable channel that is showing horse racing or featuring a breed like the American Quarter Horse. However, I do not recommend running an equine-specific ad during general programming; research shows that only four percent of the general population owns horses. However, public service announcements regarding a benefit trail ride may get good results on a local country music station.

For every rule, there is an exception. As a horse owner, you are probably very busy. Concentrate your efforts where you think you will get the best results.

Advertising Placement

Each publication sets its own rates based on the readership and demographics. Just as important as the number of copies printed is the number of publications mailed directly to readers. That is the subscriber base, and they are willing to pay for the publication. Many publications boast a large print number, only to distribute the publications to tack stores or other outlets that may just set the copies behind the counter or throw many away each month.

The demographics describe the average reader by their average age, income level, family size, number of horses owned, family income, geographic area, occupation, other hobbies and the types of goods and services purchased.

The price of the ad varies by size; prices are higher for premium space, like the inside front cover, back page, or a right-hand placement. Special sections might bring more readers to your ad; That is why publications do feature stories on fencing, for example, feature stories on fencing, new trucks, or any other product or service that can be advertised in the publication.

From an ethical standpoint, and from my training as a serious newswriter, the editorial department and the advertising department should be kept separate. Who is placing advertising in a publication should not influence the news. A daily newspaper is designed to give readers the truth about any topic, regardless of whether it might hurt advertising sales. This is the basis of freedom of the press. So, I have a clear distinction between newspapers and many horse-related publications.

Should you consider running advertising to correspond with editorial highlights? In December and January, you can expect to see editorials about selecting a stallion, foaling, pest control or dehydration issues, etc. Just as the horse calendar has a natural rhythm, so do publications. I place advertising in special section issues and make myself available to any writer working on one of the special sections. It is always better to be included rather than forgotten.

The cost of placing a message on radio and television is much higher and varies with the number of viewers (ratings). Cable stations in your area may offer some type of programming related to the horse industry, animal husbandry or agriculture in general. Some horse events are picked up nationally, like horse racing, national finals rodeo and equestrian events at the Olympics. As an industry, I think a great deal of effort should go to the promotion of horses to the general public. Credit should go to productions like Cheval Theatre, but again, placing advertising to the general public is not cost-effective. Some cable stations may work with you to create feature stories for non-profit groups or regarding trail riding or land use issues. Working with cable stations is usually considered free promotion if you have a concept of public interest.

Placing advertising in a publication can take on a different form, like inserts, or subscription cards, that are blown into the publication. Most publications and many catalog companies rent their mailing lists through brokers. Clubs and organizations may rent their lists, but are usually more comfortable running your ad in their publication. Compare the cost of each option available and measure this against the number of quality prospects.

Each publication has specific guidelines (mechanical requirements) regarding the actual production of an ad. Do not try to guess your way through this. Even if you have to hire a professional ad agency to create the ad, you want the ad produced correctly. You are ultimately responsible for the content and correct format of the ad. Some publications produce the ads, but again you have to provide the information and materials, such as logos and photos. Many of these publications assist with ad productions, but will charge for their time and resources.

When planning your ad, first consider the amount of information you want to provide and determine what space you can afford. Your budget should include all of the avenues your message can be placed in a year. Do not run a big ad at the beginning of your campaign and expect it to work all year.

A small company might begin an affordable presence with classified advertising in some publications, combined with a public relations campaign. Also, when a publication announces a special rate, know their regular rate and how much of a discount is offered. Research long-term commitment rates; these discounts can help you gain the exposure you need over your annual marketing plan. Ask if they have charges for copy changes, because you might want to change the copy of a longer duration ad.

Some publications offer links and advertising opportunities on the Internet. Some have an additional charge and some simply paste your ad on their web site. Be sure you understand any additional charges and ask how many "hits" or times their site is being looked at by potential customers. All general rules of marketing and advertising apply to placing your message on the Internet.

Some publications offer an agency discount when you provide a "camera ready" ad. The ad must already been created to their mechanical standards. Price break are usually up to 15%.

In the world of publications, deadlines are firm. They will not hold the presses for you, that only happens in the movies. Train your mind to think a month or two in advance. Think about what you want your customers to do in three months. If you want them to buy a lot of your product before you take inventory, you need to plan your sale at least three months in advance.

Tearsheets are the actual ad as it appears, sent to you as proof of production, along with a bill. Since you have studied and understood the terms and conditions of the publication, before placing the ad, you should not find any surprise charges. The publisher is not responsible or liable for the copy you provide nor for any promises or statements in the ad. The fine print in the advertising contract stipulates that the publisher is not responsible for items such as plagiarism, defamation, libel, or copyright infringement. Have a qualified proofreader examine the copy for content, grammar, spelling and punctuation. Always proofread the information you know by heart, like your phone number and address. Too often, people assume that since they know their address and phone number that they do not need to proof read that information.

Ask your advertising representative any questions you have before you sign the contract and pay for the ad. As with any legally binding contract, read it and understand it before you sign on the dotted line.

How to Measure Results
In advertising, it is not how much you spend but how you spend your money that makes the difference. Most business consultants agree that it is best to consider your advertising budget as a regular expense, just as rent and utility bills.

Another saying in the industry is that about half of your advertising dollar is wasted. It's just hard to figure out which half.

You must earn a certain level of profit to stay in business, and advertising helps to achieve this goal. The profit margin can be in terms of the return on investment (ROI). Learn how to calculate your own ROI. When you invest in an ad, can you count on more sales? Consult with someone familiar with your type of business and evaluate your ROI; this could be a volunteer with the SBA, an adult education course, a consultant or your accountant.

"Riding is a partnership. The horse lends you his strength, speed and grace, which are greater than yours. For your part you give him your guidance, intelligence and understanding, which are greater than his. Together you can achieve a richness that alone neither can."

Determining how much to spend on advertising depends upon several factors and is not an exact science. Experts recommend a budget of three to ten percent of your annual expenses for advertising.

An informal ways to measure results includes asking people where they heard about your business. Many websites provide information regarding how many people look at your web page call "hits." You may want to run slightly different offers or coupons in the different mediums you are using. Or you may want to code your ads in some way to determine which ad the prospect is responding to.

High-tech telephone systems provide the exact cities from which prospects call (a form of caller I.D). If you have more questions regarding tracking advertising results, ask your ad representative, or consult the Small Business Administration services in your area. These ideas, along with hard work and research, will help you develop a cash-winning marketing program.

🐴 CUSTOMER SERVICE

Customer service is the interaction with others in a business environment in such a manner that they will do business with you again.

Back to Basics

Much has been written and said about customer service. What can you do that will make a difference? Lack of customer service can cost you customers, even if you are just selling horses or operating a small boarding stable. Plus, as a customer yourself, you may feel entitled to better service even in the horse industry, because it revolves around expendable income and people's passion for horses.

Customer service is the root of all good and long-term business practices. Most businesses rely on repeat customers or word-of-mouth advertising to succeed. Customer service makes a business thrive or die, and it is an integral part of a Marketing Plan. Think of customer service as the follow-through such as with a golf swing. Without proper follow-through you may fall on your face.

It is a law of nature, that when a light is cast upon an object, it casts an image. The more a business is in the limelight, the more it casts an image seen by others. What is your image? It takes longer to build a good image than to tarnish one. And it takes longer to improve a tarnished image than either of the above. So, what does all this have to do with the horse industry?

Customer Service Is About Delivering More Than You Promise

We have to stop and examine the horse industry to come up with specific examples of customer service and the following should help paint a picture of good service. Since most horse-related businesses are sole-proprietorship, then what clients are reacting to, is in a sense, you the business owner. In the case of a boarding or training stable, is a business driven by personalities, including the needs of the horse and owner. Other influences include the economy, access to expendable income and trends in the industry.

"Everything is easier when you keep moving forward."

Pamela C. Biddle and Joel E. Fishman, All I Need to Know I learned From My Horse.

251

The best rule of thumb in customer service is always deliver more than you promise. A boarding facility usually offers stall cleaning, feeding, and access to trainers. Delivering more could mean offering clinics, tack-up service, child-care, access to trails even personal tack lockers. An example regarding stallion management is measuring by the vial. If it is common practice to send two straws of cooled semen to the owner of a broodmare, what happens if only one vial is sent? This could mean the veterinarian with the responsibility to inseminate the mare at the best time may be called on to work on the mare during the evening, therefore outside regular business hours; charging the client with after hours fees. It may also result in a lower conception rate. The first question is: What is standard procedure or what is normally provided or expected? Customers do compare what each business offers.

Customer service is the accumulation of small things that add up. Spelling a person's name correctly and listening to the customer's needs makes a large difference. One stable even has a "Board of Boarders" as a sounding board to bring new ideas to the boarding facility.

Whether you are operating a small boarding stable, training outside horses, repairing blankets or own a retail tack store, the challenge to is how to offer more than promised.

It Starts At the Top

The standard business hierarchy has the owner at the top, followed by managers, then employees at the bottom. Even if only a few people are on your chart, stop and think about the hierarchy of your business. If this is the manner in which your business operates, you may want to rethink–no, actually, burn the chart.

Place the customers at the top of the new organizational chart. Let the customers determine the direction of the business. Survey what they want, establish what they will pay, then develop your product in such a manner that it is profitable. Profit is not a dirty word. If you are not profitable, you will not be able to stay in business.

Another top is be to lead by example. Employees watch the owners and managers of the business to determine how they themselves should act, dress, work and treat customers. Since many people are involved with the horse industry-because it is a passion or way of life - leadership by example should be easy. An employer who is happy is much easier to work with.

Some key questions to ask yourself as an owner or manager:

- When do you arrive and leave the office?

- When you are away from the office, does someone know how to reach you and how to handle problems that arise?

- How long does an employee's request or memo sit on your desk before you get back to him/her?

Hire, Train and Retain Quality People

As the owner of a business you may already know that your most valuable resource is people. It takes time and energy to hire and train people, but this time is well-spent when customers continue to use your product or service.

When hiring a person who will have contact with your customers, it is your responsibility to ask the right questions. Ask role-playing questions. During the interview process, use examples of situations that actually have happened. Look for individuals who have a strong self-image, who are upbeat and look at the world with a little humor.

A big challenge in the horse industry is to fill entry-level positions with employees who will stay for awhile. Some companies offer a signing bonus that might be $100 payable after the employee stays for anywhere from a month to a year. Some companies offer profit-sharing and/or health benefits. Many in the horse industry even offer employee housing. Many of these options are best planned for when developing your business plan.

I once overheard a bank president say he would rather hire young people who have worked for a fast food place, then train them to work in a bank, because these employees have already been trained to give service with a smile and to count change correctly.

When looking over prospective employees' applications and resumes look for experience that may have trained them to be better employees for you. This may not necessarily mean they have performed the same duties somewhere else. Ask questions to determine if they can think on their feet and solve problems. Ask for and call references.

Training an employee is one of the most time-consuming aspects for any manager. A training program and employee handbook, even a very small one, is helpful. Employees will fail if you do not let them know what you expect of them. The program should be complete with a timetable and goals so the new employees have a realistic grasp of the job. If you hire a new bookkeeper, he/she needs to know if taxes need to be paid quarterly, if statements go out at the end of the month, or if accounts need to be paid by the 10th, and if you have a customer who always questions the billing or a client who pays late. If your company imposes interest charges to late payments, how are they equally applied?

This training program should also prepare the employees to work independently and make decisions on their own. Most employees are eager to take on new challenges and want more responsibility. When people are trained well and are given the freedom to make decisions, they are willing and able to help the customers. Nothing is more frustrating than to have an exchange or return and waiting 15 or more minutes for a manager's approval. Unfortunately, some managers do not understand the importance of training or they feel threatened by eager employees. A successful manger hires and trains people to do the job better than he/she could do the job.

Retaining quality employees can be difficult unless you know what motivates them. Mary Kay Ash built a huge cosmetics company, in part, because she realized what was important to the women who worked for her. Not only did these women want to be able to earn their own pay, but they wanted a flexible work schedule so that they could spend time with their families; and they wanted recognition. This recognition even comes in the form of pink Cadillacs!

You may want to ask prospective employees what they hope to gain by working for you, not just today but five years from now. Ask what they expect to excel at within the job description provided. When the employee does excel, give recognition, especially when the employee excels at something difficult.

If you have more W-2 forms to mail out at the end of the year than you have employees, you have a turnover problem. Of course, it is generally impossible to have no turnover, but it is important to know who is leaving and why. Many companies conduct exit interviews to learn why good employees leave and what it would take to keep them.

Although pay is only one ingredient employees look at, it is the easiest to measure. In a competitive employment environment, employees look at everything that could be beneficial, such as, health insurance, day care, continuing education, housing. What will it take to bring in and keep the best employees to your horse business.

Each employee should feel he/she is important to the overall goal of your business. Your employees are important to your success and should be reminded of this often. Most wins in life require a team effort.

To get employees to feel involved in the success of a company, many employers tie pay to performance. Profit sharing, commission, or any other benefit designed to motivate employees can be used.

And last, but not least, fire people when needed. It is always a good idea to document employee behavior and have adequate reason to fire an individual documented in their personnel files. It is a difficult decision, but if employees are unable or unwilling to perform the duties listed in the job description, they must be let go.

Give your business the competitive edge with good customer service

Good Customer Service Practices

Customers can be defined as anyone you do business with. This could be people who purchase a horse from you, board at your stable, or have a horse in training with you. The key to keeping customers satisfied is when they perceive they are receiving something of equal value to what they are paying with their hard-earned money. Customer service is partly derived from the personality of the boss and the overall environment of the business. Sometimes a person may have the desire and financial backing to open a business, but lacks the "people skills" to make it work. It is almost easier to hire someone with the skills to interact with customers than to change major personality traits.

The following ideas help improve customer service for any business:

- *Take all returns or exchanges with a smile.* This is difficult in the horse industry because horses are usually sold "as is." However, to have a customer file a lawsuit, call a customer protection group, call a television or radio advocate, or tell everyone about a bad experience, can be very damaging. To keep customers happy, it is advisable to offer a few lessons with horses that are sold, or encourage people to "test ride" the horse more than once before making a buying decision. While pre-purchase examinations made by a qualified veterinarian are important, many vets protect themselves by stating that no horse is 100 percent sound.

- *Maintain eye contact and take interruptions only when necessary.* A riding instructor with good customer service ethics does not talk to other customers, eat lunch, talk on the phone, ignore students, or leave a rider posting without stirrups indefinitely.

- *The customer you are currently with is always the most important.* People resent being put on hold while you take another call. If you are busy, simply tell the customer something like, "I see you need to think about this for awhile, so I'll be over here working... Can we meet to discuss this further? I will check back with you to see if you have any other questions..." or, "you can call me (set a time)." Business people are busy. So are your customers.

- *Set a good example.* Take time to train all of your employees regarding how to dress and address people. Customers form opinions of a trainer who wears a clean shirt with a collar as opposed to a dirty, old t-shirt.

- *Deliver more than you promise.* This is the best guideline to good customer service. If an instructor is to give a 45-minute lesson, but always stops at 30 minutes, the customer makes a mental note of this. Customers also notice empty water buckets and unclean horses. Take the time to see your business through the customers' eyes.

CASE STUDY

Customer service endears customers to you in the long run. Customer service is the accumulation of small things that all up to big sales. Spelling a customer's name correctly and listening to the customer's needs makes a big difference, but what more can be done?

A manager of a large commercial boarding stable changed the way she did business to benefit everyone in the horse industry. She worked above and beyond the expectations of her boarding stable customers and others. Connie Kimbrel, manager of Table Mountain Ranch in Golden, Colorado, worked to get the law for limiting liability passed. Kimbrel became involved with horses when her children began taking lessons at a local stable through a recreational program. Soon they owned horses and six years later Kimbrel became secretary/ bookkeeper for the largest commercial boarding stable in the area, Table Mountain Ranch (TMR). By this time her daughters were boarding at TMR. Seven years later, she became the manager. She worked hard with many programs, newsletters and shows; she blossomed in grass roots politics and was instrumental in passing the equine civil liability act in Colorado.

When Kimbrel became the manager, she also became active with the state horse council. She spent a great deal of time traveling to the state capitol to testify and observe the process. She traveled to speak to many horse groups throughout the state and opened her facility for meetings, demonstrations and receptions for city employees, elected officials, anyone the horse industry needed to impress. This involved a great deal of volunteer time. When she initiated an office charge each year to her boarders – so they automatically became members of the county and state horse council, 99% of her boarders understood the importance and accepted the charge. Thus changing the way she ran the boarding stable.

Kimbrel sees the value of the local and state horse council and believes in their mission so strongly that she encourages people to join. Most horse people have told her they always meant to join those organizations but 'never got around to it' or 'lost the application...'

Kimbrel offers an objection clause, but states it was only used once by a person who objected to being required to pay the fee. This person joined the councils independently because he realized how important they were to the whole equine community. Kimbrel's boarders respect her for her outspokenness and realize she is working on their behalf.

Connie Kimbrel stated of her dedicated practices, "Unless we become powerful and speak out, we will lose more rights for horse owners every year."

Customer service is one of the secrets of a successful horse business. It means gaining people's respect and convincing them to continue doing business with you in the future. It may vary with the economic environment and changing business standards, but it must always benefit all parties involved.

How can *you* deliver more than you promise?

HOW TO SELECT AN ATTORNEY

ow to find an attorney who is capable and competent to represent a horse owner or an equine business is challenging. Although there is no shortage of lawyers, in only a few states are lawyers certified as specialists in certain fields and no state certifies attorneys as an expert in equine law.

Among the lists of attorneys available including their education, background and experience the oldest and most highly regarded is a multi-volume work called *"Martindale Hubbell Law Directory."* This directory is published each year, covers the United States and aspires to list lawyers throughout the world.

The most interesting feature of the law directories is its system used to rate lawyers. Although no rating system can rate the ability and integrity of an attorney perfectly, the system is based on "peer review." Lawyers who are already established are asked to rate other lawyers.

The first question asked of the rating attorney is regarding the candidate's integrity. Unless the rater can give a "very high" mark to integrity, the rating process goes no further. Once a "very high" or "v" rating is is given to the candidate, the rater considers his/her ability as an attorney. A range of "a" for excellent, or "b" for very good, and "c" for good are the options available. If the rater does not know enough about the candidate's ability as an attorney, or feels that at least a good rating is not warranted, no rating is given. The highest rating an attorney can receive is "av" or excellent ability and very high integrity. The majority of attorneys are not rated for a number of reasons, including simply not being known to the attorneys asked to rate them. The *Martindale Hubbell* system is not perfect, but it does give some indication of the professional standing of particular lawyers.

In addition to their ratings of ability and integrity, some lawyers choose to pay for biographical listings in *Martindale Hubbell*. The listings include the types of law practiced by the attorney and may include a representative list of his/her clients. A biography is helpful in selecting a

"Don't corner a frightened hose unless you know what to do with him."

Pamela C.

Biddle and

Joel E.

Fishman, All I

Need to Know

I learned From

My Horse.

lawyer for representation in a specific area of law, such as equines; although, the listed lawyer furnishes the copy so there is no independent verification of the accuracy of the information.

Martindale Hubbell is available through both printed volumes and its web site *(www.martindale.com)*. They also offer a service to subscribing lawyers and law firms, whereby web sites are created giving extensive information about the lawyers, their practices, experience, and other information. These home pages are available at HYPERLINK *http://www.lawyers.com*. Printed volumes are available in some public libraries and are commonly part of most law libraries.

Other law lists are available including some computer listings of attorneys and law firms. However, availability of these lists is often a problem for the general public; they are created for and used principally by lawyers.

There is very little regulation of advertising by lawyers. Bar associations and regulatory bodies have tried to set standards for attorney advertising; however, misrepresentation and bad taste are difficult to regulate, because the purpose of advertising is to get business. Advertisements are not the most accurate or reliable source for selecting an attorney.

Look for an attorney with wisdom and knowledge in the horse industry.

What is the best source of finding an attorney with some background in equine law? Probably the best way to find an attorney is by "word-of-mouth" recommendations. Receiving a recommendation of an attorney from a satisfied client carries a great deal of credibility. When a lawyer has withstood the test of fire with a client, and the client is satisfied with the representation, a recommendation from that client is worthy of serious consideration.

Most state and local Bar Associations maintain a free lawyer referral service. Usually an advertisement of the service appears in the yellow pages. The names of attorneys with experience in general areas requested are released to the caller. Each attorney on the list should be called and questioned regarding his/her experience in the particular area needed, e.g., fees, etc. Some attorneys have prepared a letter or brochure that answers frequently asked questions. Before selecting an attorney research is the best policy.

Another source of referral for an attorney is from other attorneys. Most attorneys realize their limitations and ethical responsibility not to represent clients in areas of the law in which they are not experienced. Additionally, attorneys usually know or have access to referrals of attorneys who are experienced in equine or related legal areas. Referrals from other attorneys is a good way to obtain legal representation.

"Why is it important to have an attorney?" Most people, at some time, will need the assistance of a qualified attorney. Having a good attorney on your team is as important as having a qualified accountant and a trusted veterinarian. The lawyer's role is to advise his/her clients; counsel and aid in business planning, assist with the structure of the client's business, and work to avoid legal pitfalls.

Attorney's Fees
There are several ways an attorney may bill a client. The manner of charges varies, depending on the type of case and the lawyer.

Hourly Fees are frequently used and vary greatly in amount. The method and amount, or rate, charged by an attorney should be discussed in the initial meeting. Attorneys charge for the time they spend on the client's matter, including writing letters, meetings with you and with others regarding your case, research phone calls, and preparing documents. Other costs, such as filing fees, travel expenses, long distance telephone calls and copy charges are generally added to the hourly fee.

A **Flat Fee** is appropriate for certain types of work. A simple will, for example, may cost a flat fee of $350. This means the charge for the particular matter is set, and there is no additional charge for additional time spent in doing the job. Flat fees are usually not subject to additional costs and expenses that should be clarified ahead of time.

"A camel is a
horse planned by
a committee."

Retainer Fees are when a business, or individual, "retains" a lawyer to represent them for a specific matter or to represent them on all legal matters that may occur in the future. The retainer amount is generally paid prior to the attorney undertaking the representation and is drawn on by the lawyer on an hourly charge after the legal service is performed. Retainers are very common when an attorney is hired at the beginning of a case or when there has been no prior attorney-client relationship.

Contingent Fees are not common in the horse industry, because they apply mainly to personal injury and other cases involving litigation. In these cases, the attorney represents the client for a percentage of the amount recovered either from a settlement or an award by a judge or jury. In contingent fee cases, the client is responsible for and must pay the costs and expenses separately and in addition to the fee.

Probably the most important role of a lawyer is to practice preventive law. That is, get the client to come to the lawyer before there is a problem, before signing the contract, before changing the business's structure, before taking a bank loan to buy new stock or equipment, before doing any activity that could end in legal controversy. A lawyer's role in the horse business is to shut the barn door *BEFORE* the horse is stolen.

 # GLOSSARY

a

Acceptance - In contract law, the offeree's notification to the offer, or that the offeree agrees to be bound by the terms of a proposal.

Accrual method - Method of accounting in which income is reported when earned and expenses are reported when incurred.

Affirmative action - Job-hiring policies that give special consideration to minority groups.

Agent - A person authorized by another to act for or in place of another person.

Agreement - A meeting of two or more minds. Often used as a synonym for contract.

Ampersand - In typesetting, the short or commercial symbol "&" use for the word *and*.

Appreciation - The increase in the value of a property over time.

Arbitration - The settling of a dispute by submitting it to a disinterested third party for decision.

Articles of partnership - A written agreement that sets forth each partner's rights in, and obligations to, the partnership.

Ascender - The portion of a letter which rises above the main body of a letter, such as the top half of the vertical line in the letter "b."

Assets - Property that could be sold or have a cash value.

Assigns - Any person who has been given an interest or full ownership in a property via a will, trust, or gift.

Assumption of risk - A doctrine whereby a plaintiff may not recover for injuries or damages suffered from the inherent risks of equine sports.

Award - As a noun, not a trophy or ribbon, defines the amount of money, settlement or decision given to an injured party in a judicial proceeding.

B

Bailee - The person charged with the responsibility of caring for another's personal property. The individual who entrusts his/her property or animals to another is called a Bailor. The agreement between these two is the Bailment.

Binder - A written, temporary insurance policy; also, an extension of a current policy.

Bleed - In printing, when the printed image or color extends past the trimmed edge of the paper.

Bullets - Usually solid round typographic characters, but may be any shape; used to call attention to copy.

Business entity - A separate entity, distinct from its owner(s) and from other business(es).

Business tort - Wrongful interference with a business or contractual relationships of others, unfair competition.

C

Callouts - Arrows, lines, or any graphic elements used to call attention to the components within an advertisement.

Camera-ready - Type and/or illustrations ready to be photographed to print by offset lithography/printing. Many printers can accept digital or PDF files at a reduced cost.

Capital - Money or resources used to begin or maintain a business.

Capital expenditure - The amount of money used to purchase business property.

Capital gain - Gain from the sale or exchange of business property.

Capital loss - The loss from sale(s) of business property.

Caption or Cutline - The words printed, under or next to an illustration, explaining the contents or relevance of the illustration/photo.

Cash method - The method of accounting where income is reported when received and expenses reported when paid.

Casualty loss - The loss of purchased property that is sudden, unexpected and usual. May be deducted from other ordinary income.

Center spread or Double truck - An ad that covers two pages, jumping the fold or stitching in the center of the publication.

Color separation - The process of separating full-color originals into primary colors.

Color specifications - Color printing uses cyan, magenta, yellow and black (CMYK) to create a full range of color by changing the density and combination of millions of dots on the page.

Condition - A qualification, provision, or clause in a contractual agreement, the occurrence of which creates, suspends, or terminates the obligations of the contracting parties.

Consideration - The fee or payment for a product or service.

Consignment - A transaction in which an owner of goods (consignor) entrusts goods to be sold; as in selling a horse through a sale.

Contract - A set of promises constituting an agreement between parties, giving each a legal duty to the other; also, the right to seek a remedy in the event of a breach of contract/broken promise.

Copy - The text or written words in an advertisement.

Corporation - A legal entity created under the authority of the laws of a state or the federal government.

Covenant - To promise in a legally binding document.

Debtor - A person who owes a sum of money or other obligations to another.

Descender - The portion of a letter that extends below the line that type is set upon, like the letters, g, y, j, p.

Deduction - The amount taken as expense for tax purposes; it is subtracted from taxable income.

Default - To breach or fail to fulfill an agreement.

Depreciation - A means of recovering the cost of business a property that has a useful life of more than one year.

Dissolution - The formal disbanding of a partnership or corporation. It can take place by (1) agreement of the parties or the shareholders and board of directors, (2) by the death of a partner, (3) by the expiration of a time-period stated in the agreement, (4) or by court order.

Dividend - A distribution to corporate shareholders, disbursed in proportion to the number of shares held.

Dots per inch (DPI) - The number of dots per inch that a press is able to print at one time. Increasing the number of dots per inch increases the quality of the reproduction.

Dummy - A rough advance plan of any printed piece; also Mock-up or Layout.

Employee - A person or persons who perform services for another, in which the employer dictates what the job is, when, and how it will be accomplished.

Employment discrimination - Treating employees or job applicants unequally on the basis of race, gender, nationality, religion, or age; prohibited by Title VII of the Civil Rights Act of 1964 as amended.

Encumbrance - A lien or legal claim on property, which might interfere with the sale of a property.

Entrepreneur - One who initiates and assumes the financial risks of a new enterprise and manages the undertaking.

Estate - Everything a person owns, including animals, real estate, tack, jewelry. . . everything.

Executor (Executrix) - The person responsible for administering a will.

Expenses - The money spent on ordinary and necessary items used in the operation of a business.

Express contract - A contract, either oral or written; varies from an implied contract.

Express warranty - An express warranty can be either orally or written specifically stating what an animal or product can do.

F

Fair market value - The estimated value, or amount of money the property may bring on the open market; usually determined by the market (competition) or an appraiser.

Font(s) - The selection of letters and symbols of any particular type size and/or typeface.

Four-color process - Printing with four colors (cyan, magenta, yellow, black, CMYK) to create a range of colors.

G

Gain - The difference between the base cost of goods and the sale of said goods.

General partner - In a limited partnership, a partner who assumes responsibility for managing of the partnership and liability for all partnership debts.

Good faith purchaser - A purchaser who buys without notice of any circumstance, which would cause a person of ordinary prudence to inquire whether the seller has valid ownership or title to the horse or property being sold.

Grandfather clause - A phrase used when zoning property; means when the property is sold, it must be used as the zoning requires. Often, when a horse property is sold, the new owner is not able to have a horse on the property because of prior zoning.

Gross income - The total amount of income before expenses are deducted.

Gutter - The area on the page which is left blank between columns or between pages.

H

Halftone - A picture (photograph) that has been separated into lines made up of dots to fit the dot resolution of the press to be used.

Homestead exemption - A law allowing an owner to designate his/her house and adjoining land as a homestead, which exempts it from liability for general debts.

"Don't crack the whip before you check the harness."

Pamela C. Biddle and Joel E. Fishman, All I Need to Know I learned From My Horse.

Implied warranty - A warranty that the law implies either through the situation of the parties or the nature of the transaction.

Income - Money in exchange for products or services as a normal business activity.

Independent contractor - A person who offers a service and is not an employee or under the direct control of another.

Insert - A separate sheet or section inside a publication, added to the publication during collation or binding.

Installment sale or payments - Money paid over time; interest may be charged on the balance.

Insurance - A contract in which, for a price, the insurer can be reimbursed for loss, medical costs, and liability costs.

Insurance proceeds - Compensation received from insurance policies for property that has been stolen or lost.

Intestate - One who dies without having created a valid will.

Investment - May include time, money, or effort that goes into building a business.

Invoice - A written statement of money owed.

Joint tenancy - Ownership between two or more individuals. Upon the death of one of the joint tenants, his/her interest automatically passes to the others and cannot be transferred by the will of the decreased.

Jurisdiction - The authority of a court to hear and decide a specific action.

L

Law - A body of rules of conduct with legal force and effect.

Layout - A drawn or pasted-up example for a printer to follow in designing a page; also referred to as a dummy.

Leading - In type composition, the insertion of space between the lines of type.

Lease - A transfer by the lessor to a lessee for a period of time for consideration (usually payment). Upon termination of the lease, the property reverts to the lessor.

Liability - The legal responsibility for a person, property, animal, or situation.

Lien - An encumbrance placed upon property to satisfy or protect a claim for payment of a debt.

Limited partnership - A partnership consisting of one or more general partners, who manage the business and are liable to the full extent of their personal assets for debts of the partnership; and of one or more limited partners, who contribute only assets and are liable only up to the amount contributed by them.

Logo - The nameplate, with the name and any artwork designed to identify that specific company or group.

m

Mechanical - The pasted-up version of artwork and type ready for printing. Should be camera-ready, and may be accompanied by overlays that separate color.

Medium - In this book, refers to where an advertisement or article is placed; newspapers, magazines, radio, television, signs, etc.

Mock-up - A rough advance plan of any printed material.

n

Negligence - The failure to exercise the standard of care that a reasonable person would exercise in similar circumstances.

Net income - The amount of income after expenses are deducted.

Notice - The formal warning of the intent or change or end of an agreement.

o

Offer - An offeror's proposal to do something, which creates in the offeree accepting the offer a legal power to bind the offer to the terms of the proposal by accepting the offer.

Offeree - A person to whom an offer is made.

Offeror - A person who makes an offer.

Offset - A system of printing that is chemical, planographic, and indirect. An inked image on a flat plate is transferred to a rubber surface before being pressed to paper. Part of the surface is treated to accept ink.

Overlay - Transparent plastic sheet(s) that are secured over the artwork, providing mechanical color separation or instructions.

$\mathcal{P}$

Partnership - An association of two or more persons involved in a business, usually for profit.

Performance - In contract law, the fulfillment of one's duties arising under a contract with another.

Personal property - Property that is movable; any property that is not real property.

Premiums - The amount of money charged for insurance coverage.

Pica - A printer's unit of measurement in typesetting. One pica equals 12 points.

Point - A unit of measurement equal to .013837 inch. The American Point System was developed in 1886.

Point-or-purchase display or P.O.P. - Displays created to promote a product within a retail environment, such as cardboard stands; should complement the overall marketing campaign.

Power of attorney - A document or instrument authorizing another person to act as an agent on his/her behalf.

PMT or STAT - A high quality reproduction complete with the appropriate line screen.

Precedent - A court decision that furnishes an example or authority for deciding subsequent cases in which identical or similar facts are presented.

Probate court - A court having jurisdiction over proceedings concerning the settlement of a person's estate.

Process color - Realistic color achieved by printing from four separate plates created by separating the primary colors plus black.

Profit - The amount of income after expenses are deducted.

Promissory note - A written instrument signed by a maker unconditionally promising to pay a certain sum of money to a payee or a holder on demand, or on a specified date.

Property - Any item a person or business owns or is using.

Real property - Legal description for land.

Register - To precisely fit two or more images together, a cross imposed over a circle is used; may also have the color register.

Release - The relinquishment, concession, or giving up of a right, claim, or privilege; by the person in whom it exists or to whom it accrues, to the person against whom it might have been enforced or demanded.

Reverse - Generally black letters or images placed on a white background. Reverse this would be to place white letters or images on a black background.

Revise - A proof made after corrections have been marked.

Risk management - Planning undertaken to protect the insured's interest and to lower insurance premiums.

Sale - The passing of title to property from the seller to the buyer for a price.

Sales contract - A contract by means of which the ownership of goods is transferred from a seller to a buyer for a fixed price.

S corporations - A form of business that has met certain requirements as set out by the Internal Revenue Code, which qualifies for special income-tax treatment. Essentially, an S Corporation is taxed the same as a partnership, except it owners enjoy the privilege of limited liability.

Sans serif - The family of type without serifs. Serifs are the stroke marks at the beginning and ending of letters.

Script - Type resembling handwriting in which letters are not connected, as opposed to cursive in which letters are joined.

Serif - Tiny finishing strokes at the end of main strokes of letters. Serifs are sometimes referred to as "feet."

Sole proprietorship - Business organization in which all the firm's assets are owned by one individual. The owner, or sole proprietor, is entitled to all profits earned by the business and is personally liable for any losses or other obligations of the firm.

Spot color - Any color used in a designated area other than process color.

Stet - A proofreader's mark which indicates to the typesetter to skip the marking and leave it as originally written.

Strict liability - Liability regardless of fault. In tort law, strict liability is imposed on a merchant who introduces into commerce a good that is reasonably dangerous when in a defective condition.

Storyboards - A layout showing the coordination of script and visuals on a pasteboard.

T

Tax basis - The cost of business property, plus additions or improvements, less depreciation.

Tearsheet - A single page of newspaper or a page from a magazine given to an advertiser as proof that the ad had been printed. The tearsheet usually accompanies the bill.

Text - The typewritten message in an article or ad.

Title - Evidence of ownership, like a deed.

Tort - In civil law, when wrongs arise from a breach of contract.

Typo - Abbreviation for typographical error.

V

Valid contract - A properly constituted contract having legal strength or force.

Velox - A screen made from a photograph, film, or negative used for the actual final paste-up or to be printed.

W

Waiver - An express warranty included either written or orally, usually in reference to the performance of goods sold. An implied warranty is the general assumption that a horse has four legs, a head, and tail, and is reasonably fit.

Warranty - A guarantee or assurance of a condition either express or implied to make a sale.

White space - Space unoccupied by type, photograph, or illustration.

Will - An instrument directing what is to be done with the testator's property upon his/ her death, made by the property owner(s) and revocable during his/ her lifetime.

♞ INDEX OF CASES

"A horseman can show neither fear, nor anger."

TABLE OF ILLUSTRATIONS

INDEX